2A

FOCUS ON GRAMMAR

AN INTEGRATED SKILLS APPROACH

2A

FOCUS ON GRAMMAR

AN INTEGRATED SKILLS APPROACH

THIRD EDITION

IRENE E. SCHOENBERG

PEARSON
Longman

FOCUS ON GRAMMAR 2A: An Integrated Skills Approach

Pearson Education, 10 Bank Street, White Plains, NY 10606

Vice president, multimedia and skills: Sherry Preiss
Executive editor: Laura Le Dréan
Development manager: Paula H. Van Ells
Vice president, director of design and production: Rhea Banker
Executive managing editor: Linda Moser
Production supervisor: Christine Edmonds
Production editor: Laurie Neaman
Art director: Ann France
Marketing director: Oliva Fernández
Senior manufacturing buyer: Nancy Flaggman
Photo research: Aerin Csigay
Cover design: Rhea Banker
Cover images: Large shell, Alan Kearney, RM; background, Comstock Images, RF
Text design: Quorum Creative Services, Rhea Banker
Text composition: ElectraGraphics, Inc.
Text font: 11/13 Sabon, 10/13 Myriad Roman

Photo credits: see p. xii.

Illustrators: Steve Attoe pp. 280, 310; A. J. Garces pp. 148, 179, 186; Chris Gash pp. 45, 53, 76, 87, 129 (bottom), 130, 142, 145, 146, 231; Dave Klug pp. 88, 94, 265; Jock MacRae, pp. 198–199; Paul McCusker pp. 85, 256–257; Suzanne Mogensen p. 54; Tom Newsom pp. 12, 15, 122, 126, 395, 428; Chris Pappas, pp. 38, 46, 129 (top), 159, 162–163, 180, 340, 342; Dusan Petricic pp. 20, 229, 347, 350, 390; Steve Schulman pp. 400, A-5; Dave Sullivan, pp. 80, 358; Gary Torrisi, pp. 56, 164, 304, 353; Meryl Treatner pp. 77, 116.

Library of Congress Cataloging-in-Publication Data

Focus on grammar. An integrated skills approach — 3rd ed.
p. cm.
ISBN 0-13-147466-9 (v. 1 : student book : alk. paper) — ISBN 0-13-189971-6 (v. 2 : student book : alk. paper) — ISBN 0-13-189984-8 (v. 3 : student book : alk. paper) — ISBN 0-13-190008-0 (v. 4 : student book : alk. paper) — ISBN 0-13-191273-9 (v. 5 : student book : alk. paper)
1. English language—Textbooks for foreign speakers. 2. English language—Grammar—Problems, exercises, etc.
PE1128.F555 2005
428.2'4—dc22

2005007655

ISBNs: 0-13-189979-1 (Student Book A)
0-13-193923-8 (Student Book A with Audio CD)

Printed in the United States of America

1 2 3 4 5 6 7 8 9 10—WC—12 11 10 09 08 07 06 05

CONTENTS

PART VI THE SIMPLE PAST

APPENDICES

ABOUT THE AUTHOR

Irene E. Schoenberg has taught ESL for more than two decades at Hunter College's International English Language Institute and at Columbia University's American Language Program. She has trained ESL and EFL teachers at Columbia University's Teachers College and at the New School University. She has given workshops and academic presentations at conferences, English language schools, and universities in Brazil, Chile, Dubai, El Salvador, Guatemala, Japan, Mexico, Nicaragua, Peru, Taiwan, Thailand, and throughout the United States.

Ms. Schoenberg is the author of *Talk about Trivia*; *Talk about Values*; *Speaking of Values 1: Conversation and Listening*; *Topics from A to Z*, Books 1 and 2; and the basic level of *Focus on Grammar*. She is the co-author with Jay Maurer of the *True Colors* series and the introductory level of *Focus on Grammar 1*.

Ms. Schoenberg holds a master's degree in TESOL from Columbia University.

CREDITS

Grateful acknowledgment is given to the following for providing photographs:

p. 3 Patrick Olear/PhotoEdit; **p. 4** *(left)* Russell Boyce/Reuters/Corbis, *(right)* Reuters/Corbis; **p. 8** *(top)* Mike Powell/Getty Images, *(bottom)* Bend It Films/Film Council/ The Kobal Collection/ Parry, Christine; **p. 10** *(Matsui)* Reuters/Corbis, *(Hamm)* Darren McCollester/Getty Images, *(Lee)* Rufus F. Folkks/Corbis, *(Spielberg)* Rufus F. Folkks/Corbis, *(Rubio)* Frank Trapper/Corbis, *(Beyonce)* Reuters/Corbis, *(Rowling)* Rune Hellestad/Corbis, *(Marquez)* Jorge Uzon/AFP/Getty Images; **p. 19** Getty Images; **p. 22** Annebicque Bernard/Corbis Sygma; **p. 38** *(top)* RubberBall Productions, *(bottom left)* Reuters/Corbis, *(bottom right)* Henri Cartier-Bresson /Magnum Photos; **p. 41** Ron Chapple/Getty Images; **p. 42** Henri Cartier-Bresson /Magnum Photos; **p. 44** Henri Cartier-Bresson /Magnum Photos; **p. 48** Walter Bibikow/Index Stock Imagery; **p. 50** www.Gamirasu.com; **p. 51** Tom Bean/Corbis; **p. 59** Christie's Images/Corbis, ©C. Herscovici, Brussels; **p. 62** Bettmann/Corbis, ©Salvador Dali, Gala-Salvador Dali Foundation/Artists Rights Society (ARS), New York; **p. 70** Catherine Karnow/Corbis; **p. 75** Ryan McVay/Getty Images; **p. 90** Omni-Photo Communications, Inc.; **p. 102** *(top)* Gary Conner/PhotoEdit, *(bottom)* Stephanie Maze/Corbis, *(right)* Bob Krist/Getty Images, *(left)* Martin Barraud/Getty Images; **p. 107** Dorling Kindersley; **p. 112** Will Hart; **p. 119** Digital Vision; **p. 122** Timothy O'Keefe/Index Stock Imagery; **p. 128** Sally Brown/Index Stock Imagery; **p. 150** Peter Samuels/Getty Images, *(left)* Reuters/Corbis, *(right)* TM and ©Twentieth Century Fox Film Corp./Photofest, *(bottom)* AP/Wide World Photos; **p. 151** CBS Photo Archive/Getty Images; **p. 158** Michele Burgess/Index Stock Imagery; **p. 167** Dorling Kindersley; **p. 173** Dr. Ronald H. Cohn/ The Gorilla Foundation; **p. 174** *(left)* Nektarios Pierros/Reuters/Corbis, *(right)* Greg Epperson/Index Stock Imagery, *(bottom)* Snuba® diving in Hawaii/www.snuba.com; **p. 188** *(right)* Sally Brown/Index Stock Imagery, *(top)* Walter Bibikow/Index Stock Imagery, *(left)* Michele Westmorland/Corbis; **p. 197** Nik Wheeler/Corbis; **p. 206** Newline Cinema/ Photofest; **p. 212** Bettmann/Corbis; **p. 222** James Marshall/Corbis; **p. 239** *(left)* Gary Buss/Getty Images, *(right)* Greg Ceo/Getty Images; **p. 249** www.CartoonStock.com; **p. 256** Javier Pierini/Getty Images; **p. 266** Art Wolfe/Getty Images; **p. 274** *(right)* David Chalk/ Omni-Photo Communications, Inc., *(middle)* Will & Deni McIntyre/ Photo Researchers, Inc., *(left)* ATC Productions/ImageQuest, *(1)* Kevin Peterson/Getty Images, *(2)* RubberBall Productions, *(3)* Kevin Peterson/Getty Images, *(4)* Barbara Penoyar/Getty Images; **p. 275** *(left)* RubberBall Productions, *(right)* Barbara Penoyar/Getty Images; **p. 284** Museum of the City of New York/Corbis; **p. 286** Bettmann/Corbis; **p. 319** Jeff Greenberg/PhotoEdit; **p. 344** *(top)* Getty Images, *(bottom)* Niall Benvie/Corbis; **p. 345** *(top to bottom)* Kevin Peterson/ Getty Images, RubberBall Productions, RubberBall Productions, Kevin Peterson/Getty Images, Barbara Penoyar/Getty Images, Kevin Peterson/Getty Images; **p. 354** Royalty-Free/ Corbis; **p. 376** RubberBall Productions; **p. 385** *(top)* Stockbyte, *(bottom)* Tony Freeman/ PhotoEdit; **p. 386** *(left)* Judd Pilossof/Getty Images, *(right)* Royalty-Free/Corbis; **p. 412** *(top)* Alan Becker/Getty Images, *(bottom)* Richard Cummins/Corbis; **p. 422** Jacobs Stock Photography/Getty Images; **p. 433** *(left)* Barbara Penoyar/Getty Images, *(right)* RubberBall Productions, *(bottom)* RubberBall Productions; **p. 438** Paul A. Souders/Corbis.

INTRODUCTION

The *Focus on Grammar* series

Written by ELT professionals, ***Focus on Grammar: An Integrated Skills Approach*** helps students to understand and practice English grammar. The primary aim of the course is for students to gain confidence in their ability to speak and write English accurately and fluently.

The **third edition** retains this popular series' focus on English grammar through lively listening, speaking, reading, and writing activities. The new ***Focus on Grammar*** also maintains the same five-level progression as the second edition:

- Level 1 (Beginning, formerly Introductory)
- Level 2 (High-Beginning, formerly Basic)
- Level 3 (Intermediate)
- Level 4 (High-Intermediate)
- Level 5 (Advanced)

What is the *Focus on Grammar* methodology?

Both controlled and communicative practice

While students expect and need to learn the formal rules of a language, it is crucial that they also practice new structures in a variety of contexts in order to internalize and master them. To this end, ***Focus on Grammar*** provides an abundance of both controlled and communicative exercises so that students can bridge the gap between knowing grammatical structures and using them. The many communicative activities in each Student Book unit provide opportunity for critical thinking while enabling students to personalize what they have learned in order to talk to one another with ease about hundreds of everyday issues.

A unique four-step approach

The series follows a four-step approach:

Step 1: Grammar in Context shows the new structures in natural contexts, such as articles and conversations.

Step 2: Grammar Presentation presents the structures in clear and accessible grammar charts, notes, and examples.

Step 3: Focused Practice of both form and meaning of the new structures is provided in numerous and varied controlled exercises.

Step 4: Communication Practice allows students to use the new structures freely and creatively in motivating, open-ended activities.

Thorough recycling

Underpinning the scope and sequence of the ***Focus on Grammar*** series is the belief that students need to use target structures many times, in different contexts, and at increasing levels of difficulty. For this reason, new grammar is constantly recycled throughout the book so that students have maximum exposure to the target forms and become comfortable using them in speech and in writing.

A complete classroom text and reference guide

A major goal in the development of ***Focus on Grammar*** has been to provide students with books that serve not only as vehicles for classroom instruction but also as resources for reference and self-study. In each Student Book, the combination of grammar charts, grammar notes, a glossary of grammar terms, and extensive appendices provides a complete and invaluable reference guide for students.

Ongoing assessment

Review Tests at the end of each part of the Student Book allow for continual self-assessment. In addition, the tests in the new ***Focus on Grammar*** Assessment Package provide teachers with a valid, reliable, and practical means of determining students' appropriate levels of placement in the course and of assessing students' achievement throughout the course. At Levels 4 (High-Intermediate) and 5 (Advanced), Proficiency Tests give teachers an overview of their students' general grammar knowledge.

What are the components of each level of *Focus on Grammar*?

Student Book

The Student Book is divided into eight or more parts, depending on the level. Each part contains grammatically related units, with each unit focusing on specific grammatical structures; where appropriate, units present contrasting forms. The exercises in each unit are thematically related to one another, and all units have the same clear, easy-to-follow format.

Teacher's Manual

The Teacher's Manual contains a variety of suggestions and information to enrich the material in the Student Book. It includes general teaching suggestions for each section of a typical unit, answers to frequently asked questions, unit-by-unit teaching tips with ideas for further communicative practice, and a supplementary activity section. Answers to the Student Book exercises and audioscripts of the listening activities are found at the back of the Teacher's Manual. Also included in the Teacher's Manual is a CD-ROM of teaching tools, including PowerPoint presentations that offer alternative ways of presenting selected grammar structures.

Workbook

The Workbook accompanying each level of ***Focus on Grammar*** provides additional exercises appropriate for self-study of the target grammar for each Student Book unit. Tests included in each Workbook provide students with additional opportunities for self-assessment.

Audio Program

All of the listening exercises from the Student Book, as well as the Grammar in Context passages and other appropriate exercises, are included on the program's CDs. In the book, the symbol 🎧 appears next to the listening exercises. Another symbol 🎧, indicating that listening is optional, appears next to the Grammar in Context passages and some exercises. All of these scripts appear in the Teacher's Manual and may be used as an alternative way of presenting the activities.

Some Student Books are packaged with a separate Student Audio CD. This CD includes the listening exercise from each unit and any other exercises that have an essential listening component.

CD-ROM

Focus on Grammar Interactive, Version 2, provides students with individualized practice and immediate feedback. Fully contextualized and interactive, the activities broaden and extend practice of the grammatical structures in the reading, writing, listening, and speaking skills areas. This CD-ROM includes grammar review, review tests, score-based remedial practice, games, and all relevant reference material from the Student Book. It can also be used in conjunction with the *Longman Interactive American Dictionary* CD-ROM.

Assessment Package (NEW)

An extensive, comprehensive Assessment Package has been developed for each level of the third edition of ***Focus on Grammar***. The components of the Assessment Package are:

1. **Placement, Diagnostic, and Achievement Tests**
   - a Placement Test to screen students and place them into the correct level
   - Diagnostic Tests for each part of the Student Book
   - Unit Achievement Tests for each unit of the Student Book
   - Part Achievement Tests for each part of the Student Book
2. **General Proficiency Tests**
   - two Proficiency Tests at Level 4 (High-Intermediate)
   - two Proficiency Tests at Level 5 (Advanced)

   These tests can be administered at any point in the course.
3. **Audio CD**

   The listening portions of the Placement, Diagnostic, and Achievement Tests are recorded on CDs. The scripts appear in the Assessment Package.
4. **Test-Generating Software**

   The test-bank software provides thousands of questions from which teachers can create class-appropriate tests. All items are labeled according to the grammar structure they are testing, so teachers can easily select relevant items; they can also design their own items to add to the tests.

Transparencies (NEW)

Transparencies of all the grammar charts in the Student Book are also available. These transparencies are a classroom visual aid that will help instructors point out important patterns and structures of grammar.

Companion Website

The companion website contains a wealth of information and activities for both teachers and students. In addition to general information about the course pedagogy, the website provides extensive practice exercises for the classroom, a language lab, or at home.

What's new in the third edition of the Student Book?

In response to users' requests, this edition has:

- a new four-color design
- easy-to-read color coding for the four steps
- new and updated reading texts for Grammar in Context
- post-reading activities (in addition to the pre-reading questions)
- more exercise items
- an editing (error analysis) exercise in each unit
- new writing activities
- an Internet activity in each unit
- a Glossary of Grammar Terms
- expanded Appendices

References

Alexander, L. G. (1988). *Longman English Grammar.* White Plains: Longman.

Biber, D., S. Conrad, E. Finegan, S. Johansson, and G. Leech (1999). *Longman Grammar of Spoken and Written English.* White Plains: Longman.

Celce-Murcia, M., and D. Freeman (1999). *The Grammar Book.* Boston: Heinle and Heinle.

Celce-Murcia, M., and S. Hilles (1988). *Techniques and Resources in Teaching Grammar.* New York: Oxford University Press.

Firsten, R. (2002). *The ELT Grammar Book.* Burlingame, CA: Alta Book Center Publishers.

Garner, B. (2003). *Garner's Modern American Usage.* New York: Oxford University Press.

Greenbaum, S. (1996). *The Oxford English Grammar.* New York: Oxford University Press.

Leech, G. (2004). *Meaning and the English Verb.* Harlow, UK: Pearson.

Lewis, M. (1997). *Implementing the Lexical Approach.* Hove East Sussex, UK: Language Teaching Publications.

Longman (2002). *Longman Dictionary of English Language and Culture.* Harlow, UK: Longman.

Willis, D. (2003). *Rules, Patterns and Words.* New York: Cambridge University Press.

TOUR OF A UNIT

Each unit in the ***Focus on Grammar*** series presents a specific grammar structure (or two, in case of a contrast) and develops a major theme, which is set by the opening text. All units follow the same unique **four-step approach**.

Step 1: Grammar in Context

The **reading** or **written conversation** in this section shows the grammar structure in a natural context. The high-interest text presents authentic language in a variety of real-life formats: magazine articles, web pages, questionnaires, and more. Students can listen to the text on an audio CD to get accustomed to the sound of the grammar structure in a natural context.

UNIT 20

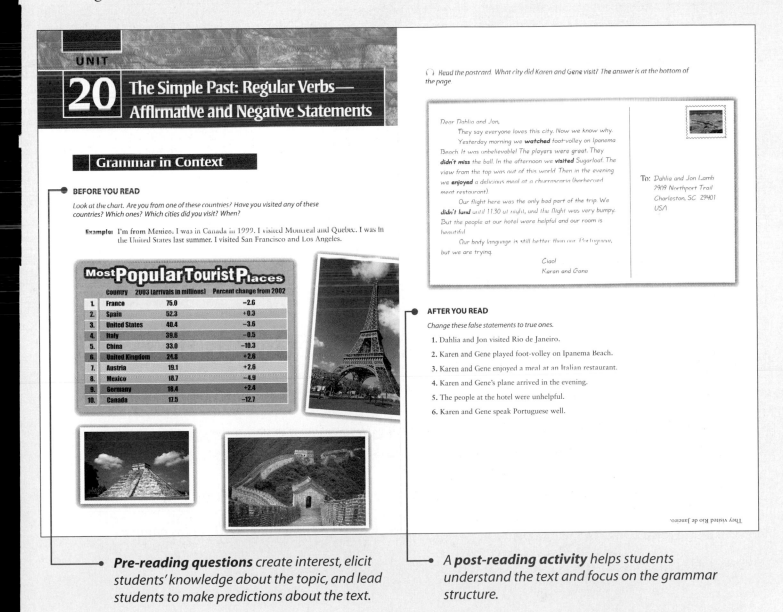

The Simple Past: Regular Verbs—Affirmative and Negative Statements

Grammar in Context

BEFORE YOU READ

Look at the chart. Are you from one of these countries? Have you visited any of these countries? Which ones? Which cities did you visit? When?

Example: I'm from Mexico. I was in Canada in 1999. I visited Montreal and Quebec. I was in the United States last summer. I visited San Francisco and Los Angeles.

Most Popular Tourist Places

	Country	2003 (arrivals in millions)	Percent change from 2002
1.	France	75.0	–2.6
2.	Spain	52.3	+0.3
3.	United States	40.4	–3.6
4.	Italy	39.6	–0.5
5.	China	33.0	–10.3
6.	United Kingdom	24.8	+2.6
7.	Austria	19.1	+2.6
8.	Mexico	18.7	–4.9
9.	Germany	18.4	+2.4
10.	Canada	17.5	–12.7

Read the postcard. What city did Karen and Gene visit? The answer is at the bottom of the page.

Dear Dahlia and Jon,

They say everyone loves this city. Now we know why.

Yesterday morning we **watched** foot-volley on Ipanema Beach. It was unbelievable! The players were great. They **didn't miss** the ball. In the afternoon we **visited** Sugarloaf. The view from the top was out of this world. Then in the evening we **enjoyed** a delicious meal at a churrascaria (barbecued meat restaurant).

Our flight here was the only bad part of the trip. We **didn't land** until 11:30 at night, and the flight was very bumpy. But the people at our hotel were helpful and our room is beautiful.

Our body language is still better than our Portuguese, but we are trying.

Ciao!

Karen and Gene

To: Dahlia and Jon Lamb
2909 Northport Trail
Charleston, SC 29401
USA

AFTER YOU READ

Change these false statements to true ones.

1. Dahlia and Jon visited Rio de Janeiro.
2. Karen and Gene played foot-volley on Ipanema Beach.
3. Karen and Gene enjoyed a meal at an Italian restaurant.
4. Karen and Gene's plane arrived in the evening.
5. The people at the hotel were unhelpful.
6. Karen and Gene speak Portuguese well.

They visited Rio de Janeiro.

Pre-reading questions *create interest, elicit students' knowledge about the topic, and lead students to make predictions about the text.*

*A **post-reading activity** helps students understand the text and focus on the grammar structure.*

Step 2: Grammar Presentation

This section is made up of grammar charts, notes, and examples. The **grammar charts** focus on the forms of the grammar structure. The **grammar notes** and **examples** focus on the meanings and uses of the structure.

*Clear and easy-to-read **grammar charts** present the grammar structure in all its forms and combinations.*

Grammar Presentation

PRESENT PROGRESSIVE: *YES/NO* QUESTIONS AND *WH-* QUESTIONS

Yes/No Questions		
Be	Subject	Base Form of Verb + *-ing*
Am	I	
Are	you	
Is	he she it	**working**?
Are	we you they	

Short Answers						
Affirmative			Negative			
	you	**are**.		you'**re**	
	I	**am**.		I'**m**	
Yes,	he she it	**is**.	No,	he'**s** she'**s** it'**s**	**not**.
	you we they	**are**.		you'**re** we'**re** they'**re**	

Wh- Questions			
Wh- Word	*Be*	Subject	Base Form of Verb + *-ing*
Why	are	you	staying home?
What	are	you	watching?
Who	is	he	meeting?
Where	are	they	going?

Answers
I'm sick.
The *I Love Lucy* show.
His teacher. He's meeting his teacher.
To the movies. They're going to the movies.

Wh- Questions about the Subject		
Wh- Word	*Be*	Base Form of Verb + *ing*
Who	is	reading?
What	is	happening?

Answers
My friend (is).
They're making candy.

*Each **grammar note** gives a short, simple explanation of one use of the structure. The accompanying **examples** ensure students' understanding of the point.*

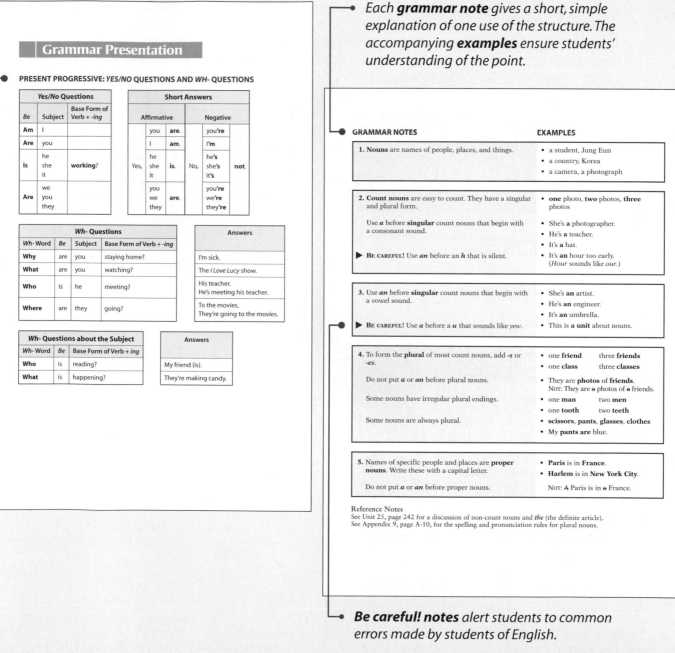

GRAMMAR NOTES	EXAMPLES
1. **Nouns** are names of people, places, and things.	• a student, Jung Eun • a country, Korea • a camera, a photograph
2. **Count nouns** are easy to count. They have a singular and plural form.	• **one** photo, **two** photos, **three** photos
Use *a* before **singular** count nouns that begin with a consonant sound.	• She's **a** photographer. • He's **a** teacher. • It's **a** hat.
▶ BE CAREFUL! Use *an* before an *h* that is silent.	• It's **an** hour too early. (*Hour* sounds like *our*.)
3. Use *an* before **singular** count nouns that begin with a vowel sound.	• She's **an** artist. • He's **an** engineer. • It's **an** umbrella.
▶ BE CAREFUL! Use *a* before a *u* that sounds like *yew*.	• This is **a unit** about nouns.
4. To form the **plural** of most count nouns, add *-s* or *-es*.	• one **friend** three **friends** • one **class** three **classes**
Do not put *a* or *an* before plural nouns.	• They are **photos** of **friends**. NOT: They are ~~a~~ photos of ~~a~~ friends.
Some nouns have irregular plural endings.	• one **man** two **men** • one **tooth** two **teeth**
Some nouns are always plural.	• **scissors**, **pants**, **glasses**, **clothes** • My **pants are** blue.
5. Names of specific people and places are **proper nouns**. Write these with a capital letter.	• **Paris** is in **France**. • **Harlem** is in **New York City**.
Do not put *a* or *an* before proper nouns.	NOT: ~~A~~ Paris is in ~~a~~ France.

Reference Notes

See Unit 25, page 242 for a discussion of non-count nouns and *the* (the definite article).
See Appendix 9, page A-10, for the spelling and pronunciation rules for plural nouns.

***Be careful!* notes** *alert students to common errors made by students of English.*

Step 3: Focused Practice

This section provides students with a variety of contextualized **controlled exercises** to practice both the forms and the uses of the grammar structure.

*Focused Practice always begins with a "for recognition only" exercise called **Discover the Grammar**.*

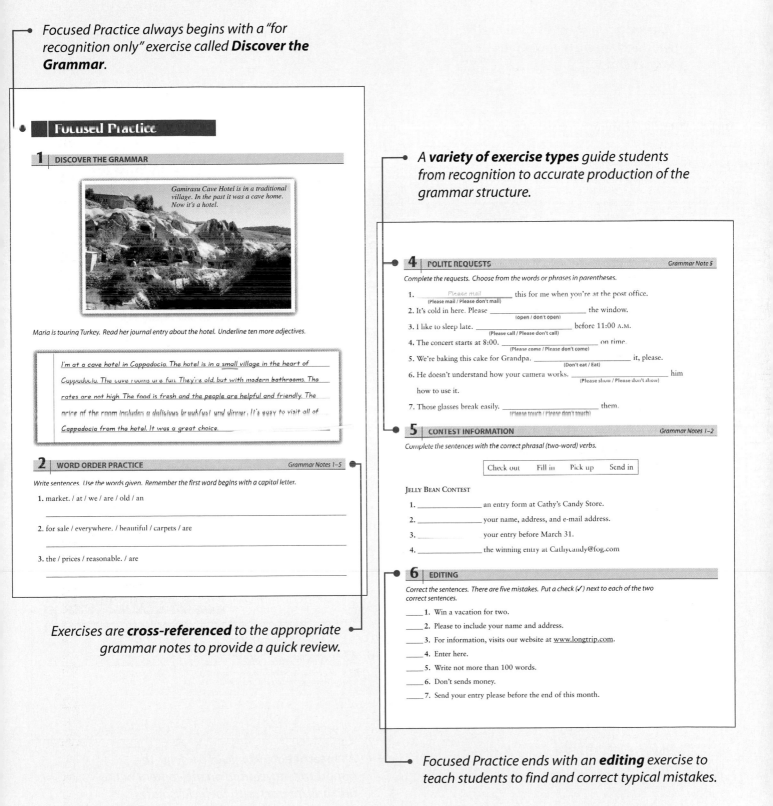

Focused Practice

1 | DISCOVER THE GRAMMAR

Gamirasu Cave Hotel is in a traditional village. In the past it was a cave home. Now it's a hotel.

Maria is touring Turkey. Read her journal entry about the hotel. Underline ten more adjectives.

> I'm at a cave hotel in Cappadocia. The hotel is in a small village in the heart of Cappadocia. The cave rooms are fun. They're old, but with modern bathrooms. The rates are not high. The food is fresh and the people are helpful and friendly. The price of the room includes a delicious breakfast and dinner. It's easy to visit all of Cappadocia from the hotel. It was a great choice.

2 | WORD ORDER PRACTICE — *Grammar Notes 1–5*

Write sentences. Use the words given. Remember the first word begins with a capital letter.

1. market. / at / we / are / old / an
____
2. for sale / everywhere. / beautiful / carpets / are
____
3. the / prices / reasonable. / are
____

*Exercises are **cross-referenced** to the appropriate grammar notes to provide a quick review.*

*A **variety of exercise types** guide students from recognition to accurate production of the grammar structure.*

4 | POLITE REQUESTS — *Grammar Note 5*

Complete the requests. Choose from the words or phrases in parentheses.

1. ___*Please mail*___ (Please mail / Please don't mail) this for me when you're at the post office.
2. It's cold in here. Please _______________ (open / don't open) the window.
3. I like to sleep late. _______________ (Please call / Please don't call) before 11:00 A.M.
4. The concert starts at 8:00. _______________ (Please come / Please don't come) on time.
5. We're baking this cake for Grandpa. _______________ (Don't eat / Eat) it, please.
6. He doesn't understand how your camera works. _______________ (Please show / Please don't show) him how to use it.
7. Those glasses break easily. _______________ (Please touch / Please don't touch) them.

5 | CONTEST INFORMATION — *Grammar Notes 1–2*

Complete the sentences with the correct phrasal (two-word) verbs.

Check out	Fill in	Pick up	Send in

JELLY BEAN CONTEST

1. _______________ an entry form at Cathy's Candy Store.
2. _______________ your name, address, and e-mail address.
3. _______________ your entry before March 31.
4. _______________ the winning entry at Cathycandy@fog.com

6 | EDITING

Correct the sentences. There are five mistakes. Put a check (✓) next to each of the two correct sentences.

____ 1. Win a vacation for two.
____ 2. Please to include your name and address.
____ 3. For information, visits our website at www.longtrip.com.
____ 4. Enter here.
____ 5. Write not more than 100 words.
____ 6. Don't sends money.
____ 7. Send your entry please before the end of this month.

*Focused Practice ends with an **editing** exercise to teach students to find and correct typical mistakes.*

Step 4: Communication Practice

This section provides open-ended **communicative activities** giving students the opportunity to use the grammar structure appropriately and fluently.

- *A **listening** activity gives students the opportunity to check their aural comprehension.*

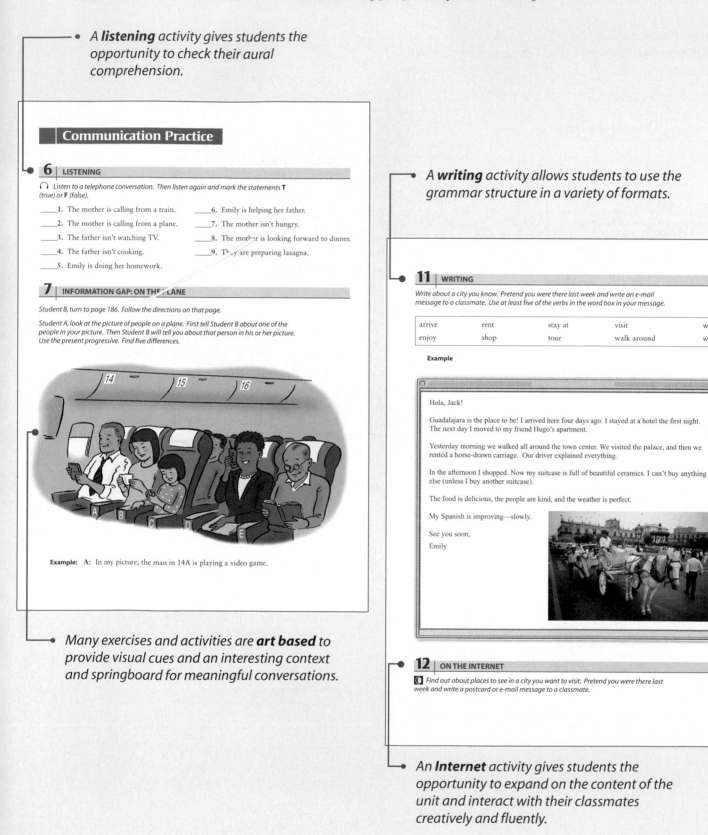

Communication Practice

6 | LISTENING

Listen to a telephone conversation. Then listen again and mark the statements **T** *(true) or* **F** *(false).*

_____1. The mother is calling from a train.
_____2. The mother is calling from a plane.
_____3. The father isn't watching TV.
_____4. The father isn't cooking.
_____5. Emily is doing her homework.
_____6. Emily is helping her father.
_____7. The mother isn't hungry.
_____8. The mother is looking forward to dinner.
_____9. They are preparing lasagna.

7 | INFORMATION GAP: ON THE PLANE

Student B, turn to page 186. Follow the directions on that page.

Student A, look at the picture of people on a plane. First tell Student B about one of the people in your picture. Then Student B will tell you about that person in his or her picture. Use the present progressive. Find five differences.

Example: A: In my picture, the man in 14A is playing a video game.

- *Many exercises and activities are **art based** to provide visual cues and an interesting context and springboard for meaningful conversations.*

- *A **writing** activity allows students to use the grammar structure in a variety of formats.*

11 | WRITING

Write about a city you know. Pretend you were there last week and write an e-mail message to a classmate. Use at least five of the verbs in the word box in your message.

arrive	rent	stay at	visit	want
enjoy	shop	tour	walk around	watch

Example

Hola, Jack!

Guadalajara is the place to be! I arrived here four days ago. I stayed at a hotel the first night. The next day I moved to my friend Hugo's apartment.

Yesterday morning we walked all around the town center. We visited the palace, and then we rented a horse-drawn carriage. Our driver explained everything.

In the afternoon I shopped. Now my suitcase is full of beautiful ceramics. I can't buy anything else (unless I buy another suitcase).

The food is delicious, the people are kind, and the weather is perfect.

My Spanish is improving—slowly.

See you soon,
Emily

12 | ON THE INTERNET

Find out about places to see in a city you want to visit. Pretend you were there last week and write a postcard or e-mail message to a classmate.

- *An **Internet** activity gives students the opportunity to expand on the content of the unit and interact with their classmates creatively and fluently.*

TOUR BEYOND THE UNIT

In the ***Focus on Grammar*** series, the grammatically related units are grouped into parts, and each part concludes with a section called **From Grammar to Writing** and a **Review Test** section.

From Grammar to Writing

This section presents a point which applies specifically to writing, for example, avoiding sentence fragments. Students are guided to practice the point in a **piece of extended writing**.

- *An **introduction** relates the grammar point to the writing focus.*
- ***Writing formats** include business letters, personal letters, notes, instructions, paragraphs, reports, and essays.*

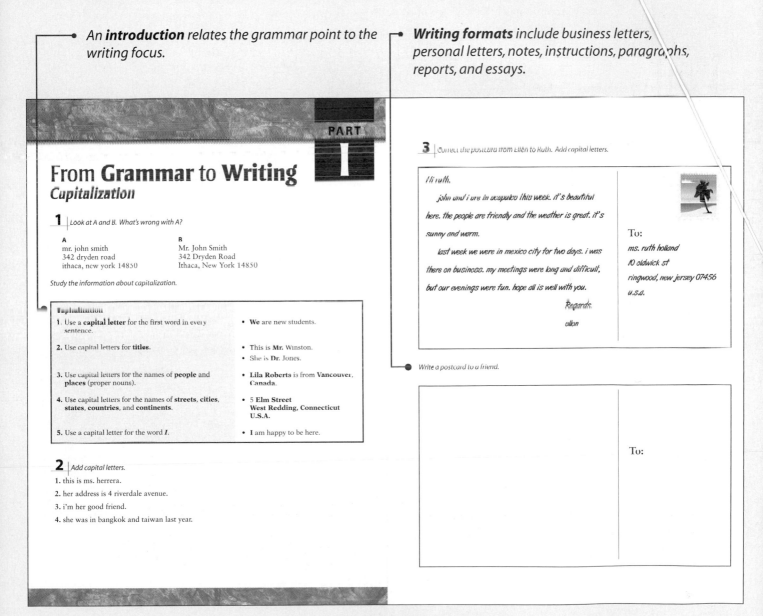

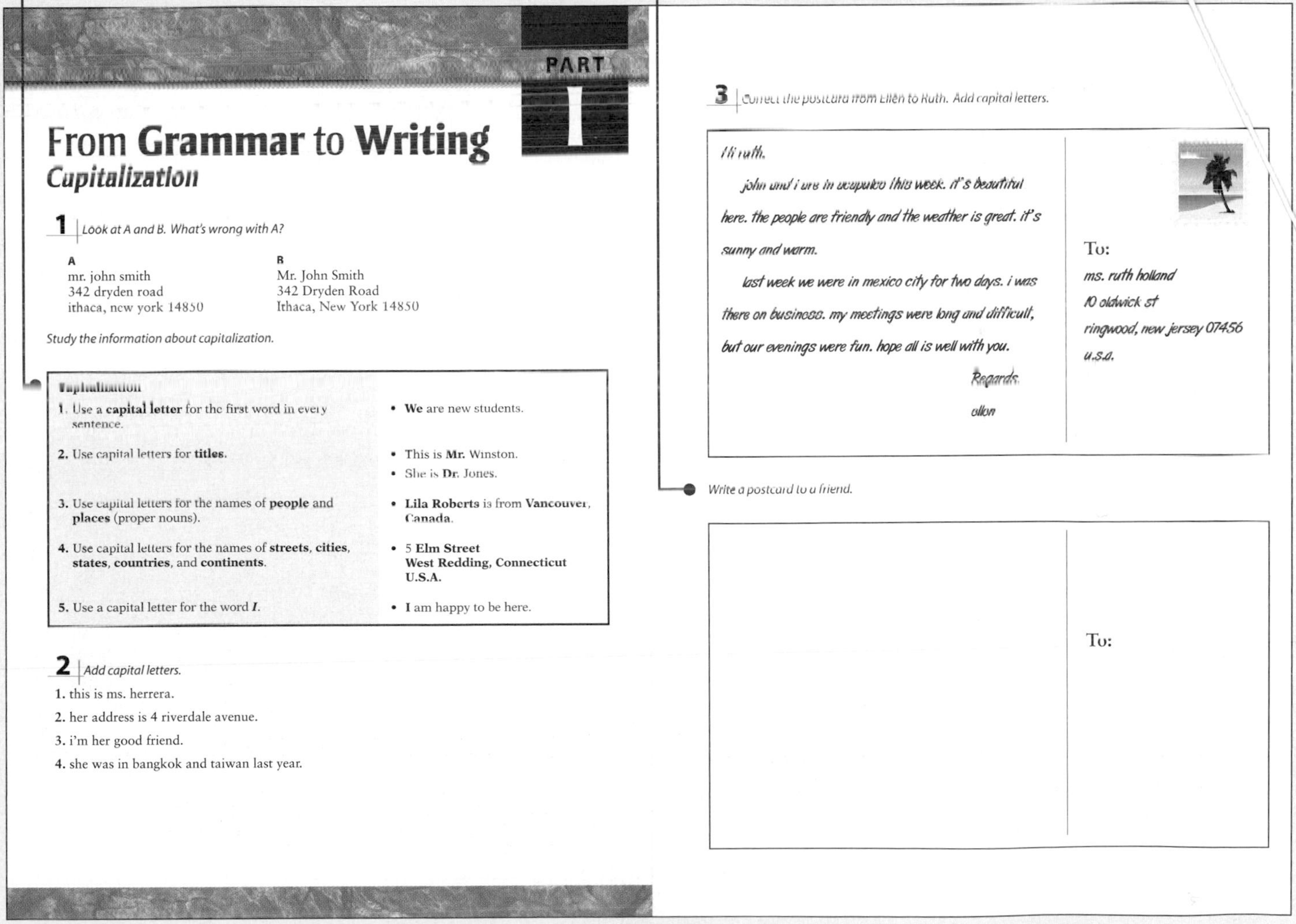

PART I

From Grammar to Writing
Capitalization

1 Look at A and B. What's wrong with A?

A	B
mr. john smith 342 dryden road ithaca, new york 14850	Mr. John Smith 342 Dryden Road Ithaca, New York 14850

Study the information about capitalization.

Capitalization	
1. Use a **capital letter** for the first word in every sentence.	• **We** are new students.
2. Use capital letters for **titles**.	• This is **Mr.** Winston. • She is **Dr.** Jones.
3. Use capital letters for the names of **people** and **places** (proper nouns).	• **Lila Roberts** is from **Vancouver**, **Canada**.
4. Use capital letters for the names of **streets**, **cities**, **states**, **countries**, and **continents**.	• 5 **Elm Street** **West Redding**, **Connecticut** **U.S.A.**
5. Use a capital letter for the word *I*.	• **I** am happy to be here.

2 Add capital letters.

1. this is ms. herrera.
2. her address is 4 riverdale avenue.
3. i'm her good friend.
4. she was in bangkok and taiwan last year.

3 Correct the postcard from Ellen to Ruth. Add capital letters.

Hi ruth,
john and i are in acapulco this week. it's beautiful here. the people are friendly and the weather is great. it's sunny and warm.
last week we were in mexico city for two days. i was there on business. my meetings were long and difficult, but our evenings were fun. hope all is well with you.
Regards,
ellen

To:
ms. ruth holland
10 oldwick st
ringwood, new jersey 07456
u.s.a.

Write a postcard to a friend.

To:

Review Test

This review section, covering all the grammar structures presented in the part, can be used as a test. An **Answer Key** is provided at the back of the book.

The Review Tests *include* ***multiple-choice questions*** *in standardized test formats, giving students practice in test taking.*

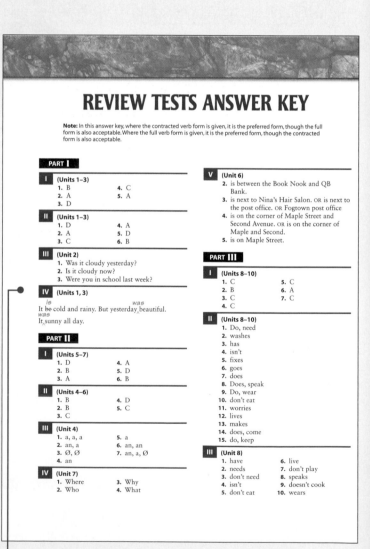

PART VIII

Review Test

I *Read each conversation. Circle the letter of the underlined word or group of words that is not correct.*

1. A: I don't know [A] him very well. Does he work [B] on Mondays? — A B C D
   B: I don't think [C] so. He works usually [D] on Tuesdays and Thursdays.

2. A: Does she like black coffee [A]? — A B C D
   B: No, she doesn't [B]. She prefers [C] drink [D] coffee with milk and sugar.

3. A: How often [A] do you changing [B] the oil? — A B C D
   B: Every three months [C]. I usually check [D] my tires too.

4. A: What did [A] he do [B] after the concert? — A B C D
   B: He met [C] some friends and go to a club [D].

II *Circle the letter of the correct word(s) to complete the sentences.*

1. Where ____ last night? — A B C D
   (A) you went
   (B) are you going
   (C) did you go
   (D) did you went

2. Who ____ you at the airport yesterday? — A B C D
   (A) did meet
   (B) is meeting
   (C) met
   (D) meets

REVIEW TESTS ANSWER KEY

Note: In this answer key, where the contracted verb form is given, it is the preferred form, though the full form is also acceptable. Where the full verb form is given, it is the preferred form, though the contracted form is also acceptable.

PART I

I (Units 1–3)
1. B
2. A
3. D
4. C
5. A

II (Units 1–3)
1. D
2. A
3. C
4. A
5. D
6. B

III (Unit 2)
1. Was it cloudy yesterday?
2. Is it cloudy now?
3. Were you in school last week?

IV (Units 1, 3)
It ~~be~~ *is* cold and rainy. But yesterday *was* beautiful. It *was* sunny all day.

PART II

I (Units 5–7)
1. D
2. B
3. A
4. A
5. D
6. B

II (Units 4–6)
1. B
2. B
3. C
4. D
5. C

III (Unit 4)
1. a, a, a
2. an, a
3. Ø, Ø
4. an
5. a
6. an, an
7. an, a, Ø

IV (Unit 7)
1. Where
2. Who
3. Why
4. What

V (Unit 6)
2. is between the Book Nook and QB Bank.
3. is next to Nina's Hair Salon. OR is next to the post office. OR Fogtown post office
4. is on the corner of Maple Street and Second Avenue. OR is on the corner of Maple and Second.
5. is on Maple Street.

PART III

I (Units 8–10)
1. C
2. B
3. C
4. C
5. C
6. A
7. C

II (Units 8–10)
1. Do, need
2. washes
3. has
4. isn't
5. fixes
6. goes
7. does
8. Does, speak
9. Do, wear
10. don't eat
11. worries
12. lives
13. makes
14. does, come
15. do, keep

III (Unit 8)
1. have
2. needs
3. don't need
4. isn't
5. don't eat
6. live
7. don't play
8. speaks
9. doesn't cook
10. wears

The Review Tests Answer Key *provides* ***cross-references*** *to the appropriate unit(s) for easy review.*

ACKNOWLEDGMENTS

A series requires the coordination of many people. Managing all aspects of a series is a daunting task. Laura Le Dréan, the series director, put her heart and soul into managing this project. I thank her for her superb handling of the series, and for her commitment to this book. Her grammar expertise and thoughtful comments were invaluable. It has been my pleasure to work with her.

I also wish to thank my development editor Paula Van Ells. Her good ear for language helped to refine many activities. In addition, I am particularly grateful for her input in developing the new Internet and writing activities.

Aerin Csigay researched and found great photos to make the pages come alive. In the production department, Laurie Neaman, Ann France, Linda Moser, and Rhea Banker put a great deal of effort into making the art and page makeup useful and appealing. To all of them, I am grateful.

I thank my colleagues at the International English Language Institute, Michelle Thomas and Gretchen Irwin, for their enthusiastic response to my changes from the second edition, as well as for their excellent suggestions.

My former student, Hye Won Paik Mohanram, who has recently become a teacher herself, gave excellent suggestions based on her knowledge of English language problems for Korean speakers.

Ellen Shaw reviewed the first few units. Her insight into what should be modified from the second edition was always on target. In addition, I thank the many reviewers of this new edition.

I am ever grateful to Joanne Dresner. The series would not have existed had it not been for her foresight.

As always, I thank my family—Dan, and Dahlia and now Jonathan—for their love and support. And I dedicate this book to Harris, whose love of language and encouragement have always been an inspiration.

I. E. S.

PART I

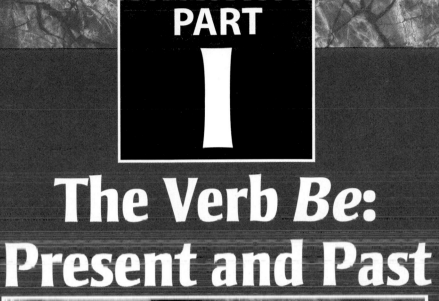

The Verb *Be*: Present and Past

Introducing Yourself

THE FIRST DAY OF CLASS

Two students meet outside an English class. Read their conversation.

SHANA: Is this room 2? Basic English?

MARCY: Yes, it is.

SHANA: Great. I'm Shana McCabe.

MARCY: Hi, I'm Marceline Costa.

SHANA: Nice to meet you.

MARCY: Nice to meet you too.

SHANA: So, your first name is Marceline?

MARCY: Yes, but everyone calls me Marcy.

SHANA: OK, Marcy. Is that M-A-R-C-Y?

MARCY: Yes, it is.

THE ALPHABET

Listen and repeat the letters of the alphabet.

Aa Bb Cc Dd Ee Ff Gg Hh Ii Jj Kk Ll Mm Nn Oo Pp Qq Rr Ss Tt Uu Vv Ww Xx Yy Zz

CONVERSATION PRACTICE

Read this conversation. Work with a partner. Practice the conversation. Use your own name.

A: What's your name?

B: Marceline Costa, but everyone calls me Marcy.

A: OK, Marcy. How do you spell that?

B: M-A-R-C-Y.

A: Nice to meet you.

B: Nice to meet you too.

Write the names of your classmates in a notebook.

UNIT

1 The Present of *Be*: Statements

Grammar in Context

BEFORE YOU READ

Mark these statements **T** *(true) or* **F** *(false). Put a* **?** *(question mark) if you don't know.*

__T__ David Beckham is a soccer player.

__F__ David Beckham is from Brazil.

__F__ Posh Spice is a soccer player.

__F__ Posh Spice is from the United States.

__F__ David and Posh are friends.

Read this article about the people in the photos.

POP Culture News

TALENTED PEOPLE

David Beckham **is** a soccer player. He**'s** from England. David**'s** married to Posh Spice. Her real name **is** Victoria Adams. Their home **is** in England. It**'s** big. They call their home Beckingham Palace. David and Victoria **are** rich and famous. They**'re** popular all over the world.

Ramon Gomes **is** from Rio de Janeiro. He likes Beckham and he likes soccer. But Beckham **isn't** his favorite soccer player. And soccer **isn't** his favorite sport. His favorite player **is** Ronaldo. His favorite sport **is** foot-volley.

Foot-volley **is** a new game. It**'s** a combination of soccer and volleyball. Ramon plays foot-volley every day. His dream **is** to become the world foot-volley champion.

AFTER YOU READ

A *Mark these statements* **T** *(true) or* **F** *(false).*

__F__ **1.** David Beckham is from Korea.

__T__ **2.** Ramon Gomes is from Brazil.

__T__ **3.** Ramon is a foot-volley player.

B *Complete the sentences.*

1. David and Victoria: They __'re__ **('re / 're not)** from England.
2. Foot-volley: It __'s__ **('s / isn't)** a combination of soccer and volleyball.
3. Ramon says: "Soccer __is not__ **(is / is not)** my favorite sport."

Grammar Presentation

THE PRESENT OF *BE*: STATEMENTS

AFFIRMATIVE STATEMENTS

Singular		
Subject	***Be***	
I	**am**	popular.
You	**are**	
David He	**is**	
Victoria She		
Soccer It		

Plural		
Subject	***Be***	
Masami and I We	**are**	students.
You and Josh You		
Ivona and Juan They		
Seoul and London They		cities.

Contractions			
I am →	**I'm**	we are →	**we're**
you are →	**you're**	you are →	**you're**
he is →	**he's**	they are →	**they're**
she is →	**she's**	David is →	**David's**
it is →	**it's**		

(continued)

NEGATIVE STATEMENTS AND CONTRACTIONS (SHORT FORMS)

Singular	
Subject + *Be/Not*	
I **am not** I'**m not**	from London.
You **are not** You'**re not** You **aren't**	from London.
His **is not** He'**s not** He **isn't**	from London.
She **is not** She'**s not** She **isn't**	from London.
It **is not** It'**s not** It **isn't**	new.

Plural	
Subject + *Be/Not*	
We **are not** We'**re not** We **aren't**	in London.
You **are not** You'**re not** You **aren't**	in London.
They **are not** They'**re not** They **aren't**	in London.

GRAMMAR NOTES / EXAMPLES

1. Sentences have a **subject** and a **verb**.

The **subject** is a noun or a pronoun.

Subject pronouns (*I, you, he, she, it, we, you, they*) replace subject nouns.

▶ **BE CAREFUL!** You cannot make a sentence without a subject. You cannot make a sentence without a verb. You cannot put a subject pronoun right after a subject noun.

subject verb
- **Ramon Gomes is** from Brazil.

subject noun
- **David Beckham is** a soccer player.

subject pronoun
- **He is** from England.

NOT: ~~Is from~~ England.

NOT: ~~He from~~ England.

NOT: David ~~he~~ is from England.

2. The **present of *be*** has three forms: ***am, is, are***.

- I **am** a student.
- He **is** from Brazil.
- They **are** famous.

3. Use the verb ***be*** before **nouns**, **adjectives**, or **prepositional phrases**. A noun can be **singular** (one) or **plural** (more than one). Plural nouns usually end in *-s*.	singular noun • He is a **singer**. plural noun • They are **singers**. adjective • It is **big**. prepositional phrase • Emiko is **in New York**.
4. Use the correct form of ***be*** + ***not*** to make a **negative statement**.	• I **am not** from England. • It **is not** popular. • We **are not** famous.
5. Use **contractions** (short forms) in speaking and informal writing. There are two negative contractions for ***is not*** and ***are not***.	• I**'m** from Mexico. • I**'m not** from Ecuador. • Mr. Crane**'s** from Los Angeles. • It**'s not** popular. OR It **isn't** popular. • We**'re not** single. OR We **aren't** single.

Notes

For definitions and examples of grammar terms, see Glossary on page G-1.

Focused Practice

1 DISCOVER THE GRAMMAR

Check (✓) the negative statements. Circle the contractions (short forms).

__✓__ 1. David is not in England.

_____ 2. He's in Spain.

_____ 3. His eyes are blue.

__✓__ 4. They're not brown.

__✓__ 5. His hair is not black.

_____ 6. It's blond.

__✓__ 7. Ramon is not from England.

_____ 8. He's not a singer.

2 | THE VERB *BE* — *Grammar Note 2*

Complete the sentences with **am, is,** *or* **are**.

1. Ronaldo ___is___ a soccer player. He ___is___ from Brazil.
2. Soccer ___is___ popular in Brazil. It ___is___ the number one sport there.
3. I ___am___ not a soccer player. I ___am___ a soccer fan.
4. My friends and I ___are___ soccer fans. We love the game.

3 | *BEND IT LIKE BECKHAM* — *Grammar Notes 1–4*

Complete the sentences. Use the full form.

Parminder Nagra ___is___ (1.) an actor. She ___is___ (2.) the star of the movie *Bend It Like Beckham*. It ___is___ (3.) a comedy. In the movie, Nagra ___is___ (4.) a young Indian girl in England. She ___is___ (5.) a good soccer player and she loves soccer. But her parents ___are___ (6.) traditional. They ___aren't___ (7. (not)) happy. They don't want her to play soccer. They say, "Soccer ___is not___ (8. (not)) for girls. Marriage ___is___ (9.) for girls. Look at your sister." She says, "I ___am not___ (10. (not)) my sister."

Listen and check your work.

4 WHAT'S TRUE?

Grammar Notes 1–5

Write true sentences. Use the words in parentheses. Use contractions.

1. (I / a student.) I'm a student.
2. (I / from London.) I'm not from London.
3. David Beckham is a soccer player. (He / famous in this country.) He's famous in this country.
4. Soccer is a great game. (It / popular in my country.) It is popular in my country.
5. Ronaldo is from Rio. (He / Brazilian.) He is from Brazilian.
6. Ronaldo and Beckham are famous. (They / great soccer players.) They are great soccer players.
7. (My friend and I / big soccer fans.) My friend and I are big soccer fans.

5 PRONOUNS

Grammar Note 5

Change the underlined nouns to pronouns. Use contractions of **be**.

1. Ronaldo is from Brazil. ~~Ronaldo is~~ He's a great soccer player.
2. Mr. Smith is a soccer fan. ~~Mr. Smith is~~ He's a baseball fan too.
3. My partner and I are new students. ~~My partner and I are~~ We're not in class now.
4. Soccer is a great sport. ~~Soccer is~~ It's popular all over the world.
5. Parminder Nagra and Halle Berry are actors. ~~Nagra and Berry are~~ They're talented.
6. Ms. Brown is an English teacher. ~~Ms. Brown is~~ She's a supervisor too.
7. Tennis and ping-pong are my favorite sports. ~~Tennis and ping-pong are~~ They're exciting games.

6 EDITING

Correct this short paragraph. There are seven mistakes. The first mistake is already corrected.

My family is in Brazil. My parents ~~they~~ are teachers. Alessandra is my sister. She is an engineer. Marco ~~be~~ is my brother. ~~Is~~ He's a businessman. They are far away, but thanks to e-mail, ~~we~~ we're close.

Communication Practice

7 | LISTENING

Work with a partner. Look at the chart. Do you know these talented people? Try and complete the chart with words from the box. Follow the example. Then listen and check your guesses.

Example: A: Who is Hideki Matsui?
B: He's a soccer player from Japan.
A: He's from Japan, but he's not a soccer player. He's a baseball player.

baseball player	Japan	singer	the United States
Colombia	Mexico	soccer player	writer
England	movie director	Taiwan	

Person	 *Hideki Matsui*	 *Mia Hamm*	 *Ang Lee*	 *Steven Spielberg*
Job	*baseball player*	soccer player	movie director	movie director
Country	Japan	the United states	Taiwan	the United states.

Person	 *Paulina Rubio*	 *Beyoncé*	 *J.K. Rowling*	 *Gabriel Garcia Marquez*
Job	singer	singer	writer	writer
Country	Mexico	the united states.	England	colombia

8 | GEOGRAPHY GAME

Work with a partner. Student A reads sentences 1–4. Student B reads sentences 5–8. After each sentence, your partner says, **That's right** *or* **That's wrong** *and corrects the wrong sentences. (See the map in Appendix 1, page A-1).*

Examples: **A:** São Paulo is in Brazil.
B: That's right.

A: France is in Paris.
B: That's wrong. France isn't in Paris. Paris is in France.

Student A

1. Great Britain is in Africa.
2. Mongolia is near China.
3. The United States is in Argentina.
4. Australia is near the United States.

Student B

5. Mali is in Asia.
6. France is not near Spain.
7. Taiwan is near Hong Kong.
8. Canada is in Vancouver.

Now use the map and make more statements about the world. Your partner answers **That's right** *or* **That's wrong** *and corrects the wrong statements.*

9 | WRITING

Write about a talented person.

Example: Pedro is my brother. He's 19 years old. He's in Mexico. He's a musician. He plays the guitar. He's talented. I think his music is great. Pedro is not famous now. But one day everyone will know him.

10 | ON THE INTERNET

Search for information about one of the people in Exercise 7. Write two new things about that person. Read your sentences to the class. Do not say the name of the person. The class guesses who it is.

Example: **A:** This person is the director of *Jaws*, *Jurassic Park*, *Indiana Jones and the Temple of Doom*, and *Schindler's List*. George Lucas, the director of *Star Wars*, is his friend. They made the film *Raiders of the Lost Ark* together.
B: It's Steven Spielberg.

UNIT

2 The Present of *Be*: *Yes/No* Questions

Grammar in Context

BEFORE YOU READ

Are you usually early? Are you late? Are you on time?

It's the first day of an English class. Read this conversation.

ARRIVING IN CLASS

CLAUDIA OLIVERA: Excuse me. **Am I** late for class?

AL BROWN: **No, you're not.**

CLAUDIA: Whew! **Is the teacher** here?

AL: **Yes, he is.**

CLAUDIA: **Are you** new here?

AL: **Yes, I am.**

CLAUDIA: Me, too.

AL: What's your name?

CLAUDIA: I'm Claudia Olivera.

AL: Nice to meet you. I'm Al Brown. **Are you** from Latin America?

CLAUDIA: **Yes, I am.** I'm from Mexico. What about you?

AL: I'm from Michigan.

CLAUDIA: Michigan? Michigan's in the United States. So you're American. Then you're not a student in this class.

AL: You're right. I'm not a student. I'm a teacher. I'm your new English teacher.

Now read the conversation with a partner.

AFTER YOU READ

Answer the questions with **Yes, No,** *or* **I don't know.**

1. Are the man and woman late? No, they aren't
2. Is the woman from Mexico? Yes, she is
3. Is Michigan in the United States? Yes, it is
4. Are the man and woman students? The woman is a student. The man isn't.
5. Is the school in Michigan? I don't know

Grammar Presentation

THE PRESENT OF *BE*: *YES/NO* QUESTIONS AND SHORT ANSWERS

YES/NO QUESTIONS

verb	Singular	
Be	**Subject**	
Am	I	in room 2?
Are	you	
Is	he	
	she	
	it	

verb	Plural	
Be	**Subject**	
Are	we	on time?
	you	
	they	

SHORT ANSWERS

Singular			
Yes		***No***	
Yes,	you **are**.	**No,**	you**'re not**. you **aren't**.
	I **am**.		I**'m not**.
	he **is**.		he**'s not**. he **isn't**.
	she **is**.		she**'s not**. she **isn't**.
	it **is**.		it**'s not**. it **isn't**.

Plural			
Yes		***No***	
Yes,	you **are**.	**No,**	you**'re not**. you **aren't**.
	we **are**.		we**'re not**. we **aren't**.
	they **are**.		they**'re not**. they **aren't**.

(continued)

OTHER SHORT ANSWERS

Yes.	Yes, I think so.
No.	No, I don't think so.
I don't know.	

GRAMMAR NOTES	EXAMPLES
1. In ***yes/no* questions with *be***, a form of *be* comes before the subject.	*be* / *subject* • **Are** you from Canada? • **Is** he late? • **Am** I on time?
2. We usually answer *yes/no* questions with **short answers**. ▶ **BE CAREFUL!** Don't use contractions in short answers with *yes*.	**A:** Are you new here? **B: Yes.** OR **Yes, I am.** **C: No.** OR **No, I'm not.** NOT: YES, ~~I'm.~~
3. We sometimes answer *yes/no* questions with **long answers**. You can use contractions in long answers with *yes*.	**A:** Are they students? **B: Yes, they are students.** OR **Yes, they're students.**
4. When we are not sure of an answer, we say, **"I don't know."** When we think something is true, we say, **"Yes, I think so."** or **"I think so."** When we think something is not true, we say, **"No, I don't think so."** or **"I don't think so."**	**A:** Is Sydney the capital of Australia? **B: I don't know.** **A:** Is she a good athlete? **B: Yes, I think so.** OR **I think so.** **A:** Is it hot today? **B: No, I don't think so.** OR **I don't think so.**

Focused Practice

1 DISCOVER THE GRAMMAR

Look at the picture. Match the questions and answers.

f	1. Is the door open?	a. Yes, he is.
c	2. Is it ten o'clock on September 1?	b. I don't know.
a	3. Is the teacher a man?	c. Yes, it is.
h	4. Are the students hungry?	d. Yes, I think so.
e	5. Are the books open?	e. Yes, they are.
g	6. Is the woman at the door early?	f. No, it's not.
d	7. Is the woman at the door unhappy?	g. No, she's late.

2 ASKING *YES/NO* QUESTIONS

Grammar Note 1

Write **yes/no** *questions about the statements in parentheses.*

1. **A:** (It's September 2.) *Is it September 2?*
   B: No, it's not. It's the first.
2. **A:** (Today is Tuesday.) Is today Tuesday?
   B: Yes, it is.
3. **A:** (We are in the right room.) Are we in the right room?
   B: I think so.

(continued)

4. **A:** (You are a new student.) Are you a new student?
   B: No, I'm not. This is my second year.
5. **A:** (She is the teacher.) Is she the teacher?
   B: I'm not sure. I think so.
6. **A:** (It's ten o'clock.) Is it ten o'clock?
   B: Yes. It's ten.
7. **A:** (They are in our class.) Are thay in our class?
   B: I don't know.
8. **A:** (This is your pen.) Excuse me, Excuse me, Is this your pen?
   B: No, I don't think so.
9. **A:** (Kaori and Marco are here.) Are Kaori and Marco here?
   B: Kaori is here, but Marco is absent.
10. **A:** (I'm in the right room.) Am I in the right room?
    B: Yes, you are.

* 3 | WORD ORDER PRACTICE *Grammar Notes 1–2*

*Write **yes/no** questions. Use the words given. Then answer the question. Write true short answers. Use contractions (short forms) when possible.*

1. you / Are / usually early
   A: *Are you usually early?*
   B: *Yes, I am.* OR *No, I'm not.*
2. your watch / from Switzerland / Is
   A: Is your watch from Switzerland?
   B: No, It isn't.
3. comfortable / Are / your shoes
   A: Are your shoes comfortable?
   B: Yes, they are.
4. Are / expensive / camera phones / in your country
   A: Are camera phones expensive in your country?
   B: Yes, they are.
5. your name / Is / easy to pronounce (say)
   A: Is your name easy to pronounce?
   B: Yes, It is.

6. Tasmania / in Australia / Is

   A: Is Tasmania in Australia?

   B: No, It isn't!

7. different cities / Are / from / you and your classmates

   A: Are you and your classmates from different cities?

   B: Yes, we are.

8. busy / Are / your classmates / now

   A: Are your classmates busy now?

   B: Yes, they are.

ทำไมเด็กที่
คนที่เค้ามีปัญหาและเขียนจดหมายไปในหนังสือพิมพ์

4 | LETTERS TO AND FROM A PSYCHOLOGIST

Grammar Notes 1–2, 4

A *Read the e-mail message. Write* **yes/no** *questions. Use the words given. Then answer the questions with short answers.*

Dear Dr. Brown,

I have two good friends. I like them a lot. They're fun and interesting. But there's one problem. They're always late. You're a psychologist. Please, tell me why. Thank you.

Molly

1. Molly / always late

   A: *Is Molly always late?*

   B: *No, she's not.* OR *No, she isn't.*

2. her friends / interesting and fun

   A: Is her friends intersting and fun?

   B: Yes, they are.

3. her friends / on time

   A: Is her friends on time?

   B: No, they aren't.

4. Dr. Brown / a psychologist

   A: Is Dr. Brown a psychologist?

   B: Yes, he is.

B *Now read Dr. Brown's answer. Write* **yes/no** *questions. Use the words given. Then answer the questions with* **Yes, I think so., No, I don't think so.,** *or* **I don't know.**

Dear Molly,

You're unhappy because your friends are late.

There are different reasons why people are late. Maybe they think, "I'm late. That means I'm important." It's hard to do something about that. But maybe your friends are late, and they don't know it's a problem for you. Tell them. They may change. Or perhaps your friends are bad at planning their time. Try and help them.

Good luck.

Sincerely,

Maria Brown, Ph.D.

1. Molly / unhappy

   A: *Is Molly unhappy?*

   B: *Yes, I think so.*

2. her friends / unhappy

   A: Is her friend unhappy?

   B: I don't know.

3. her friends / important

   A: Is her friends inportant?

   B: No, I don't think so.

4. her friends / good at planning their time

   A: Is her friends good at planning their time?

   B: No, I don't think so.

5. the psychologist's answer / good

   A: Is the psychologist answer good?

   B: Yes, I think so.

5 | EDITING

Correct these conversations. There are seven mistakes. The first mistake is already corrected.

1. A: Are you tired?
   B: Yes, ~~I'm~~ *I am*.
2. A: Is late?
   B: No, it's early.
3. A: He Korean?
   B: No, he's isn't.
4. A: Am I in the right room?
   B: You are yes.
5. A: Is this English 3?
   B: Yes, I think.
6. A: Are they in room 102?
   B: I no know.

Communication Practice

6 | LISTENING

Listen to the conversation about Hugo's English class. Read the questions. Then listen again and circle the correct answer to each question.

1. Is the teacher from the United States?
   a. Yes, he is. He's from California.
   b. No, he's not. He's Canadian.
   c. No, he's not. He's Cambodian.
2. Is the teacher 40 years old?
   a. Yes, he is.
   b. No, he's not.
   c. I don't know.
3. Are all the students from the same country?
   a. Yes, they are.
   b. No, they're not.
   c. Yes, I think so.
4. Are the students good at different skills?
   a. Yes, they are.
   b. No, they're not.
   c. No, I don't think so.
5. Is Hugo good at writing?
   a. Yes, he is.
   b. Yes, I think so.
   c. No, I don't think so.

7 | OCCUPATIONS

A *Check (✓) your occupation and the occupations of people in your family.*

- ☐ a businessman
- ☐ a businesswoman
- ☐ a salesperson
- ☐ a student
- ☐ a teacher
- ☐ an actor

☐ a nurse

☐ a homemaker

☐ a doctor

☐ an athlete

☐ an electrician

☐ a detective

☐ a plumber

☐ a writer

☐ a lawyer

☐ a carpenter

B *Have a conversation with a partner. Tell about the occupations of your family and friends. Use the words from the box.*

boring	exciting	hard
dangerous	fun	interesting
easy		

Examples: **A:** My cousin is a detective.
B: Is his work dangerous?
A: I think so.

8 | CARS

A *Match the cars and the countries. Then work in small groups. Check your answers with others in your group.*

_____	1. Toyotas	a. Swedish
_____	2. Ferraris	b. Italian
_____	3. Hyundais	c. British
_____	4. Hummers	d. Japanese
_____	5. Jaguars	e. Korean
_____	6. Volvos	f. American

Example: A: Are Hyundais Japanese cars?
B: No, they're not. They're Korean.

B *Study these words and phrases.*

big	comfortable	economical	expensive	fast	safe	small
roomy	good for a single person		good for a family		good for rough roads	

Ask **yes / no** *questions about cars.*

Examples: A: Are Hummers very big?
B: Yes, they are.

9 | ON THE INTERNET

C *Find information about a car. Your classmates ask* **yes / no** *questions about the car. Answer their questions. They then guess the car.*

Example: A: Is it expensive?
B: I think so. A new one in the U.S. is between $16,000 and $24,000.
A: Is it comfortable?
B: Yes. It seats five.
A: Is it good for a single person?
B: No, I don't think so. I think it's a good family car.
A: Is it a Japanese car?
B: Yes, it is.
A: Is it a Honda Accord?
B: Yes, it is!

UNIT

3 The Past of *Be*

Grammar in Context

BEFORE YOU READ

Read the sentences. Check **yes** *or* **no.**

	Yes	No
I have an answering machine.	☑	☐
I use e-mail.	☐	☑
I have Caller ID.	☑	☐

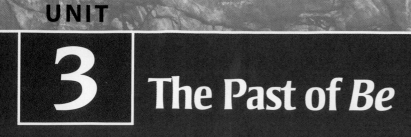

Read these telephone messages.

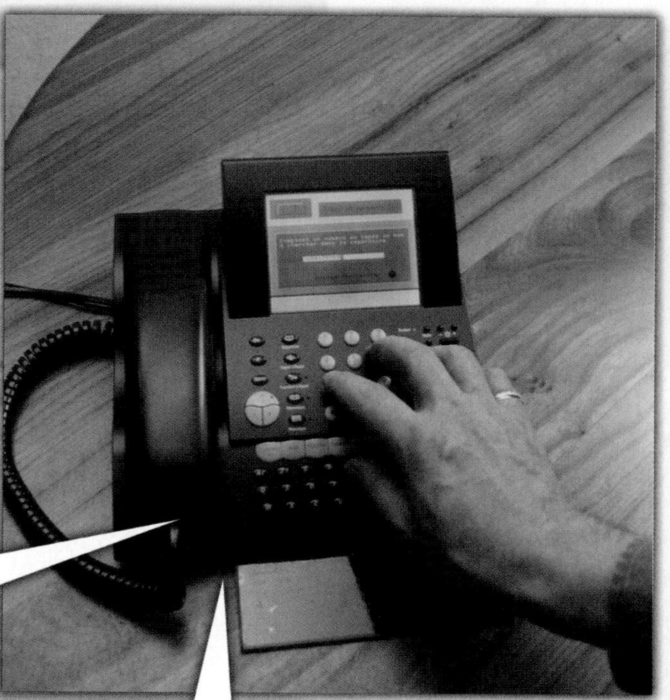

Message 1—Hi, Jay. This is Emily. **I**'m calling to thank you. The party **was** great. We **were** so happy to meet Gina. She's a special person. We're happy for both of you.

Message 2—Hello, Jay. This is Dave. I'm sorry I **wasn't** at the party last night. The weather in Ottawa **was** terrible. My plane **was** late. I **was** at the airport for four hours. I'm home now. Please call me at 879-0089.

AFTER YOU READ

Read the questions. Check **yes** *or* **no.**

	Yes	No
1. Was Emily at the party with someone?	☑	☐
2. Are Emily and Gina old friends?	☐	☑
3. Was Dave at the party?	☐	☑
4. Was Dave in Ottawa?	☑	☐

Grammar Presentation

THE PAST OF *BE*; PAST TIME MARKERS

AFFIRMATIVE STATEMENTS

Singular			
Subject	***Be***		**Time Marker**
I	**was**	in Kyoto	**last year**.
You	**were**		
He She It	**was**		

Plural			
Subject	***Be***		**Time Marker**
We You They	**were**	in Toronto	**two weeks ago**.

NEGATIVE STATEMENTS

Singular			
Subject	***Be/Not***		**Time Marker**
I	**was not** **wasn't**	at the party	**last night**.
You	**were not** **weren't**		
He She It	**was not** **wasn't**		

Plural			
Subject	***Be/Not***		**Time Marker**
We You They	**were not** **weren't**	at the party	**last night**.

YES/NO QUESTIONS

Singular			
Be	**Subject**		**Time Marker**
Was	I	at the party	**last night**?
Were	you		
Was	he she it		

Plural			
Be	**Subject**		**Time Marker**
Were	we you they	at the party	**two weeks ago**?

PAST TIME MARKERS

yesterday
the day before yesterday
last _____ (night, week, year)
(a week, two weeks, a month, two months) _____ ago

GRAMMAR NOTES	EXAMPLES
1. The past of ***be*** has two forms: ***was*** and ***were***.	• She **was** at the airport. • They **were** late.
2. Use ***was*** or ***were*** + ***not*** to make negative statements.	• He **was not** at the party. • They **were not** in class.
3. In informal writing and speaking, use the contractions ***wasn't*** and ***weren't*** in negative statements and negative short answers.	• He **wasn't** at the party. • They **weren't** in class. • **No, he wasn't.** • **No, they weren't.**
4. To ask a ***yes/no*** question, put ***was*** or ***were*** before the subject.	subject • **Was she** at the airport? • **Were you** in Spain?
5. **Time markers** are usually at the end of statements. Time markers are sometimes at the beginning of statements. Time markers go at the end of a question.	• We were in Toronto **yesterday**. • **Yesterday** we were in Toronto. • Was he in Toronto **yesterday**?

Focused Practice

1 DISCOVER THE GRAMMAR

Read this thank-you note. Underline the past of **be**.

Dear Emily and Rob,

I was happy to meet you finally. Jay was right—you are both very special. Thanks for the CD. It was a good idea. The songs were perfect for the party.

Sincerely,

Gina

2 | CONVERSATIONS *Grammar Notes 1–5*

Put the sentences in the correct order. Read the conversations.

Example

- No, it was terrible.
- Were you at the party?
- Was it any good?
- No, I wasn't. I was at a concert.

A: *Were you at the party?*

B: *No, I wasn't. I was at a concert.*

A: *Was it any good?*

B: *No, it was terrible.*

1.
- She's not in the photos.
- Yes, she was. Why?
- Was Emily at the party?
- She was the photographer.

A: Was Emily at the party?

B: Yes, she was. Why?

A: She's not in the photos.

B: She was the photographer.

2.
- Yes, they were. Why?
- Were Ali and Mo in school on Monday?
- Their names are not on the attendance sheet.
- I think they were late.

A: Were Ali and Mo in school on Monday?

B: Yes, they were. Why?

A: Their names are not on the attendance sheet.

B: I think they were late.

3.
- It's cold. It was cold yesterday too.
- How's the weather in Montreal? → canada
- Was it cold the day before?
- I think so.

A: How's the weather in Montreal?

B: It's cold. It was cold yesterday too.

A: Was it cold the day before?

B: I think so.

Now listen and check your answers.

3 | AFFIRMATIVE AND NEGATIVE OF *BE*

Grammar Notes 1–3

A *Look at yesterday's attendance record. Complete the sentences. Use* **was, wasn't, were**, *or* **weren't**.

Attendance Record

	April 5
Pierre	✓
Juan	✓
Gloria	✓
Emiko	absent
Anna	✓

1. Pierre ___was___ here yesterday. He ___wasn't___ absent.
2. Emiko ___wasn't___ here yesterday. She ___was___ absent.
3. Juan and Gloria ___were___ here yesterday. They ___weren't___ absent.

B *Complete the sentences. Use* **was, wasn't, were**, *or* **weren't**. *Make true sentences.*

1. Our school ___was___ open yesterday. It ___wasn't___ closed.
2. I ___wasn't___ absent yesterday. I ___was___ in school.
3. My friend and my teacher ___weren't___ absent last week. They ___were___ in school.
4. Our English homework ___was___ easy yesterday. It ___wasn't___ hard.
5. It ___was___ sunny yesterday. It ___wasn't___ cloudy.

4 | A GREAT WEEKEND

Grammar Notes 1–4

Complete the conversation. Use the affirmative or negative of **was** *or* **were**.

A: How ___was___ (1.) your weekend?

B: Great. I ___was___ (2.) at the park on Saturday and at the art museum on Sunday.

A: ___Were___ (3.) you with Joe?

B: Yes, I ___was___ (4.). We ___were___ (5.) together all day Saturday and Sunday.

A: Joe ___was___ (6.) in class this morning. ___Was___ (7.) he at an interview?

B: No, he ___wasn't___ (8.). He ___was___ (9.) at the airport. His parents ___were___ (10.) there for a few hours. They ___were___ (11.) on their way to Mexico.

A: ___Were___ (12.) his brothers with them?

B: No, they ___weren't___ (13.). They were at home with their grandparents.

5 | NOW AND THEN — *Grammar Notes 1–3*

Complete the sentences. Change from the present to the past.

1. They are busy now. Last month <u>they were busy</u> too.
2. Today it's cold. Yesterday <u>It was cold</u> too.
3. My friend is in Seoul now. <u>My friend was in Seoul</u> last year too.
4. It's not sunny today. <u>It wasn't sunny</u> yesterday.
5. She's not in class this week. <u>She wasn't in class</u> last week.
6. He's at the airport this morning. <u>He was at the airport</u> yesterday morning.
7. I'm in Lima this week. I <u>was in Lima</u> last week too.
8. His phone is busy. It <u>was busy</u> yesterday evening too.

6 | YES/NO QUESTIONS AND ANSWERS — *Grammar Notes 4–5*

Write questions and answers. Use the words given.

1. Dave / at the party Friday night — **A:** <u>Was Dave at the party Friday night?</u>
   No, he / in Ottawa — **B:** <u>No, he was in Ottawa.</u>
2. Dave / in Ottawa on business — **A:** <u>Was Dave in Ottawa on business?</u>
   Yes, he / at a meeting there — **B:** <u>Yes, he was at a meeting there.</u>
3. **A:** The weather was terrible in Ottawa.
   the airport / closed — <u>Was the airport closed?</u>
   No, but all the planes / late — **B:** <u>No, but all the planes were late.</u>
4. Emily and Rob / at the party — **A:** <u>Were Emily and Rob at the party?</u>
   Yes, they / there for hours — **B:** <u>Yes, they were there for hours.</u>
5. you / at home last night — **A:** <u>Were you at home last night?</u>
   No, I / at a party — **B:** <u>No, I was at a party.</u>

7 WORD ORDER PRACTICE

Grammar Notes 1–5

Write statements or questions. Use the words and punctuation given.

1. in Toronto / He / . / last week / was

   He was in Toronto last week.

2. cold / . / It / in Toronto / yesterday / was

   It was cold in Toronto yesterday.

3. wasn't / It / two days ago /. / cold

   It wasn't cold two days ago.

4. in Toronto / ? / last month / Were / you

   Were you in Toronto last month?

5. in Toronto / ? / Were / they / last year

   Were they in Toronto last year?

6. weren't / . / there / we / A week ago

   A week ago we weren't there.

8 EDITING

Correct this message. There are six mistakes. The first mistake is already corrected.

Hi Victor,

Right now Bob and I are in a taxi on our way home from the airport. We ~~was~~ were in Mexico all last week. It ~~were~~ was great. The weather ~~it~~ was dry and sunny. The people were warm and friendly. Last night we ~~was~~ were at the Ballet Folklorico. The dancers ~~was~~ were terrific. There was only one problem. My Spanish ~~no was~~ wasn't good. See you soon.

Rina

Communication Practice

9 LISTENING

Listen to the telephone messages. Listen again and complete the messages.

Message #	From	Message
1	Dan	The concert it's great and the seat it's super.
2	Emiko	I was out of town all of week. I'm bad now. Please call me. My number is (917) 8654821.
3	John	I'm sorry I wasn't at the meeting. Please call me at (846) 4910090.

10 INFORMATION GAP: WEATHER AROUND THE WORLD

Learn these words for weather.

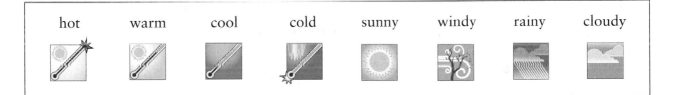

hot warm cool cold sunny windy rainy cloudy

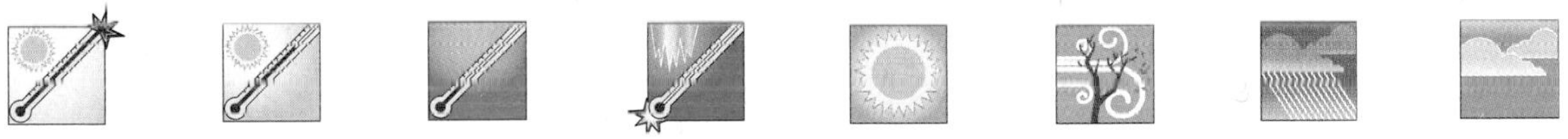

Work in pairs. Student B, turn to page 35. Student A, look at this page.

Student A, ask your partner questions to complete your chart.

Example: A: It's sunny in Istanbul today. Was it sunny yesterday too?

City	Yesterday	Today
Bangkok	sunny	cloudy
Beijing	cloudy	partly cloudy
Budapest	cloudy	cloudy
Guadalajara	sunny	sunny
Istanbul	cloudy	sunny
Rio de Janeiro	sunny	sunny
Seoul	sunny	rainy
Vancouver	cloudy	sunny

11 | WRITING

A *Work with a partner. Complete the e-mail message.*

Hi Irina,

I hope you understand my message. My homework was: Write an e-mail message in English. Well, here goes.

I ___am___ in a level two English class at Hunter College in New York City. My classmates ___are___ from different countries—Korea, Taiwan, Colombia, Italy, Poland, and Thailand. We ___are___ a class of ten women and four men! :-(My teacher ___is___ very good. :-) She ___is___ from Canada.

I ___was___ nervous and worried last week. It ___was___ my first week of classes. ___I___ was the only new student. But now I ___'m___ fine.

I ___was___ at a party Saturday night. It ___was___ a classmate's 21st birthday. The party ___was___ fun.

It ___is___ warm and sunny now. ___It___ was cold and cloudy yesterday. That's New York weather. It ___is___ hard to speak English all the time. It ___is___ hard to be a "foreigner." But it ___is___ also exciting to be here.

I hope you ___are___ OK. Please say hi to everyone.

Best,

Ingrid

B *Write your own e-mail message to a friend. Tell your friend about your life now. Say something about last weekend. Say something about the weather. Use contractions when possible.*

12 | ON THE INTERNET

In 1876, Alexander Graham Bell invented the telephone. Find out more about him. Report to the class.

OR

Find out about Kazuo Hashimoto. Where is he from? What did he invent? Report to the class.

PART I

From **Grammar** to **Writing**

Capitalization

1 *Look at A and B. What's wrong with A?*

A	B
mr. john smith 342 dryden road ithaca, new york 14850	Mr. John Smith 342 Dryden Road Ithaca, New York 14850

Capital ตัวใหญ่

Study the information about capitalization.

Capitalization	
1. Use a **capital letter** for the first word in every sentence.	• **We** are new students.
2. Use capital letters for **titles**.	• This is **Mr.** Winston. • She is **Dr.** Jones.
3. Use capital letters for the names of **people** and **places** (proper nouns).	• **Lila Roberts** is from **Vancouver**, **Canada**.
4. Use capital letters for the names of **streets**, **cities**, **states**, **countries**, and **continents**.	• 5 **Elm Street** **West Redding, Connecticut** **U.S.A.**
5. Use a capital letter for the word ***I***.	• **I** am happy to be here.

2 *Add capital letters.*

1. this is ms. herrera. This is Ms. Herrera.
2. her address is 4 riverdale avenue. Her address is A Riverdale Avenue.
3. i'm her good friend. I'm her good friend.
4. she was in bangkok and taiwan last year. She was in Bangkok and Taiwan last year.

3 *Correct the postcard from Ellen to Ruth. Add capital letters.*

Hi ruth,

john and i are in acapulco this week. it's beautiful here. the people are friendly and the weather is great. it's sunny and warm.

last week we were in mexico city for two days. i was there on business. my meetings were long and difficult, but our evenings were fun. hope all is well with you.

Regards,

ellen

To:

ms. ruth holland
10 oldwick st
ringwood, new jersey 07456
u.s.a.

Write a postcard to a friend.

Hi Ruth,

John and I are in Acupulco this week. It's beautiful here. The people are friendly and the weather is great. It's sunny and warm.

Last week we were in Mexico city for two days. I was there on business. My meetings were long and difficult, But our evening were fun. Hope all is will with you

Regards,

Ellen

To:

Ms. Ruth Holland
10 Oldwick St.
Ringwood, New Jersey
07456 U.S.A.

PART I

Review Test

I *Read each conversation. Circle the letter of the underlined word or group of words that is not correct.*

1. CLAUDIA: Are you a (A) new student? — A B C D

ALEXANDER: Yes, I'm (B). I'm from Ecuador. Where are you (C) from?

CLAUDIA: I'm (D) from Mexico.

2. JUAN: You're old student (A). — A B C D

YOKO: No, you're wrong. We aren't (B) old students. Emiko and I are (C) new (D) students.

3. VIVIAN: It's (A) hot here. — A B C D

PHIL: No, it's not (B). It's 60 degrees. It's cold (C).

VIVIAN: Well, I hot (D).

4. JUAN: Was (A) it hot in your room last night (B)? — A B C D

BILL: No, it isn't (C). It (D) was cold.

5. JAMES: Was (A) Alexander and Nuray in class yesterday (B)? — A B C D

STEVE: I don't know (C). I was (D) absent.

II *Circle the letter of the correct word(s) to complete the sentences.*

1. Last week we _______ in Turkey. — A B C D

(A) was **(C)** is

(B) are **(D)** were

2. Mike and Ivona _______ absent last week. — A B C D

(A) were **(C)** are

(B) was **(D)** is

(continued)

3. _______ a photographer? A B (C) D

(A) Is you **(C)** Are you

(B) You **(D)** You are

4. Andrew _______ the United States. (A) B C D

(A) is from **(C)** are from

(B) am from **(D)** were from

5. Are you tired? Yes, _______. A B C (D)

(A) we tired **(C)** we be

(B) we're **(D)** we are

6. _______ Wendy and Mi Young home last night? A (B) C D

(A) Was **(C)** Are

(B) Were **(D)** Be

III *Write **yes/no** questions. Use the words in parentheses.*

A: (cloudy / yesterday) Was It clouldy yesterday?
1.

B: No, it wasn't. It was sunny.

A: (cloudy / now) Is It cloudy now?
2.

B: Yes.

A: (you / in school / last week) Were you in school last week?
3.

B: Yes, I was.

IV *Correct this e-mail from Jill to her father. There are three mistakes.*

Hi Dad,

Thanks for the money. Books are always expensive. Today the weather is terrible. It ~~be~~ is cold and rainy. But yesterday was beautiful. It is sunny all day. How's is the weather in New York? Autumn is usually very nice.

Love,

Jill

▶ *To check your answers, go to the Answer Key on page RT-1.*

INFORMATION GAP FOR STUDENT B

Unit 3, Exercise 10

Learn these words for weather.

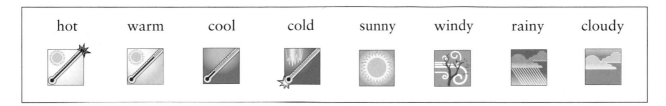

hot warm cool cold sunny windy rainy cloudy

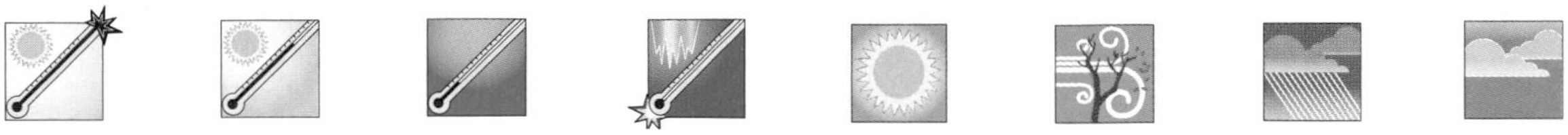

Student B, ask your partner questions to complete your chart.

Example: B: It's cloudy in Bangkok today. Was it cloudy yesterday too?

City	Yesterday	Today
Bangkok	sunny	cloudy
Beijing	cloudy	partly cloudy
Budapest	cloudy	cloudy
Guadalajara	sunny	sunny
Istanbul	cloudy	sunny
Rio de Janeiro	sunny	sunny
Seoul	sunny	rainy
Vancouver	cloudy	sunny

PART II

Nouns, Adjectives, Prepositions, *Wh*-Questions

UNIT

4 Count Nouns; Proper Nouns

Grammar in Context

BEFORE YOU READ

What's in your wallet? Check (✓) true statements.

__✓__ 1. I have photos of friends or family.

__✓__ 2. I have a photo of myself.

_____ 3. I don't have any photos in my wallet.

Talk about a photo in your wallet.

Example: A: This is a photo of my sister. She's a dancer. She's 20 years old.
B: What's her name?

Read about this photographer and this photo.

A PHOTOGRAPHER AND A PHOTO

Henri Cartier-Bresson was **a photographer** and **an artist.** He was born in **France** in 1908. He died in 2004. His **photos** are famous all over the **world.**

This is a **photo** by **Henri Cartier Bresson.** It's **a photo** of **a man** and **a woman.** The **woman** is beautiful. The **man** is looking at her. They are in **Harlem,** in **New York.** It is 1947.

AFTER YOU READ

Complete the sentences. Use the words in the box.

artist	France	photographer	photos

1. Henri Cartier-Bresson was a photographer.
2. He was an artist too.
3. He was from France.
4. His photos are famous all over the world.

Grammar Presentation

SINGULAR AND PLURAL COUNT NOUNS; PROPER NOUNS

Singular Nouns (one)
He is **a photographer**. He is **an artist**.

Plural Nouns (more than one)
They are **photographers**. They are **artists**.

Irregular Plural Nouns

Singular	Plural
man	men
woman	women
child	children
foot	feet
tooth	teeth
person	people

Nouns That Are Always Plural
pants scissors clothes glasses

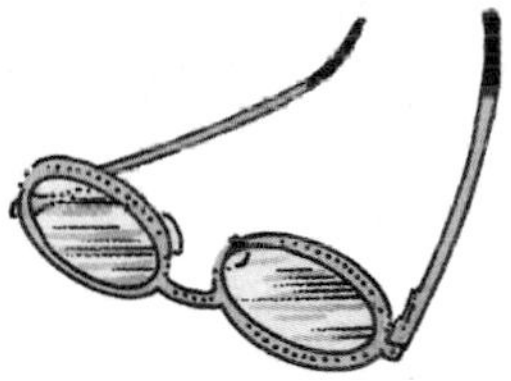

Proper Nouns
Harlem is in **New York City**. **Maya Angelou** has a home in **Harlem**.

GRAMMAR NOTES	EXAMPLES
1. **Nouns** are names of people, places, and things.	• a student, Jung Eun • a country, Korea • a camera, a photograph
2. **Count nouns** are easy to count. They have a singular and plural form.	• **one** photo, **two** photos, **three** photos
Use ***a*** before **singular** count nouns that begin with a consonant sound.	• She's **a** photographer. • He's **a** teacher. • It's **a** hat.
▶ **BE CAREFUL!** Use ***an*** before an ***h*** that is silent.	• It's **an** hour too early. (*Hour* sounds like *our*.)
3. Use ***an*** before **singular** count nouns that begin with a vowel sound.	• She's **an** artist. • He's **an** engineer. • It's **an** umbrella.
▶ **BE CAREFUL!** Use ***a*** before a ***u*** that sounds like *yew*.	• This is **a unit** about nouns.
4. To form the **plural** of most count nouns, add ***-s*** or ***-es***.	• one **friend** three **friends** • one **class** three **classes**
Do not put ***a*** or ***an*** before plural nouns.	• They are **photos** of **friends**. NOT: They are ~~a~~ photos of ~~a~~ friends.
Some nouns have irregular plural endings.	• one **man** two **men** • one **tooth** two **teeth**
Some nouns are always plural.	• **scissors**, **pants**, **glasses**, **clothes** • My **pants are** blue.
5. Names of specific people and places are **proper nouns**. Write these with a capital letter.	• **Paris** is in **France**. • **Harlem** is in **New York City**.
Do not put ***a*** or ***an*** before proper nouns.	NOT: ~~A~~ Paris is in ~~a~~ France.

Reference Notes

See Unit 25, page 242 for a discussion of non-count nouns and ***the*** (the definite article).
See Appendix 9, page A-10 for the spelling and pronunciation rules for plural nouns.

Focused Practice

1 DISCOVER THE GRAMMAR

Read the conversation.

MIKE: Is that you?

DOUG: Yes, it is. It's a photo of me with friends from high school.

MIKE: Where are they now?

DOUG: Well, Jasmine's in Brazil.

MIKE: Really?

DOUG: Uh-huh. She's a teacher there. And Bob's on the right. He's an accountant. He's here in New York.

MIKE: Who's she?

DOUG: That's Amy. She's a photographer. What a life! She travels all over the world. Last month she was in India. Her photos are in a show at the library this month.

MIKE: I'd love to see them.

DOUG: Them? Or her?

Find:

1. One noun that begins with a vowel: an accountant
2. Two nouns that begin with a consonant (no proper nouns): a teacher, a photographer, a life, a show
3. Two proper nouns: Brazil, New York
4. Two plural nouns: friends, photos

2 | HARLEM, 1947

Grammar Notes 2–3

A *Write* **a** *or* **an** *before each word.*

1. a man
2. a hand
3. a hat
4. an earring
5. a flower
6. a suit
7. an eye
8. an ear
9. a lip
10. a woman

B *Look at the photo,* Harlem, 1947, below. *Find the items from the list. Label the photo. Use the words from the list. Number them 1–10.*

3 | *A OR AN* — *Grammar Notes 2–5*

Complete the sentences with **a** *or* **an**. *Write* **Ø** *if you don't need* **a** *or* **an**.

1. Henri Cartier-Bresson was __a__ photographer.
2. Henri Cartier-Bresson and Ansel Adams were __Ø__ photographers.
3. Henri Cartier-Bresson was __an__ artist, too.
4. All good photographers are __Ø__ artists.
5. Ansel Adams was __a__ pianist before he was __a__ photographer.
6. Ansel Adams was born in __Ø__ San Francisco, California.
7. For Adams, photography began with __a__ trip to Yosemite National Park.
8. __Ø__ Henri Cartier-Bresson was born in __Ø__ Normandy.
9. __Ø__ Normandy is in __Ø__ France.
10. Henri Cartier-Bresson was the first photographer with __Ø__ pictures in the Louvre Museum.

4 | PEOPLE, PLACES, AND THINGS — *Grammar Note 4, Appendix 9*

Look at the spelling rules for plural nouns on page 40. Complete the sentences. Use the correct form of one of the nouns in the box.

~~city~~	clothes	fish	husband	person	wife
class	country	flower	museum	watch	

1. San Francisco and Los Angeles are __*cities*__ in California.
2. Brazil and France are __countries__.
3. The Louvre and the Prado are __museums__.
4. Seiko and Rolex are kinds of __watches__.
5. The __clothes__ of Issey Miyake and Ralph Lauren are beautiful.
6. Salmon and tuna are __fish__.
7. Jason is a teacher. His __classes__ are interesting.
8. The men are on a business trip. Their __wives__ are at home.
9. The women are on a business trip. Their __husbands__ are at home.
10. There are two __people__ in the photo *Harlem, 1947* by Henri Cartier-Bresson.
11. The woman in *Harlem, 1947* has a hat with __flowers__.

5 | PROPER NOUNS *Grammar Note 5*

Change small letters to capital letters where necessary.

MIKE: Hi, are you amy smith?

AMY: Yes, I am.

MIKE: I'm mike cho. doug and I work together.

AMY: Nice to meet you, mike.

MIKE: It's nice to meet you.

AMY: So, mike, are you from phoenix?

MIKE: No, I'm not. I'm from san francisco.

AMY: Oh, san francisco is beautiful. I was there last year.

MIKE: Doug says you travel a lot.

AMY: Yes, I do. I was in india last year. And the year before that I was in kuwait, turkey, jordan, and egypt.

MIKE: That's great.

6 | EDITING

Correct these sentences. There are six mistakes. The first mistake is already corrected.

1. Cartier-Bresson's photos are often of famous ~~person~~ people.
2. This is photo of Henri Matisse.
3. Henri Matisse was artist.
4. Matisse's paintings are in museum all over the world.
5. We see four bird in this photo.
6. In this photo Matisse was in the south of france.

Communication Practice

7 | LISTENING

Complete the sentences with the words in the box. Then listen and check your work. See Appendix 9 on page A-10 for more about plural endings. Listen again and check the sound of the endings.

books	boxes	classes	glasses	pants	~~photos~~	scissors

	/s/	/z/	/ɪz/
1. The ___photos___ are ready.		✓	
2. Our ___classes___ are from 10:00 to 1:00.			✓
3. Be careful. The ___scissors___ are sharp.		✓	
4. The ___boxes___ are full of old clothes.			✓
5. My ___pants___ have two pockets.	✓		
6. I don't see well without ___glasses___.			✓
7. Our ___books___ are open to page 20.	✓		

8 | DRAW MY PICTURE

A *Choose five things. Draw a picture with the five things in it. You don't have to be an artist. Your picture does not have to look real!*

a photo	a camera	five people	three children
an apple	an ice cream cone	flowers	earrings

B *Work with a partner. Tell your partner about your picture. Your partner draws your picture. Compare pictures.*

Example: *My picture has three children—a boy and two girls. It has an apple with earrings. It has flowers everywhere.*

9 | CLASSROOM OBJECTS

A *Work with a partner. Label the pictures. Ask your partner about things you don't know.*

Example: A: What's this? OR What's this called in English?
B: It's an eraser.
A: What are these?
B: They're CDs.

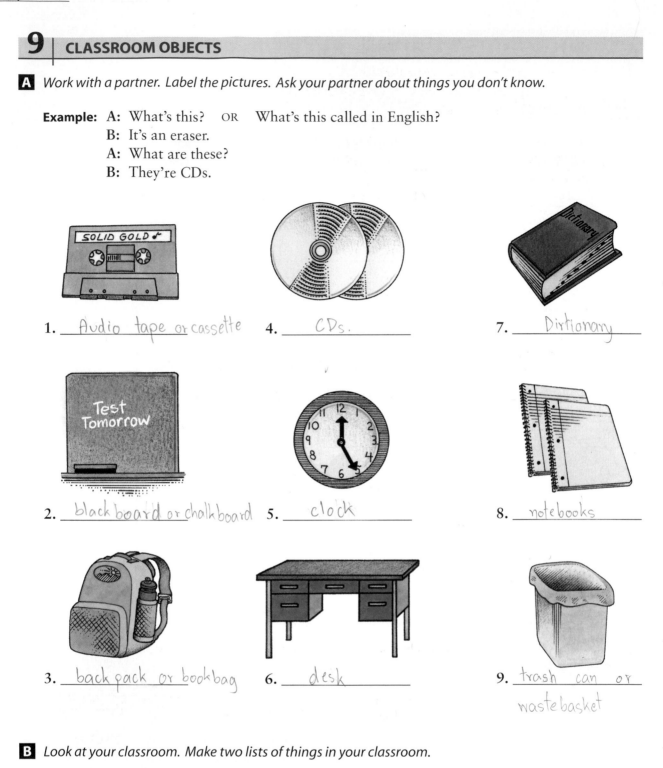

1. Audio tape or cassette

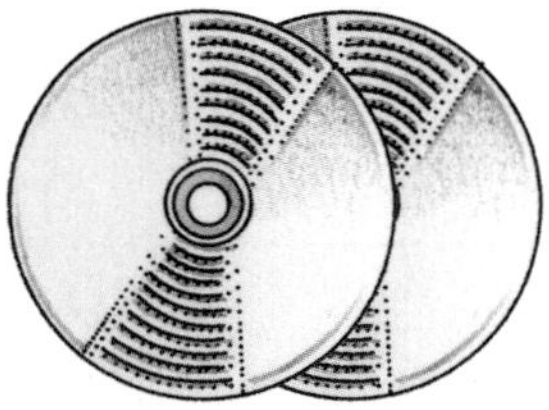

4. CDs.

7. Dirtionary

2. blackboard or chalkboard

5. clock

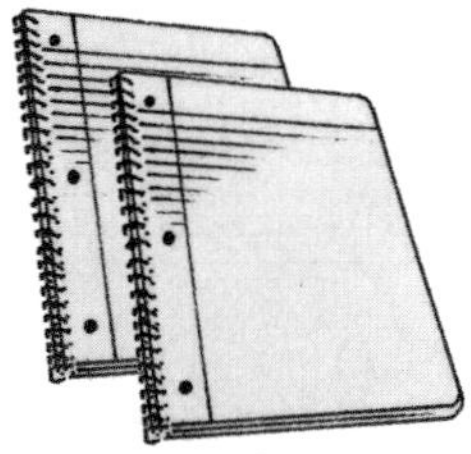

8. notebooks

3. backpack or bookbag

6. desk

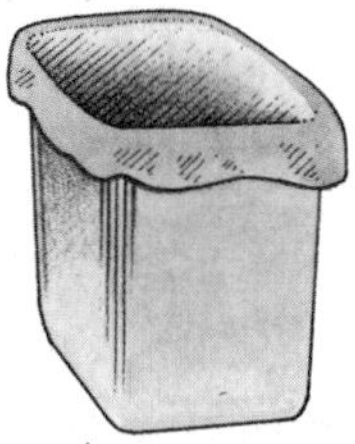

9. trash can or wastebasket

B *Look at your classroom. Make two lists of things in your classroom.*

Our Classroom			
We have:		We have two or more:	
a board	an overhead	erasers	chairs
a thash can	a projector	desks	windows
a clock	a table	notebooks	students
a computer	a pencil sharpener	back packs	
a T.V. / VCR		book bags	

C *Compare your lists.*

Example: A: Are erasers on your list?
B: Yes, they are. Are windows on your list?
A: No, they aren't.

10 | WRITING

Work with a partner. Write sentences about people and places. Remember to use **a** *or* **an** *with singular count nouns.*

1. Henri Matisse was an artist.
2. Henri Matisse was a photographer.
3. Bangkok is a city.
4. The United State and Thailand are countries.
5. J. K. Rowling and Gabriel Garcia Marquez are writers.
6. Tom Cruise and Evan are actors.
7. Diana and I are students.
8. Ms. Marshall is a teacher.

Read each sentence to a partner. Your partner asks a question. Try to answer it.

Example: A: Henri Matisse was an artist.
B: Was he from France?
A: Yes, he was. OR I don't know.

11 | ON THE INTERNET

Look on the Internet for photos by Henri Cartier-Bresson. Print one if possible. Tell the class about the photo.

Example: This is a photo by Henri Cartier-Bresson. The place is Kashmir, India. It's 1948. The women are wearing long dresses. The photo is beautiful.

UNIT

5 Descriptive Adjectives

Grammar in Context

BEFORE YOU READ

Look at the photograph. What words describe this place?

beautiful—ugly

interesting—boring

usual—strange

Example: It's interesting.

Were you ever in a place like this? When? Where?

Read about Cappadocia, Turkey.

AN UNUSUAL PLACE

Cappadocia is in the center of Turkey. It is an **unusual** place. It has underground cities and cave homes. It's a **great** place to hike. Everywhere there are **interesting** things to see. Sometimes the landscape looks like a **different** world. That's why a *Star Wars* movie was filmed in Cappadocia. In the past, people lived in the caves. Today people from all over the world visit the caves.

The climate is **mild** in Cappadocia. The days are **sunny** and **warm**, and the nights are **cool**. It is a **beautiful** place to visit.

AFTER YOU READ

Read the statements. Mark them **T** *(true) or* **F** *(false).*

__F__ 1. Cappadocia is in the west of Turkey.

__T__ 2. It is in the center of Turkey.

__F__ 3. It has underwater cities.

__T__ 4. It has cave homes.

__F__ 5. *Lord of the Rings* was filmed in Cappadocia.

__F__ 6. The climate is tropical.

__F__ 7. The days are sunny and cold.

Grammar Presentation

DESCRIPTIVE ADJECTIVES

Noun	*Be*	Adjective
The room	is	**small.**
The rooms	are	

	Adjective	Noun
It is a	**small**	room.
They are		rooms.

GRAMMAR NOTES / EXAMPLES

1. Adjectives describe nouns.

- **Cappadocia** (noun) is **beautiful** (adjective).
- It's a **beautiful** (adjective) **place** (noun).

2. Adjectives can come:

- after the verb ***be***.
- before a noun.

Examples:

- The room is **big**.
- It's a **big** room.

NOT: It's a ~~room big~~.

3. Do <u>not</u> add ***-s*** to adjectives.

- a **sunny** day, a **cool** night
- **sunny** days, **cool** nights

NOT: ~~cools~~ nights

4. For **adjective + noun:**

Use ***a*** before the adjective if the adjective begins with a consonant sound.

- It's **a small** village.

Use ***an*** before the adjective if the adjective begins with a vowel sound.

- It's **an old** village.

5. Some adjectives end in ***-ing***, ***-ly***, or ***-ed***.

- It's **interesting**.
- They're **friendly**.
- We're **tired**.

Focused Practice

1 DISCOVER THE GRAMMAR

Gamirasu Cave Hotel is in a traditional village. In the past it was a cave home. Now it's a hotel.

Maria is touring Turkey. Read her journal entry about the hotel. Underline ten more adjectives.

I'm at a cave hotel in Cappadocia. The hotel is in a small village in the heart of Cappadocia. The cave rooms are fun. They're old, but with modern bathrooms. The rates are not high. The food is fresh and the people are helpful and friendly. The price of the room includes a delicious breakfast and dinner. It's easy to visit all of Cappadocia from the hotel. It was a great choice.

2 WORD ORDER PRACTICE

Grammar Notes 1–5

Write sentences. Use the words given. Remember the first word begins with a capital letter.

1. market. / at / we / are / old / an

   We are at an old market.

2. for sale / everywhere. / beautiful / carpets / are

   Beautiful carpets are for sale everywhere.

3. the / prices / reasonable. / are

   The prices are reasonable.

4. warm. / it / and / sunny / is /

It's sunny and warm.

5. tired / happy. / I'm / but

I'm tired but happy.

3 | EDITING

Correct these sentences. There are five mistakes. The first mistake is already corrected.

A: Is that a ~~carpet new~~ new carpet?

B: Yes, it is. It's from Turkey.

A: The colors are beautiful~~s~~.

B: Thanks. I got it at an old market in Cappadocia.

A: Were there many ~~things interesting~~ interesting things to buy?

B: Yes. These bowls are from Turkey too.

A: They're ~~colors great~~ great colors.

B: Here. This one is for you.

Communication Practice

4 | LISTENING

Emiko is on vacation at Mesa Verde National Park in Colorado. Listen to her telephone conversation. Then choose the word or phrase to complete the sentences.

1. Emiko says, "Mesa Verde is _______."
   - (a.) strange and awesome
   - b. interesting and exciting

2. The cliff dwellings are very _______.
   - a. cold
   - (b.) old

3. Emiko is at a _______ hotel.
   - (a.) clean
   - b. nice

4. The weather is _______.
   - a. warm
   - (b.) cold

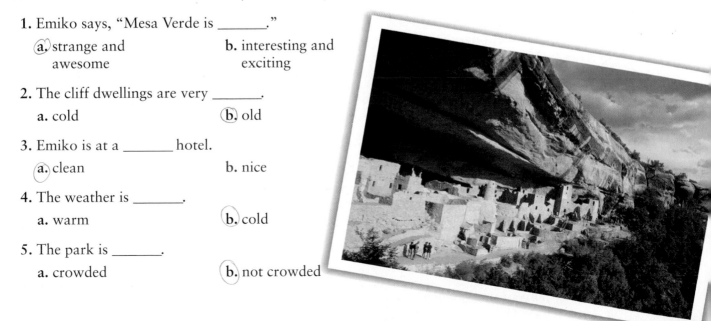

5. The park is _______.
   - a. crowded
   - (b.) not crowded

5 | MY CITY

A *Match the word on the left with its opposite on the right.*

__d__ 1. usual	a. helpful
__b__ 2. beautiful	b. ugly
__g__ 3. comfortable	c. warm
__h__ 4. expensive	d. unusual
__j__ 5. traditional	e. friendly
__i__ 6. important	f. interesting
__f__ 7. boring	g. uncomfortable
__a__ 8. unhelpful	h. cheap
__c__ 9. cold	i. unimportant
__e__ 10. unfriendly	j. modern

B *Choose ten words from A. Use each word in a sentence. Write about the city you are in.*

Examples: The houses are expensive. The buses are comfortable. The people are friendly.

C *Read your sentences to a partner. Listen to your partner's sentences. Are any of your sentences the same?*

6 | OBJECTS IN OUR CLASSROOM

Work with a partner. Look around the classroom. Describe objects in your classroom. Use the adjectives in the box.

big	heavy	long	old	thick
dark	large	new	straight	

Examples: My dictionary is thick.
My book bag is heavy.

7 | ON THE INTERNET

Find a picture of one of these cave dwellings.

- Argentina, Cueva de las Manos
- China, Longmen Grottoes
- France, Lascaux Cave
- India, Ajanta Cave
- Spain, Altamira Cave

Read about it. Tell your class about it.

UNIT 6

Prepositions of Place

Grammar in Context

BEFORE YOU READ

Look at these pictures. Answer the questions: What kind of doctor is Dr. Green? Where is his office?

Read the conversations of a patient and a receptionist and the patient and a doctor.

THE EYE DOCTOR

PATIENT: Hello. I'd like an appointment with Dr. Green.

RECEPTIONIST: OK. How about this Monday at 11?

PATIENT: Good. Uh, what's the address again?

RECEPTIONIST: We're at 7 East 89th Street. That's between Madison and Fifth Avenues. We're on the ground floor near the art museum.

PATIENT: Thanks a lot. See you Monday.

(The following Monday)

PATIENT: Dr. Green, I think I need glasses.

DR. GREEN: Well, let's see. Please look at the chart. . . . Now where's the A?

PATIENT: It's next to the D.

DOCTOR: Good. And the D?

PATIENT: It's between the A and the N.

DOCTOR: Good. How about the bottom row?

PATIENT: Sorry, I can't see anything.

DOCTOR: And now?

PATIENT: Now it's a piece of cake*—J, L, P, E, U, X, Z.

DOCTOR: Well, I guess you need glasses.

**a piece of cake*: easy

AFTER YOU READ

Complete these sentences. Choose from the words in parentheses.

1. The D is ___between___ the A and the N.
   (above / between)
2. The A is ___next to___ the D.
   (next to / under)
3. The doctor's office is ___near___ a museum.
   (near / in)
4. His office is ___on___ the ground floor.
   (on / in)
5. His office is ___at___ 7 East 89th Street.
   (on / at)

Grammar Presentation

PREPOSITIONS OF PLACE

The glasses are **between** the book and the watch.

The glasses are **next to** the newspaper.

The glasses are **behind** the box.

The glasses are **under** the table.

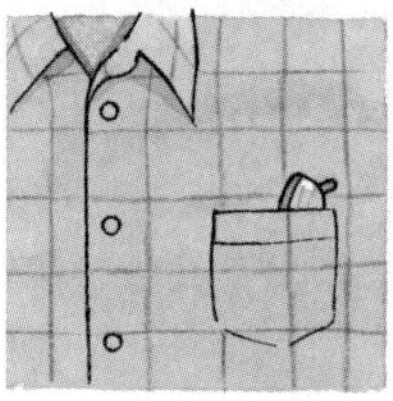

The glasses are **in** his pocket.

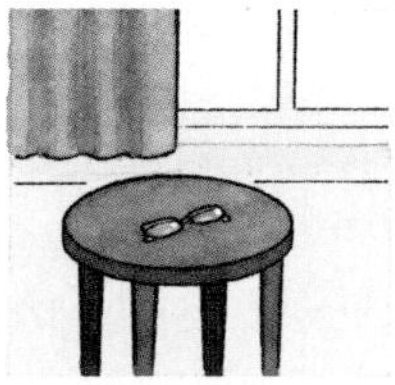

The glasses are **on** the table **near** the window.

The man is **in back of** the woman.

The man is **in front of** the woman.

GRAMMAR NOTES	EXAMPLES
1. Prepositions of place tell <u>where</u> something is. Some common prepositions of place are: ***under, behind, on, next to, between, near, in, in front of, in back of***	• My bag is **under** my seat. • Your umbrella is **near** the door.
▶ **BE CAREFUL!** *Near* and *next to* are not the same. Look at the letters of the alphabet: ABCDEFGHIJKLMNOPQRSTUVWXYZ	• The letter A is **next to** the letter B. It is **near** the letter B, too. • The letter A is **near** the letter C, but it is not **next to** the letter C. • The letter J is not **next to** the letter A. It is not **near** the letter A, either.

2. We use the following prepositions in addresses:	
in before a country, a state, a province, a city, a room number	• He's **in** Canada. He's **in** British Columbia. • He's **in** Vancouver. He's **in** room 302.
on before a street, an avenue, a road	• It's **on** Main Street. It's **on** Tenth Avenue.
at before a building number	• We're **at** 78 Main Street.
on the before a floor	• We're **on the** 2nd floor.
on the corner of before a street or streets	• It's **on the corner of** Main Street.
USAGE NOTE: In informal conversation, *street* or *avenue* is dropped.	• It's on the corner of **Main Street** and **Mott Avenue**. • It's on the corner of **Main** and **Mott**.

3. Use the following prepositions before these places:	
in school OR ***at*** school	• I'm **in** school from 9 to 11. • I'm **at** school now.
at work	• She's **at** work right now.
at home OR home	• No one is **at** home. • No one is home.

Focused Practice

1 DISCOVER THE GRAMMAR

Look at the eye chart. Read the paragraph. Find the message.

			E			
		R	T	N		
	I	L	W	O	V	
E	G	S	L	I	P	H

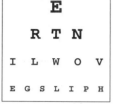

There are three words. The first word has one letter. This letter is next to an *L*. It isn't a *W* or an *S*. The second word has four letters. The first letter is between the *S* and an *I*. The second letter is under the *N*. The third letter is a *V*. A *T* is under the last letter. The third word has seven letters. A *T* is under the first letter. The second letter is an *N*. The third letter is between an *E* and the *S*. The fourth letter is an *L*. The fifth letter is an *I*. The sixth letter is between the *L* and the *G*. The last letter is an *H*.

What's the message? I L O V E E N G L I S H

2 UNDERSTANDING A MAP

Grammar Notes 1–2

Look at the map. Complete the sentences on the next page. Use the words in the box.

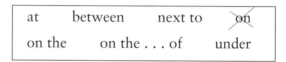

at	between	next to	~~on~~
on the	on the . . . of	under	

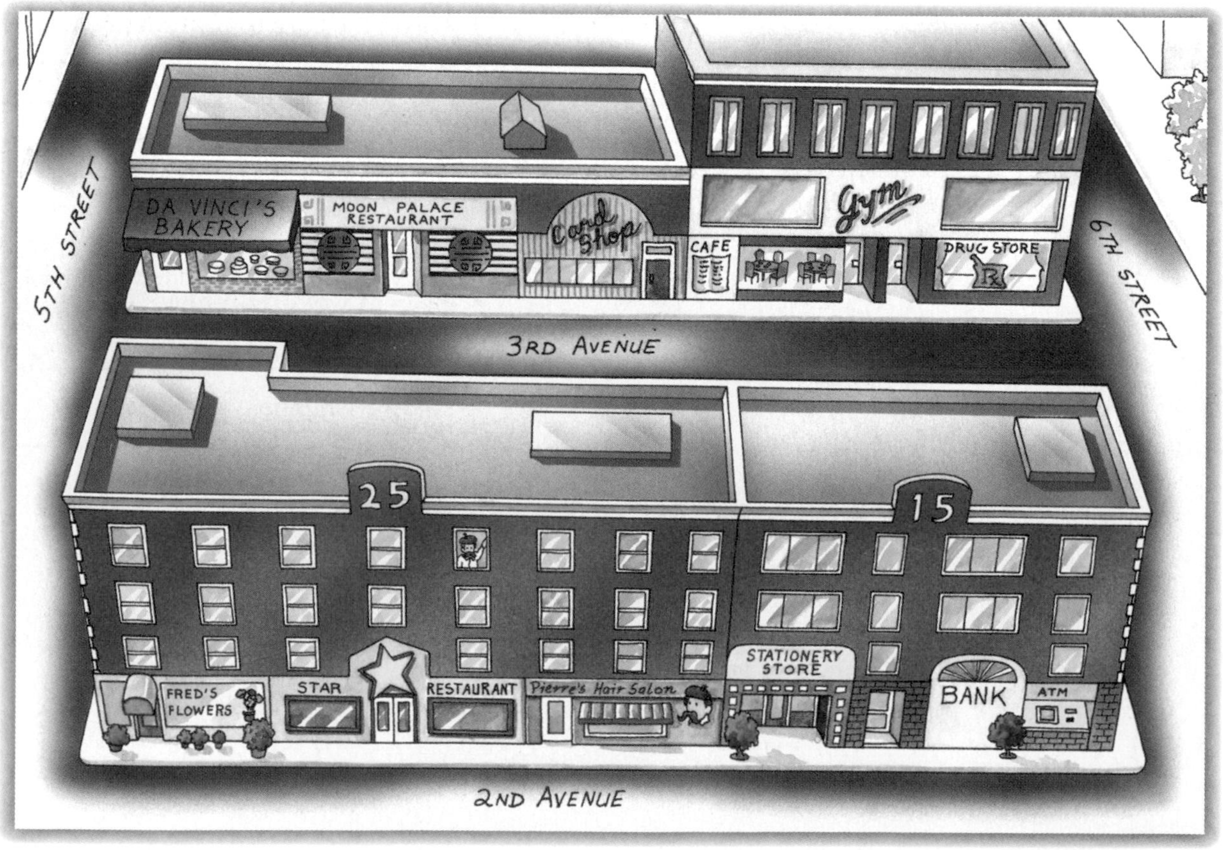

1. Fred's Flowers is ___on___ 2nd Avenue.
2. Pierre's Hair Salon is ___between___ a stationery store and a restaurant.
3. Da Vinci's Bakery is ___on the___ corner ___of___ 3rd Avenue and 5th Street.
4. The café is ___next to___ the drugstore.
5. Pierre's apartment is ___at___ 25 2nd Avenue.
6. His apartment is ___on the___ fourth floor.
7. The café and drugstore are ___under___ a gym.

3 | A PLACE TO MEET *Grammar Notes 1–2*

Look at the map. Listen to the conversation. Complete the sentences.

1. They are meeting on ___3rd___ Avenue.
2. They're meeting ___between___ 5th and 6th ___streets___.
3. They're meeting on 3rd Avenue ___in front of___ the restaurant.
4. The restaurant is ___between___ the card shop and the ___bakery___.
5. The name of the restaurant is ___Moonpalace___.

4 | I AM IN SCHOOL *Grammar Notes 1–3*

Complete the sentences. Write true sentences. Write them in class.

1. I am ___in___ school.
2. I am ___in___ room ___360___.
3. I am not ___at___ home. I'm not ___at___ work.
4. I am ___In Thailand___.
   (your country)
5. I am ___In Nakhonsawan___.
   (your city)
6. I am ___on the third floor___.
   (floor)
7. My school is ___at 3001 Nort Beauregard Street Alexandia, V.A. 22311___.
   (school address)

5 | EDITING

Put a check (✓) next to the three correct sentences. Add a word or words to correct the other sentences.

_____ 1. She's next the policeman.

_____ 2. The bookstore is on the corner Main Street.

_____ 3. He lives on first floor.

_____ 4. I'm near the museum.

_____ 5. He's not work today. He's home.

_____ 6. I'm the corner of Main and Second.

_____ 7. A man is in front the stationery store.

_____ 8. It's between the flower shop and the drugstore.

_____ 9. We're in back of the house.

_____ 10. Her office is 78 Elm Street.

_____ 11. He's Osaka now.

_____ 12. We're third floor.

Communication Practice

6 | LISTENING

A *Look at the world map in Appendix 1, page A-1. Listen to the speaker. Write the names of the countries.*

1. _ _ _ _ _

2. _ _ _ _ _ _ _ _

3. _ _ _ _ _ _ _ _ _ _ _ _

4. _ _ _ _ _ _

B *Work with a partner. Write sentences about a country's location. Use the prepositions* **between**, **near**, **next to**, *and* **in**. *Read your sentences to your partner. Your partner guesses the country. (See the map in Appendix 1, page A-1.)*

Example: This country is in Central America. It is between Costa Rica and Colombia. What country is it?

7 | A WORD GAME

Look at Exercise 1, page 56. Write your own word puzzle. Read it to the class.

8 | ON THE INTERNET

Look on the Internet. Find the official residence of the leader of a country.

Examples: The prime minister of Canada lives at 24 Sussex Drive in Ottawa, Canada.
The president of France lives on Champs Elysées Avenue at the Elysées Palace in Paris, France.

UNIT 7

Wh- Questions

Grammar in Context

BEFORE YOU READ

Look at this painting. What do you see?

A professor is speaking to his students in Art History 101. Read the questions about the painting. Then read the professor's comments and the student's test paper.

1. **Who** is the artist?
2. **Where** is the artist from?
3. **What** is the name of the painting?
4. **Why** is this painting unusual?

PROFESSOR: Today is our first test. Look at the questions. Then look at each painting. There are 12 paintings. This is the first one. You have five minutes to answer the questions about each painting. Work fast. The test is one hour long.

Name: *Tim Smith* Date: *November 2*

Painting #1

1. *The artist is René Magritte.*
2. *He is from Brussels, Belgium.*
3. *The name of the painting is The Son of Man.*
4. *It's unusual because an apple hides the man's face.*

AFTER YOU READ

*Answer the questions. Circle **a** or **b**.*

1. What is *The Son of Man*?
   a. a book — b. a painting
2. Who is René Magritte?
   a. a Belgian artist — b. the Son of Man
3. Where is Brussels?
   a. in France — b. in Belgium
4. Why is it important to work fast?
   a. There are many paintings. — b. There are many students.

Grammar Presentation

QUESTIONS AND ANSWERS WITH *WHO, WHAT, WHERE,* AND *WHY*

Questions		
Question Word	*Be*	
Who	**are**	René Magritte and Salvador Dali?
What	**is**	*The Son of Man*?
Where	**are**	Magritte and Dali from?
Why	**is**	the museum closed?

Answers	
Short Answers	Long Answers
Artists.	They're artists.
A painting.	It's a painting.
Belgium and Spain.	Magritte is from Belgium and Dali is from Spain.
It's Monday.	The museum is closed because it's Monday.

GRAMMAR NOTES

GRAMMAR NOTES	EXAMPLES
1. ***Wh-* questions** ask for **information**. They cannot be answered with a *yes* or *no*.	**Q: Where** are you from? **A:** Canada. (I'm from Canada.) NOT: ~~Yes, I am~~.
Use ***is*** for singular subjects and ***are*** for plural subjects.	• Where **is** he? • Where **are** they?
2. ***Who*** asks about people.	**Q: Who** is René Magritte? **A:** He's a Belgian artist.

3. ***What*** asks about **things**.	**Q: What** is the name of that painting? **A:** *The Son of Man.*

4. ***Where*** asks about **places**.	**Q: Where** is Magritte from? **A:** He's from Brussels.

5. ***Why*** asks for a **reason**. In long answers use *because* before the reason.	**Q: Why** is the painting strange? **A:** An apple hides the man's face. OR **A:** The painting is strange because an apple hides the man's face.

6. We often use **contractions** (short forms) for *wh-* questions with *is* in speaking and informal writing.	**Q: Who's** Salvador Dali? **Q: Where's** he from?

7. We usually give **short answers**. We can give **long answers** too.	**Q:** Where are the paintings? **A: In a museum.** **A: The paintings are in a museum.**

Focused Practice

1 DISCOVER THE GRAMMAR

This is the information under a painting. Read the information and answer the questions.

1. Who is the artist? Georgia O'Keeffe.

2. Where is the painting? In the Museum of fine Arts.

3. What is the name of her painting? White Rose with Larkspur.

4. Where is the Museum of Fine Arts? It's in Boston, Massachusetts.

2 THE HERMITAGE AND RODIN

Grammar Notes 1–7

Complete the questions. Use **Who's, What's, Where's,** *and* **Why is.**

1. **Q:** What is the Hermitage? **A:** It's a museum.
2. **Q:** Where's the Hermitage? **A:** It's in Saint Petersburg.
3. **Q:** Where's Saint Petersburg? **A:** It's in Russia.
4. **Q:** What's the name of that sculpture? **A:** *Eternal Spring.*
5. **Q:** Why is there a special Rodin room? **A:** Because he was the most famous sculptor of the early 20th century.

3 SURREALISM

Grammar Notes 1–7

Read about surrealism. Read the answers. Then write the questions. Use the question word in parentheses.

Surrealism is a painting style of the early 1900s. Surrealist artists use their dreams in their art. René Magritte and Salvador Dali are famous surrealist artists. Magritte is from Belgium. Dali is from Spain. Dali's most famous painting is *The Persistence of Memory*. Do you like it?

1. (What) **Q:** What is Surrealism ?

   A: It's a painting style.

2. (Who) **Q:** Who are Rene Magritte and Salvador Dali ?

   A: They are surrealist artists.

3. (Where) **Q:** Where are Rene Magritte and Salvador Dali from ?

   A: Magritte is from Belgium and Dali is from Spain.

4. (What) **Q:** What is Dali most famous painting ?

   A: *The Persistence of Memory.*

4 | EDITING

Read the conversation. There are four mistakes. The first mistake is already corrected.

1. **A:** What's the name of this class?
   B: Art History 101.
2. **A:** Who the teacher is?
   B: Professor Good.
3. **A:** Where he is?
   B: He's next to the board. He's the tall man with the gray beard.
4. **A:** Why the students are so quiet?
   B: There's a test today.

Communication Practice

5 | LISTENING

Listen to the conversation. Then complete the answers.

1. **Q:** What is the gift? **A:** It's a painting .
2. **Q:** Who is the artist? **A:** John's brother .
3. **Q:** Where is his gallery? **A:** It's on 2nd Avanve .
4. **Q:** Why is it closed? **A:** It all way closed on Monday .

6 | WHAT DO YOU KNOW ABOUT ART AND ARTISTS?

A *Work in small groups. One student reads the answer. The others ask the question.*

Example: **A:** She is a famous American artist. She paints large flowers.
B: Who is Georgia O'Keeffe?

1. It is a museum. It is in Saint Petersburg, Russia.
2. He is a surrealist artist. He is from Spain.
3. He is a surrealist artist. He is from Belgium.
4. It is in Boston. It is a big museum. It has a painting by Georgia O'Keeffe.
5. He is a sculptor. He is from France. Some of his sculptures are in Russia.

B *With your group, write two sentences about artists. Your class asks the questions.*

7 | ON THE INTERNET

Download a picture of a painting. Include the following information:

Who's the artist?
What's the name of the painting?
Where's he or she from?
Why is it a great painting?

Tell your class about it.

PART

II From Grammar to Writing

Connecting with And *and* But

1 *Read these sentences.*

1. a. He's tall. He's a good basketball player.

   b. He's tall, **and** he's a good basketball player.

2. a. He's tall. He's a terrible basketball player.

   b. He's tall, **but** he's a terrible basketball player.

And adds information. ***But*** shows a surprise or contrast. We usually use a comma before ***and*** and ***but*** when they connect two sentences.

Examples: The book is good, **and** it is easy to understand.
The book is good, **but** it is difficult to understand.

Do not use a comma to connect two descriptive adjectives.

Examples: I am hungry **and** tired.
He is tired **but** happy.

2 *Use* **and** *or* **but** *to complete the sentences.*

1. She's friendly ___and___ popular.
2. She's friendly ___but___ unpopular.
3. Her last name is long, ___and___ it's hard to pronounce.
4. Her last name is long, ___but___ it's easy to pronounce.

3 *Use* **and** *or* **but** *to complete the story about Henry. Then write a story about someone who made a big change in his or her life.*

Five years ago Henry was a banker. His home was big ___and___ expensive. His car was fast ___and___ fancy. His workday was long, ___and___ his work was stressful. He was rich, ___but___ he was stressed and unhappy.

Today Henry works in a flower shop. His home is small ___and___ inexpensive. His car is old ___and___ small. His workday is short, ___and___ his work is relaxing. He isn't rich, ___but___ he's relaxed and happy.

Review Test

I *Read each conversation. Circle the letter of the underlined word or group of words that is not correct.*

1. A: Where (A) is your friend (B)?
   B: She's (C) on (D) Paris. — A B C D

2. A: Is (A) Kaori in work (B) now?
   B: No, she isn't (C). She's at home (D). — A B C D

3. A: Who's (A) on (B) Elm Street?
   B: A post office (C) and a new bank (D). — A B C D

4. A: Is the bank on the corner (A) Wood Street?
   B: No, it's not (B). It's between (C) Wood Street and (D) Main Street. — A B C D

5. A: Is (A) the new bakery (B) next to (C) the building tall? (D)
   B: No, it's next to the bookstore. — A B C D

6. A: Where (A) are the olds (B) newspapers (C)?
   B: They're on the desk (D). — A B C D

II *Circle the letter of the correct word(s) to complete the sentences.*

1. It is _____. — A B C D
   (A) a day sunny
   (B) a sunny day
   (C) sunny days
   (D) sunny day

2. They are _____. — A B C D
   (A) child
   (B) children
   (C) a child
   (D) a children

(continued)

3. He is _____. **A B C D**

(A) artists **(C)** an artist

(B) a artist **(D)** an artists

4. Is this _____? **A B C D**

(A) old rug **(C)** rugs old

(B) old rugs **(D)** an old rug

5. The bank is _____. **A B C D**

(A) next the post office **(C)** next to the post office

(B) next of the post office **(D)** next at the post office

III *Complete the sentences. Use* **a** *or* **an** *or* **Ø***.*

1. He isn't __a__ teacher. He's __a__ student. He's __a__ new student in this school.
2. She isn't __an__ artist. She's __a__ dancer.
3. They're __Ø__ famous. They're __Ø__ actors.
4. Our grammar class isn't long. It's __an__ hour.
5. This is __a__ hospital. It's near the university.
6. He's __an__ uncle. She's __an__ aunt.
7. This is __an__ old photograph. It's __a__ photograph of my grandparents as children. It's __Ø__ special to me.

IV *Use the words in the box to complete the conversations.*

What	Where	Who	Why

1. **A:** __Where__ is your school?
   B: It's on Main Street.
2. **A:** __Who__ are your teachers?
   B: Ms. Thomas and Mr. James.
3. **A:** __Why__ is the school closed today?
   B: It's a holiday.
4. **A:** __What__ is the name of your textbook?
   B: *Focus on Grammar.*

V *Look at the street. Use the word(s) in parentheses to complete the sentences.*

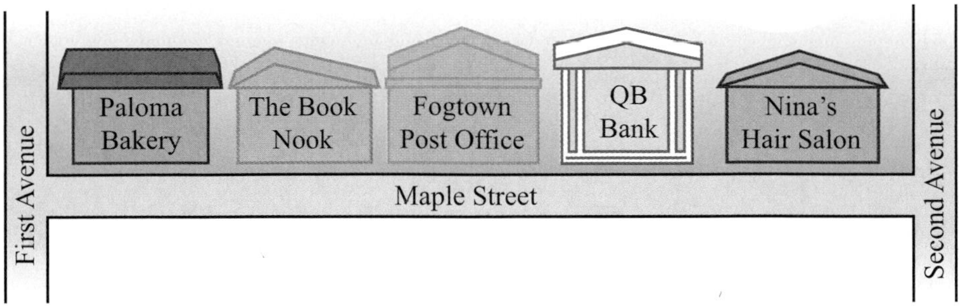

1. (corner) Paloma Bakery *is on the corner of Maple Street and First Avenue.*
2. (between) The post office is between The Book Nook and QB Bank.
3. (next to) The bank is next to Fogtown post office.
4. (corner) Nina's Hair Salon is on the corner of Maple Street and Second Avenue.
5. (on) The Book Nook is on Maple Street.

▶ ***To check your answers, go to the Answer Key on page RT-1.***

PART III

The Simple Present

UNIT

8 The Simple Present: Affirmative and Negative Statements

Grammar in Context

BEFORE YOU READ

	YES	NO
I shop for clothes often.	☑	☐
I don't shop for clothes often.	☐	☑
I look at the labels.	☑	☐
I don't look at the labels.	☐	☑

Complete the sentences.

I like to buy clothes at Potomac Mills

I buy most of my clothes at Potomac Mills

TEENAGE GIRLS' FAVORITE STORES

UK	*Topshop*
France	*H&M*
Germany	*H&M*
United States	*Old Navy*

Read a magazine article about teenage shoppers in Japan.

stye

TEEN TRENDS

Yumi **is** seventeen years old. She**'s** a senior in high school in Japan. Yumi **wears** "kawaii" boots, jeans, and sunglasses. And she **carries** a "kawaii" camera phone. "Kawaii" **is** a Japanese word. It **means** cute. Yumi **uses** the word a lot. She **doesn't buy** "non-kawaii" things.

Businesses **look** at Yumi and her friends. They **study** their clothes. Companies **know** that Yumi **is** not alone. There **are** many other teens like Yumi.

Yumi and her friends **buy** the same things. They **want** to look the same. Their clothes **don't** always **cost** a lot. But the number of teenage shoppers **is** big. And that **means** a lot of money for businesses.

In the 1990s, college girls were the trendsetters—they were the first to start a trend. Now it**'s** high school girls. Maybe in the future it will be junior high school girls. And it**'s** not just girls. Nowadays guys **shop** and **want** a certain "look" too.

AFTER YOU READ

A *Mark these statements* **T** *(true) or* **F** *(false).*

__T__ 1. Yumi wears boots.

__F__ 2. Yumi works for a company.

__T__ 3. Yumi has friends.

__T__ 4. "Kawaii" means cute.

__F__ 5. Yumi doesn't look like her friends.

__F__ 6. Teenage boys don't like clothes.

B *In Japan girls like "kawaii" things. In the United States teens want "cool" things. Korean teens want "zahng" things. Mexican teens say, "Esta padre." In the Dominican Republic they say, "Que chulo." What do people say in your country to describe something they like? Tell your class.*

Grammar Presentation

THE SIMPLE PRESENT: AFFIRMATIVE AND NEGATIVE STATEMENTS

Affirmative Statements	
Subject	**Verb**
I You* We They	**work**.
He She It	**works**.

Negative Statements		
Subject	***Do not / Does not***	**Base Form of Verb**
I You* We They	**do not** **don't**	**work**.
He She It	**does not** **doesn't**	**work**.

* *You* is both singular and plural.

GRAMMAR NOTES

1. Use the **simple present** to tell about **things that happen again and again** (habits, regular occurrences, customs, and routines).

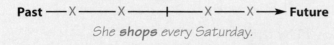

Now
Past —X——X——+——X——X——➤ **Future**
She ***shops*** *every Saturday.*

EXAMPLES

- She **drinks** green tea.
- He **shops** at the mall.
- They **give** gifts on New Year's Day.
- She **goes** to bed at midnight.

(continued)

2. Use the simple present to tell **facts**.	• This jacket **costs** sixty dollars. • The word "kawaii" **means** cute.
3. Use the simple present with **non-action verbs**.	• She **is** seventeen years old. • She **likes** that store.
4. In **affirmative statements**, use the **base form** of the verb for all persons except the third person singular. Put ***-s*** or ***-es*** on the third person singular (*he/she/it*).	• **I want** a new sweater. **You need** a new suit. **They have** a car. • **She wants** a camera phone. • **He watches** TV every day.
5. PRONUNCIATION NOTE: Pronounce the third person singular ending /s/, /z/, or /ɪz/.	• /s/ He like**s** music. • /z/ She play**s** golf. • /ɪz/ He watch**es** TV every day.
6. In **negative statements**, use ***does not*** or ***do not*** before the base form of the verb. Use the contractions ***doesn't*** and ***don't*** in speaking or in informal writing. ▶ **BE CAREFUL!** When ***or*** connects two verbs in a negative statement, we do not repeat *don't* or *doesn't* before the second verb.	• He **does not wear** ties. • We **do not shop** there. • He **doesn't wear** ties. • We **don't shop** there. • They **don't live or work** there. • He **doesn't work or study** on weekends. NOT: He doesn't work or ~~doesn't~~ study on weekends.
7. The **third person singular affirmative** forms of ***have***, ***do***, and ***go*** are <u>not regular</u>. The **third person singular negative** form of ***have***, ***do***, and ***go*** are <u>regular</u>.	• She **has** a new coat. • He **does** the laundry on Saturday. • He **goes** to the gym at ten. • She **doesn't have** a new hat. • He **doesn't do** laundry on Sunday. • He **doesn't go** to the gym at eleven.
8. The verb ***be*** has different forms from all other verbs.	• I **am** tired. I **look** tired. • You **are** tall. You **look** tall. • He **is** bored. He **looks** bored.

Reference Notes

See Unit 27, page 267 for a fuller discussion of non-action verbs.
See Appendix 16, page A-17 for spelling and pronunciation rules for the third person singular in the simple present.
See Unit 1 for a complete presentation of the verb *be*.

Focused Practice

1 DISCOVER THE GRAMMAR

Circle the correct word to complete the sentence.

1. My grandfather wear / wears a suit every day.
2. My brothers like / likes jeans and t-shirts.
3. His teacher know / knows about fashion.
4. I carry / carries my cell phone in my bag.
5. They shop / shops online.
6. The word "cool" mean / means different things.
7. You have / has a cool jacket.

2 NEGATIVE STATEMENTS *Grammar Notes 6, 8*

Underline the verb in the first sentence. Complete the second sentence in the negative. Use the same verb.

1. He shops at flea markets. He ___doesn't shop___ at chain stores.
2. We buy name brands. They ___don't buy___ name brands.
3. I like jeans. I ___don't like___ suits.
4. I need a new jacket. I ___don't need___ a new coat.
5. She likes leather. He ___doesnt like___ leather.
6. It looks good. It ___doesn't look___ tight.
7. We are twenty years old. We ___aren't___ teenagers.
8. It is expensive. It ___isn't___ on sale.

3 AFFIRMATIVE AND NEGATIVE STATEMENTS *Grammar Notes 1–4, 6, 7*

Write affirmative or negative statements. Use the verb in parentheses.

1. (cost) **a.** It's expensive. It ___costs___ a lot.
   b. It's cheap. It ___doesn't cost___ a lot.
2. (need) **a.** I'm cold. I ___need___ a sweater.
   b. I'm hot. I ___don't need___ a sweater.

3. (want) a. His jacket is old. He ___wants___ a new one.

b. His jacket is new. He ___doesn't want___ a new one.

4. (like) a. We ___like___ window shopping. We often look at store windows.

b. They ___don't like___ window shopping. They never look at store windows.

5. (have) a. He's rich. He ___has___ a lot of money.

b. She's poor. She ___doesn't have___ a lot of money.

6. (go) a. He loves to swim. He ___goes___ swimming twice a week.

b. She doesn't like to swim. She ___doesn't go___ swimming often.

4 | ADVICE COLUMN

Grammar Notes 1–4, 6–8

A *Complete the letter. Use the verbs in parentheses.*

Dear Rosa,

Our son ___is___ (1. be) fourteen years old. He ___is___ (2. be) a good student, and he ___has___ (3. have) a lot of friends. But we ___have___ (4. have) one big problem with him. He ___loves___ (5. love) clothes. He ___wants___ (6. want) all the latest styles. And he ___prefers___ (7. prefer) designer clothes. We ___aren't___ (8. be, not) poor, but I ___think___ (9. think) it is wrong to spend a lot of money on clothes, especially for a growing boy.

We ___give___ (10. give) him spending money, but he ___doesn't have___ (11. have, not) enough to buy all the clothes he wants. Now he ___wants___ (12. want) to get a part-time job. I ___don't want___ (13. want, not) him to work, but my husband ___thinks___ (14. think) it's okay. What do you think?

Worried Mom

B *Complete the letter to "Worried Mom." Use the words in the box.*

agree	sounds	thinks	want	works

Dear Worried Mom,

Most teens ___want___ *to look like their friends. It's very normal. And I* ___agree___ *with your husband. When a person* ___works___, *that person* ___thinks___ *about the cost of things. A job for your son* ___sounds___ *fine to me.*

Rosa

5 | EDITING

Correct this paragraph. There are eight mistakes. The first mistake is already corrected.

Miyuki Miyagi ~~live~~ in Japan. She work for a big advertising company. She studies teenagers. She say, "Teenagers change things. They doesn't think like the manufacturers. Manufacturers thinks of one way to use things. Teenagers find another way. For example, pagers are for emergencies. But teenagers are think they're fun and cute. They don't uses them for emergencies. They uses them for fun."

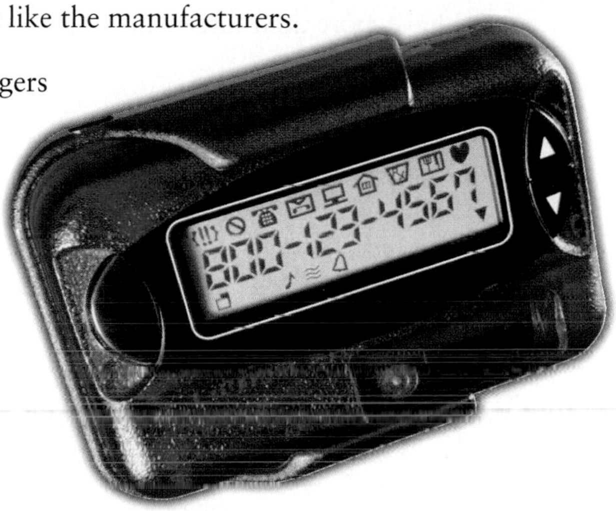

Communication Practice

6 | LISTENING

Underline the verb in each sentence. Then listen to each sentence and check (✓) the sound of the verb ending. (See Appendix 16, page A-17 for an explanation of these endings.)

	/s/	/z/	/ɪz/
1. He <u>shops</u> a lot.	✓		
2. She buys clothes at discount stores.			
3. She uses that word a lot.			
4. It costs a hundred dollars.			
5. He knows his business.			
6. She carries a cell phone.			
7. He misses her.			
8. She watches fashion shows on TV.			
9. He thinks about his clothes.			

7 | MY PARTNER AND I

Check (✓) the sentences that are true for you.

1. _____ I wear colorful clothes.   __✓__ I don't wear colorful clothes.
2. __✓__ I like leather jackets.   _____ I don't like leather jackets.
3. __✓__ I have more than three pairs of jeans.   _____ I don't have more than three pairs of jeans.
4. __✓__ I buy designer clothes.   _____ I don't buy designer clothes.
5. __✓__ I like to look at fashion magazines.   _____ I don't like to look at fashion magazines.
6. _____ I like unusual clothes.   __✓__ I don't like unusual clothes.
7. __✓__ I wear traditional clothes on holidays.   _____ I don't wear traditional clothes on holidays.

Work with a partner. In what ways are you and your partner alike? In what ways are you different?

Example: We don't wear colorful clothes. We like dark colors like black and gray.

8 | CLOTHES AND CUSTOMS FROM AROUND THE WORLD

Argentina	China	Denmark	India	Japan	Korea	the United States

Work with a partner. First circle the correct form of the verbs. Then guess the country.

1. People in __Korea__ (don't wear / doesn't wear) shoes in their homes. When Sho (come / comes) home, he (remove / removes) his shoes and (put / puts) on slippers.
2. In Southern __Denmark__, the *gauchos* [cowboys] (wear / wears) baggy pants and hats with wide brims.
3. Most women (wear / wears) saris in __India__. It (take / takes) six meters of cloth to make a sari.
4. On New Year's Day in __China__, parents and grandparents (give / gives) children money in red envelopes.

5. In the United State people usually (don't work / doesn't work) on July 4. They (have / has) barbecues and (watch / watches) fireworks.
6. Eric Olson is from Argentina. On New Year's Eve he (bang / bangs) on his friends' doors and sets off fireworks.

Now check your answers below.

9 | WRITING

Think about a person you know. Write about his or her job.

Example: Jill goes to work at 4:30 in the morning. She works for a TV news channel. She does the makeup for a news anchor. Jill works only four hours a day. People say, "Jill is good at her job. She's an artist." The news anchor says, "I only want Jill. She's the best." Jill makes a good salary and she enjoys her work. But Jill has a secret. She doesn't want to be a makeup artist forever. In the afternoons Jill studies journalism. Jill really wants to be a news anchor.

10 | ON THE INTERNET

Find information and pictures of traditional clothes from one part of the world. Tell your class about the clothes.

Example: Traditional Mexican clothes are comfortable and beautiful. Men wear cotton shirts and pants. Sombreros (hats with wide brims) protect them from the sun. In cold weather, they wear ponchos. Women wear blouses and long, full skirts. They cover their heads with shawls called rebozos. Sometimes women use their rebozos to carry their babies.

Exercise 8

1. Japan, don't wear, comes, removes, puts 2. Argentina, wear 3. wear, India, takes 4. China, give 5. the United States, don't work, have, watch 6. Denmark, bangs

UNIT

9 The Simple Present: *Yes/No* Questions and Short Answers

Grammar in Context

BEFORE YOU READ

Do you share a room? Do you live alone? Do you have a roommate? Imagine you are looking for a roommate. What questions are important to ask?

Colleges often use questionnaires to help students find the right roommate. Read this roommate questionnaire and two students' answers.

Names:	Dan		Jon		You	
	Yes	No	Yes	No	Yes	No
1. **Do** you **smoke**?	☐	☑	☐	☑	☐	☑
2. **Does** smoking **bother** you?	☑	☐	☐	☑	☑	☐
3. **Do** you **wake up** early?	☐	☑	☐	☑	☑	☐
4. **Do** you **stay up** late?	☑	☐	☑	☐	☑	☐
5. **Are** you neat?	☑	☐	☑	☐	☑	☐
6. **Does** a messy room **bother** you?	☑	☐	☑	☐	☑	☐
7. **Are** you quiet?	☐	☑	☑	☐	☑	☐
8. **Are** you talkative?	☑	☐	☐	☑	☐	☑
9. **Do** you **listen** to loud music?	☑	☐	☑	☐	☑	☐
10. **Do** you **watch** a lot of TV?	☑	☐	☑	☐	☑	☐
11. **Do** you **study** and **listen** to music at the same time?	☑	☐	☑	☐	☐	☑
12. **Do** you **study** with the TV on?	☑	☐	☑	☐	☐	☑

AFTER YOU READ

A *Mark these statements* **T** *(true) or* **F** *(false).*

_F_ 1. Dan and Jon both smoke.

_T_ 2. Dan and Jon wake up late.

_F_ 3. Dan is neat, but Jon isn't.

_F_ 4. Dan and Jon are quiet.

_T_ 5. Dan and Jon listen to loud music.

_F_ 6. Dan and Jon don't watch TV.

_T_ 7. Dan and Jon study and listen to music at the same time.

B *Discuss with a partner.*

Are Dan and Jon a good match? If so, why? If not, why not?

C *Answer the questions for yourself. Compare your answers with a partner's. Are you and your partner a good match?*

Grammar Presentation

THE SIMPLE PRESENT: *YES/NO* QUESTIONS AND SHORT ANSWERS

***Yes/No* Questions**		
Do/Does	**Subject**	**Base Form of Verb**
Do	I you* we they	**work**?
Does	he she it	

Short Answers					
Affirmative			**Negative**		
Yes,	you I/we you they	**do**.	No,	you I/we you they	**don't**.
	he she it	**does**.		he she it	**doesn't**.

* *You* is both singular and plural.

(continued)

GRAMMAR NOTES / EXAMPLES

GRAMMAR NOTES	EXAMPLES
1. For *yes/no* **questions in the simple present**, use ***do*** or ***does*** before the subject. Use the base form of the verb after the subject.	(subject / base form) • **Do** you **work**? • **Does** he **have** a roommate?
2. We usually use **short answers** in conversation. Sometimes we use **long answers**.	**Q:** Do you work at the bank? **A: Yes, I do.** OR **Yes, I work** at the bank. **Q:** Does he have a roommate? **A: Yes, he does.** OR **Yes, he has a roommate.**
3. Do not use *do* or *does* for *yes/no* questions with *be*.	• **Are** you from Ecuador? • **Is** he from France? NOT: ~~Do~~ are you from Ecuador? ~~Does~~ is he from France?

Reference Note
See Unit 2, page 14 for a discussion of *yes/no* questions with *be*.

Focused Practice

1 DISCOVER THE GRAMMAR

Read about Dan and Jon.

In many ways Dan and Jon are alike. Both Dan and Jon like music and sports, but Dan likes popular music and Jon likes jazz. Both Dan and Jon like basketball, but Jon likes tennis and Dan doesn't. Dan and Jon are both neat. They don't like a messy room. They both like to go to bed late—after midnight. They watch about two hours of TV at night, and they study with the TV on. But in one way Dan and Jon are completely different. Dan is talkative, but Jon is quiet. Dan says, "We're lucky about that. It works out nicely. I talk, he listens." Jon says, "Uh-huh."

Match the questions and answers.

__b__ 1. Do they both like music and sports?

__d__ 2. Do they like to go to bed early?

__c__ 3. Does Dan like popular music?

__e__ 4. Dan is talkative. Jon is quiet. Does it matter?

__a__ 5. Do Dan and Jon like classical music?

a. It doesn't say.

b. Yes, they do.

c. Yes, he does.

d. No, they don't.

e. No, it doesn't.

2 | *YES/NO* QUESTIONS AND SHORT ANSWERS — *Grammar Notes 1–2*

Complete the questions with **Do** *or* **Does** *and the verb in parentheses. Then complete the short answers.*

1. **Q:** (listen) __Do__ you __listen__ to music?

   A: Yes, __we do__. OR Yes, __I do__.

2. **Q:** (have) __Does__ your roommate __have__ a TV?

   A: No, she __doesn't__.

3. **Q:** (know) __Does__ he __know__ your brother?

   A: No, __he doesn't__.

4. **Q:** (like) __Do__ they __like__ Thai food?

   A: Yes, __they do__.

5. **Q:** (wear) __Does__ she __wear__ designer clothes?

   A: No, __she doesn't__.

6. **Q:** (have) __Does__ your room __have__ a big window?

   A: Yes, __it does__.

7. **Q:** (rain) __Does__ it __rain__ a lot in your city?

   A: No, __it doesn't__.

8. **Q:** (have) __Do__ I __have__ Internet access?

   A: Yes, __you do__.

9. **Q:** (go) __Does__ she __go__ to school by train?

   A: No, __she doesn't__.

3 | *YES/NO* QUESTIONS: THE SIMPLE PRESENT

Grammar Notes 1–3

Complete the **yes/no** *questions with* **Do, Does, Am, Is,** *or* **Are**. *Then complete the short answers.*

1. **Q:** ___Am___ I late? **A:** No, ___you aren't___.
2. **Q:** ___Does___ he come late? **A:** Yes, ___he does___.
3. **Q:** ___Are___ you busy? **A:** Yes, we ___are___.
4. **Q:** ___Do___ they have a lot of work? **A:** No, ___they don't___.
5. **Q:** ___Are___ they roommates? **A:** No, ___they aren't___.
6. **Q:** ___Do___ they live in a dormitory? **A:** Yes, ___they do___.
7. **Q:** ___Is___ she your sister? **A:** No, ___she isn't___.
8. **Q:** ___Do___ you live at home? **A:** Yes, I ___do___.
9. **Q:** ___Does___ your roommate play tennis? **A:** No, he ___doesn't___.
10. **Q:** ___Are___ we in the right room? **A:** Yes, you ___are___.
11. **Q:** ___Are___ you friends? **A:** Yes, ___we are___.
12. **Q:** ___Do___ you cook well? **A:** No, I ___don't___.

4 | A ROOMMATE

Grammar Notes 1–2

Complete the conversation. Write the questions and short answers. Use the words in parentheses. Use **do** *or* **does** *in every question and answer.*

Then listen and check your work.

A: So tell me about your new roommate. ___Do you like___ (1. you / like) him?

B: ___Yes, I do___ (2.). He's a really nice guy.

A: I know he speaks English fluently, but he's not American. ___Does he come___ (3. he / come) from England?

B: ___No, he doesn't___ (4.). He comes from Australia.

A: Oh? ___Does he come___ (5. he / come) from Sydney?

B: ___No, he doesn't___ (6.). He comes from Melbourne.

A: What's he studying?

B: Music.

A: Do you like the same kind of music?
7. (you / like)

B: Yes, we do. We both like classical music. He has a good CD player and hundreds of CDs.
8.

A: Does he have relatives here?
9. (he / have)

B: Yes, he does. His uncle and aunt live here. I was at their home last night.
10.

A: Really? Do you see them often?
11. (you / see)

B: Yes, I do. They invite the two of us for a meal at least once a month. They're great cooks and interesting people. He's a conductor and she's an opera singer.
12.

A: Do you bring them a small gift when you visit?
13. (you / bring)

B: No, I don't. I'm a poor student.
14.

A: Hey, you're not that poor.

5 | EDITING

Read these conversations. There are eight mistakes. The first mistake is already corrected.

1. A: Does she ~~goes~~ go to school?

   B: Yes, she ~~goes.~~ does

2. A: Does he needs help?

   B: Yes, he does.

3. A: Do they are like jazz?

   B: Yes, they do.

4. A: ~~Do~~ Does she live near the museum?

   B: Yes, she ~~lives.~~ does

5. A: Does he ~~has~~ have a roommate?

   B: Yes, he does.

6. A: Are you friends?

   B: Yes, we do. are

Communication Practice

6 | LISTENING

Andrea wants a roommate. She is talking to Valentina Gold. Ms. Gold helps people find roommates. Listen to Andrea's answers. Complete the chart. Then read Gloria's answers.

	Andrea	**Gloria**
likes	She doesn't like party	parties
listens to	Jazz	rock
plays		basketball, soccer, tennis
studies	at night, in her room	at night, in her room

Are they a good match? ☐ Yes ☑ No

Reason 1: Andrea doesn't listen to rock music, but Gloria listens to rock music.

Reason 2: Andrea doesn't like party, but Gloria likes party.

7 | FIND SOMEONE WHO . . .

Find out about your classmates. Ask these questions or add your own. Take notes. Tell the class something new about three classmates.

Yes — No — Yes

Do you _______?

- speak more than two languages — Rashida
- cook well — wacth
- know tai chi — wroong
- know sign language
- play a musical instrument
- have more than four sisters and brothers

Your question: Do you happy ?

Rashida

No

Are you _______?

- an only child — Mandy
- a good dancer — wroong
- good at a sport — wroong
- clean — wroong
- messy — wroong
- easy-going

Your question: Are you maried ?

Mandy

8 | A TREASURE HUNT

Work in small groups. Ask questions. Check (✓) the items you have. The first group to check ten items wins.

Example: Do you have a stamp? OR Does anyone have a stamp?

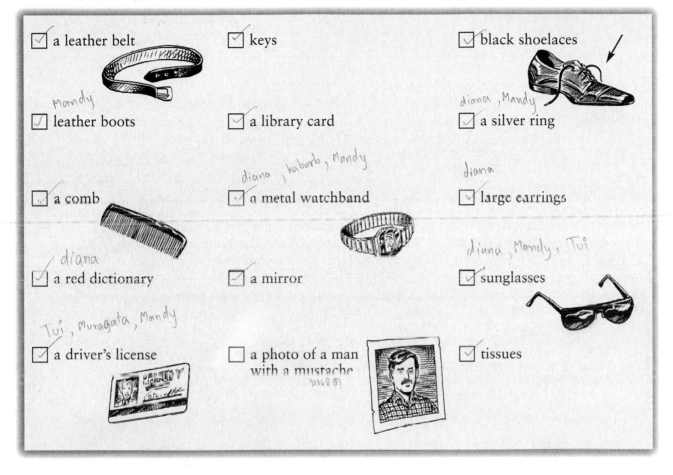

- [x] a leather belt

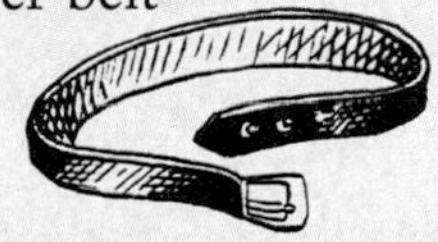

- [x] keys
- [x] black shoelaces

Mandy
- [x] leather boots
- [x] a library card

diana, Mandy
- [x] a silver ring
- [x] a comb

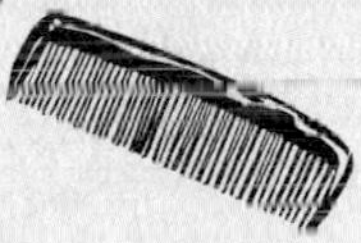

diana, kabarb, Mandy
- [x] a metal watchband

diana
- [x] large earrings

diana
- [x] a red dictionary
- [x] a mirror

diana, Mandy, Tui
- [x] sunglasses

Tui, Muragata, Mandy
- [x] a driver's license

- [ ] a photo of a man with a mustache

- [x] tissues

9 | PHRASES WITH *DO* AND *DOES*

A *Work in pairs. Complete the short conversations. Use the sentences in the box. Practice them with your partner.*

No, it's broken.	Yes, thanks. We need a salad.
No. I'm busy all afternoon.	Yes. It's 9:45.
Yes, it's more than two hundred dollars.	

1. **A:** Do you have time?
   B: No. I'm busy all afternoon.
2. **A:** I have a class at 10:00. Do you have the time?
   B: Yes. It's 9:45.

(continued)

3. **A:** Do you need any help?

   B: Yes, thanks. We need a salad.

4. **A:** Does it cost a lot?

   B: Yes, it's more than two hundred dollars.

5. **A:** Does it work?

   B: No, it's broken.

B *Use one of the conversations above in a role play with your partner.*

Example: **A:** Do you need any help?
B: Yes, thanks. We need a salad. Here's the lettuce.

10 | WRITING

You plan to study English at a school for international students during your vacation. The school matches you with a roommate. You receive this letter from your roommate. Answer the letter. Or write to the school. Explain why this person is not a good roommate for you.

Hi,

I understand you're my new roommate. I'm excited about our English language school, but I'm also a little nervous. Here's some information about me.

My name is Sonia. I'm from a small town. I love English and I love to study—especially English grammar. I don't like TV or music. I'm not very neat. I usually go to bed at nine o'clock and get up at 6:00. I exercise every morning from 6:00 to 8:00.

Please tell me about yourself. Do you come from a small town too? Do you like English grammar? Do you like to get up early?

I hope we will be good friends. I look forward to your reply.

Sincerely,

Sonia

Example

Dear Sonia,

Thanks for your letter. I'm a little nervous too. Here's some information about me . . .

11 | ON THE INTERNET

Some online services help people find roommates. Find out about a service like this. Report to the class.

UNIT 10

The Simple Present: *Wh-* Questions

Grammar in Context

BEFORE YOU READ

Do you dream? Do you remember your dreams? What do you dream about?

Ask the Expert *is a radio talk show. Today Rob Stevens is talking to dream expert Helena Lee. Read their conversation.*

DREAMS

Rob Stevens: Good afternoon. I'm Rob Stevens. Welcome to *Ask the Expert*. This afternoon my guest is Helena Lee. She's the author of *Sleep and Dreams*. Thank you for coming.

Helena Lee: Thanks, Rob. It's great to be here.

Rob: Helena, we have a lot of questions about dreams. Our first question is from Carolina Gomes. She asks, **"Why do we dream?"**

Helena: That's a good question. Actually, nobody really knows why. But I think dreams help us understand our feelings.

Rob: OK. . . . Our next question is from Jonathan Lam. He asks, "**Who dreams?** Does everyone dream?"

Helena: Yes, everyone dreams. People dream in every part of the world. And what's more, scientists believe animals dream too.

Rob: Wow! That's really interesting. **How do we know?**

Helena: We have machines. They show when people or animals dream. But, of course, no one knows what animals dream about.

Rob: Our next question is from Pablo Ortiz. He writes, "People don't remember *all* their dreams. **What dreams do they remember?**"

Helena: People remember their unusual dreams. And, unfortunately, people remember their bad dreams, or nightmares.

Rob: Beata Green says, "I have the same dream again and again. **What does that mean?**"

Helena: That dream has special meaning for you. You need to think about it.

Rob: Here's a question from Samuel Diaz. "**When do people dream?**"

Helena: They dream during deep sleep. It's called REM sleep. REM means *rapid eye movement.*

Rob: I hear REM sleep is important. **Why do we need it?**

Helena: Without it, we can't remember or think clearly.

Rob: Our last question for today is from Mike Morgan. He writes, "My roommate doesn't remember his dreams. **Why do I remember my dreams?**"

Helena: Well, a University of Iowa professor says, "Creative people remember their dreams."

Rob: Thank you so much, Helena. We look forward to reading your new book.

AFTER YOU READ

Match the questions and answers.

____ **1.** Who dreams?	**a.** Nobody knows.
____ **2.** What does *REM* mean?	**b.** Everyone does.
____ **3.** Why are dreams good?	**c.** They dream during REM sleep.
____ **4.** When do people dream?	**d.** It stands for rapid eye movement.
____ **5.** What do animals dream about?	**e.** They help us understand our feelings.

Grammar Presentation

THE SIMPLE PRESENT: *WH-* QUESTIONS; SHORT AND LONG ANSWERS

Wh- Questions				
Wh- Word	*Do/Does*	Subject	Base Form of Verb	
When	**do**	I	**sleep**?	
Where	**do**	you	**sleep**?	
What	**do**	we	**need**?	
Why	**does**	he	**get up**	late?
Who(**m**)	**does**	she	**dream**	about?
How	**does**	it	**feel**?	

Short Answers
From 10:00 P.M. to 5:00 A.M.
On the futon.
Two pillows.
He goes to bed late.
A movie star.
Good.

Long Answers
You sleep from 10:00 P.M. to 5:00 A.M.
I sleep on the futon.
We need two pillows.
He gets up late because he goes to bed late.
She dreams about a movie star.
The blanket feels good.

Wh- Questions About the Subject		
Wh- Word	Verb	
Who	**dreams**?	
What	**happens**	during REM sleep?

Answers
Everyone does.
People dream.

GRAMMAR NOTES

EXAMPLES

1. ***Wh-* questions** ask for information. Most questions use a ***wh-* word** + ***do*** or ***does*** + **a subject** + **the base form of the verb**.

	Wh- word	*do/does*	subject	base form	
Q:	When	do	you	go	to bed?
Q:	What	does	he	dream	about?

(continued)

2. To ask a question about the subject, use ***who*** or ***what*** **+ the third-person singular form of the verb**. ▶ **BE CAREFUL!** Do not use ***do*** or ***does*** with questions about the subject. Do not use the base form of the verb.	• **Who sleeps** on the futon? subject My brother sleeps on the futon. • **What helps** you fall asleep? subject • Milk helps me fall asleep. NOT: Who ~~does~~ sleeps on the futon? NOT: Who ~~do~~ sleeps on the futon? NOT: Who ~~sleep~~ on the futon?

3. ***Who*** asks questions about a <u>subject</u>. ***Who*** and ***whom*** ask questions about an <u>object</u>. USAGE NOTE: ***Whom*** is very formal.	subject • **Who** helps John? Mary does. object • **Who** does Mary help? John. object • **Whom** does Mary help? John.

Reference Note

For more about *who*, *what*, *where*, and *why*, see Unit 7, page 60.
For more about *when*, see Unit 11, page 104.

Focused Practice

1 DISCOVER THE GRAMMAR

get dressed	get up	stay up	wake up

Night owls like to stay up late at night. Early birds get up early. Read about a night owl and an early bird. Then match the questions and answers.

Doug is a night owl. He hates to get up in the morning. On weekends, he goes to bed at 1:00 A.M. and gets up at noon. Unfortunately for Doug, his first class starts at 8:15, and he needs to get up early.

At 7:00 A.M. Doug's alarm rings. He wakes up, but he doesn't get up. He stays in bed and daydreams. At 7:20 his mom comes in. She has a big smile. She says, "Dougie, it's time to get up."

Doug's mother is an early bird. Even on vacations she is up at 6:00 A.M. When his mom wakes him, Doug says, "Leave me alone. I'm tired."

Finally, at about 7:30, Doug gets up. He jumps out of bed, showers, and gets dressed. At 7:50 he drinks a big glass of juice, takes a breakfast bar, and runs to the bus stop. The bus comes at 8:00.

f 1. Who hates to get up in the morning?
b 2. How does Doug feel in the morning?
e 3. Why does Doug run to the bus stop?
d 4. What does Doug have for breakfast?
a 5. When does Doug sleep late?
c 6. What happens at 7:00?

a. On weekends.
b. Tired.
c. Doug's alarm rings.
d. A glass of juice and a breakfast bar.
e. Because he doesn't want to miss the bus.
f. Doug does.

2 WORD ORDER OF *WH-* QUESTIONS

Grammar Notes 1–3

Write questions. Use the words given.

1. do / you / usually get up / When

   A: *When do you usually get up?*

   B: At 7:00 on weekdays.

2. Where / sleep / the baby / does

   A: Where does the baby sleep ?

   B: In our bedroom.

3. at night / they / How / do / feel

   A: How do they feel at night ?

   B: They're never tired at night. They're night owls.

4. does / Who / she / dream about

   A: Who does she dream about ?

   B: She dreams about me.

5. What / he / dream about / does

   A: What does he dream about ?

   B: He dreams about cars.

6. Who /daydreams

   A: Who daydreams ?

   B: John does.

3 DOUG'S ROUTINE

Grammar Notes 1–3

Read the answers. Then ask questions about the underlined words.

1. Doug wakes up at 7:00.
   When does Doug wake up?
2. School begins at 8:15.
   When does school begin ?
3. Doug has lunch in the school cafeteria.
   Where does Doug have lunch ?
4. Doug has a hamburger and french fries for lunch on Mondays.
   What does Doug have for lunch on Mondays ?
5. Doug meets Noah at the soccer field after school.
   Who does Doug meet at the soccer field after school ?
6. Doug and Noah play soccer in West Park.
   Who plays soccer in West Park ?
7. Doug feels tired after soccer practice.
   How does Doug feel after soccer practice ?
8. Doug stays up late because he has a lot of homework.
   Why does Doug stay up late ?

4 QUESTIONS ABOUT THE SUBJECT AND OBJECT

Grammar Notes 2–3

*Label the subject **(S)** and the object **(O)** in each sentence. Write one question about the subject and one question about the object. Then answer the questions. Use short answers.*

1. On Sunday mornings Sam (S) calls his grandmother (O).
   Q: Who calls his grandmother on Sunday mornings? A: Sam does.
   Q: Who does Sam call on Sunday mornings? A: His grandmother.
2. My brother (S) sees his friends (O) after school.
   Q: Who does my brother see after school? A: His friends.
   Q: Who sees his friends after school? A: My brother does.
3. My mother (S) wakes me (O) on weekdays.
   Q: Who wakes me on weekdays ? A: My mother does.
   Q: Who does my mother wake on weekdays? A: Me.

4. Maria helps her neighbor.

   Q: Who helps her neighbor? A: Maria.

   Q: Who does Maria help? A: Her neighbor.

5. Shira and Carolina meet friends at a club on weekends.

   Q: Who meets friends at a club on weekend? A: Shira and Carolina

   Q: Who do Shira and Carolina meet at a club on weekend? A: Friends.

5 | EDITING

Correct these questions. There are six mistakes. The first mistake is already corrected.

1. Where do they ~~sleeps~~ *sleep*?
2. Why [do] they need two pillows?
3. Who ~~sleep~~ [sleeps] on the sofa?
4. When does she ~~goes~~ [go] to bed?
5. Who ~~wake~~ [wakes] you?
6. Who do you dream about?
7. How [does] he feel~~s~~ about that?

Communication Practice

6 | LISTENING

Diane often has the same dream. She tells a doctor about her dream. Listen to their conversation. Complete the answers.

1. Where is Diane in her dream? She's in ____________________.
2. What does the man in her dream look like? He's tall. He has a ____________________.
3. What does he want to do? He wants to ____________________.
4. What happens? First she walks fast. Then ____________________. She runs. Then ____________________. Then ____________________.
5. What does Dr. Fox tell Diane? "You're ____________________. You need ____________________."

7 | SLEEPING HABITS

Answer the questions. Then work with a partner. Ask your partner the questions.

	You	Your Partner
When do you go to bed?	11.00 P.M.	12.00 P.M.
What days do you sleep late?	weekends	sunday
Does anyone wake you? If so, who?	No	Yes, her sister
Do you dream? If so, what do you dream about?	Yes. I dream about my self	Yer, she dream about her family.
Are you an early bird or a night owl?	an early bird	an early bird

8 | WHO DOES WHAT?

Ask five students these questions. Take notes.

Example: You: Juan, do you snore?
Juan: No, I don't, but my sister Bianca snores.

1. Who snores?
2. Who gets up before 6:00 A.M.?
3. Who goes to bed after midnight?
4. Who needs more than eight hours of sleep?
5. Who needs less than five hours of sleep?
6. Who dreams in English?
7. Who daydreams?
8. Who has insomnia? (trouble sleeping)

Tell the class interesting results.

Example: Juan's sister snores. Nobody gets up before 6:00 A.M., but sometimes Hasan goes to bed at 5:00 A.M.

9 | INFORMATION GAP: UNDERSTANDING DREAMS

Student B, turn to page 100.

A *Student A, Student B often has a dream. Find out about Student B's dream. Ask these questions.*

In your dream:

Where are you?

Who do you see?

How does the person look?

How do you look?

What does the person say?

What do you do?

Student A, you have the following dream again and again. Read about your dream. Then answer Student B's questions about it.

You are on an airplane. The pilot comes to you. He says, "I need your help." You go with the pilot. You fly the plane. You land the plane. Everyone claps. You feel good. You wake up.

B *Talk about your dreams. What do they mean?*

10 | ON THE INTERNET

Look on the Internet for "help for insomnia." Report to the class.

Questions to answer for your report:

What do people do for insomnia?

What do they drink?

What do they eat?

Why do they get insomnia?

Where do they go for help for insomnia?

PART III

From **Grammar** to **Writing**

Time Word Connectors: First, Next, After that, Then, Finally

1 *Which paragraph sounds better,* **A** *or* **B**? *Why?*

Paragraph A

I like to watch my roommate prepare tea. She boils water and pours the boiling water in a cup with a teabag in it. She removes the teabag and adds sugar. She adds lemon. She adds ice. She sips the tea and says, "Mmm. This tea is just the way I like it."

Paragraph B

I like to watch my roommate prepare tea. First, she boils some water and pours the boiling water in a cup with a teabag in it. Next, she removes the teabag and adds some sugar. After that, she adds some lemon. Then she adds some ice. Finally, she sips the tea and says, "Mmm. This tea is just the way I like it."

You can make your writing clearer by using **time word connectors**. They show the order in which things happen. Some common ones are: ***first***, ***next***, ***after that***, ***then***, and ***finally***. We usually use a **comma** after these connectors.

Example: **First**, you add the water. **Next**, you add the sugar.

2 *Use time word connectors to show the order of things in this paragraph.*

I take a shower. I have breakfast. I drive to the train station. I take a train and a bus.

I get to work.

Now write a paragraph about a routine you follow. Use time word connectors. Here are some ideas:

Every Saturday morning . . .

Every New Year's Day . . .

Every year on my birthday . . .

PART III

Review Test

I *Read each conversation. Circle the letter of the underlined word or group of words that is not correct.*

1. A: Do (A) you have (B) a good dictionary? — A B (C) D
   B: Yes, I have (C). It's (D) on my desk.

2. A: Where (A) does he works (B)? — A (B) C D
   B: He works (C) at the bank next to (D) the supermarket.

3. A: Does (A) he need (B) a doctor? — A B (C) D
   B: Yes, he needs (C). He has (D) a terrible earache.

4. A: Why (A) do you work (B) at night? — A B (C) D
   B: When (C) I study (D) during the day.

5. A: Do (A) you have (B) any sweatshirts in medium? — A B (C) D
   B: Yes, we are (C) have (D) sweatshirts in all sizes.

6. A: Irina doesn't to (A) live (B) in California. — (A) B C D
   B: Where (C) does she live (D)?

7. A: Who (A) does (B) Carol usually eats (C) lunch with? — A B (C) D
   B: She usually eats (D) with Dan and Jon.

II *Complete the sentences. Use the present tense of the verb in parentheses.*

1. Do you need (need) a suit?
2. He washes (wash) the windows once a month.
3. Marcia has (have) a sister and a brother.

(continued)

4. Paul _____isn't_____ a lawyer.
(be, not)

5. Mrs. Smith _____fixes_____ lamps.
(fix)

6. Pete _____goes_____ to the park on Tuesdays.
(go)

7. She _____does_____ the dishes every morning.
(do)

8. _____Does_____ your sister _____speak_____ English?
(speak)

9. _____Do_____ the students _____wear_____ uniforms to school?
(wear)

10. We _____don't eat_____ turkey for breakfast.
(eat, not)

11. My uncle often _____worries_____ about his family.
(worry)

12. Who _____lives_____ next to the Salazars?
(live)

13. What _____makes_____ you happy?
(make)

14. What time _____does_____ your father _____come_____ home from work?
(come)

15. Where _____do_____ they _____keep_____ their money?
(keep)

III *Read the first sentence. Complete the second sentence. Use the affirmative or negative of the verb in parentheses.*

1. I like blue. I _____have_____ a lot of blue shirts.
(have)

2. His jacket is old and worn. He _____needs_____ a new jacket.
(need)

3. I have a lot of sweaters. I _____don't need_____ to buy any more.
(need)

4. That book is for level 8. We're in level 3. It _____isn't_____ for our class.
(be)

5. I don't like sweet things. I _____don't eat_____ a lot of cake or cookies.
(eat)

6. We don't live in an apartment. We _____live_____ in a house.
(live)

7. I only play music in the early evening. I _____don't play_____ music late at night.
(play)

8. He knows three languages. He _____speaks_____ Polish, Russian, and a little English.
(speak)

9. She eats out almost every day. She _____doesn't cook_____ often.
(cook)

10. He's a lawyer. He _____wears_____ a suit to work every day.
(wear)

IV *Use the words in parentheses to complete the questions and short answers. Use the simple present tense.*

1. A: Do you like your new roommate?
   a. (you/like)
   B: Yes, I do. I like him a lot.
   b.
2. A: Does he need a new camera?
   a. (he/need)
   B: No, he doesn't. His old camera still works.
   b.
3. A: Do they speak fluent English?
   a. (they/speak)
   B: No, they don't. They're in the first level.
   b.
4. A: Do I know her?
   a. (I/know)
   B: Yes, you do. She lives in our building.
   b.
5. A: Do you remember your dreams?
   a. (you/remember)
   B: No, I don't. I always forget them.
   b.
6. A: Does it rain a lot in your country?
   a. (it/rain)
   B: Yes, it does. That's why everything is so green.
   b.
7. A: Does your brother live near you?
   a. (your brother/ live)
   B: No, he doesn't. He lives far away.
   b.

V *Write* **yes/no** *and* **wh-** *questions. Use the simple present.*

1. "Amazing" means "surprising."

   What does "amazing" mean? It means "surprising."

2. Sachiko always wears a hat.

   a. Who always wears a hat? Sachiko does.

   b. What does Sachiko always wear? A hat.

3. Jasmine gets up at nine o'clock.

   a. Does Jasmine gets up at nine o'clock? Yes, she does.

   b. When does Jasmine get up? At nine o'clock.

   c. Who gets up at nine o'clock? Jasmine does.

(continued)

4. My friend works at a restaurant.

a. Does your friend work at a restaurant? Yes, she does.

b. Who works at a restaurant? My friend does.

c. Where does your friend work? At a restaurant.

d. What does your friend do? She works at a restaurant.

5. Bob usually goes to bed after midnight.

a. Who usually goes to bed after midnight? Bob does.

b. When does Bob usually go to bed? After midnight.

VI *Correct the sentences.*

1. Dan ~~like~~ likes soccer.
2. She ~~isn't~~ doesn't write to me often.
3. Does your friend need~~s~~ an umbrella?
4. Do they want~~s~~ any help?
5. My aunt ~~is~~ teaches Spanish.
6. Who ~~does~~ cooks in your family?
7. They don't work or ~~don't~~ live near the train station.
8. What ~~means that word~~ does that word mean?
9. How do you spell your name?
10. When ~~does~~ do you get up?
11. Why do they shop there?
12. How does he feel~~s~~ ~~he~~?

▶ ***To check your answers, go to the Answer Key on page RT-1.***

INFORMATION GAP FOR STUDENT B

Unit 10, Exercise 9

A *Student B, you have the following dream again and again. Read about your dream. Then answer Student A's questions about it.*

You are in the third grade. You see your third grade teacher. Your teacher is very big. You are small. Your teacher says, "Your schoolwork is good. You are my favorite student." You smile. Then you laugh. Then you wake up.

Student B, Student A often has a dream. Find out about Student A's dream. Ask these questions.

In your dream:

Where are you?

Who comes to you?

What does he say?

What do you do?

How do you feel?

What happens?

B *Talk about your dreams. What do they mean?*

PART IV

When, *What* + Noun; Prepositions of Time; Possessives; *This* / *That* / *These* / *Those*; *One* / *Ones* / *It*

UNIT 11 *When, What* + Noun; Prepositions of Time; Ordinal Numbers

Grammar in Context

BEFORE YOU READ

What's your favorite holiday? When is it?

Read this conversation between three high school friends.

ELECTION DAY

TONY: Hey Alex.
ALEX: Hey Tony, Dino. How're you doing?
TONY: OK. And you?
ALEX: Good. By the way, what's the next school holiday?
TONY: Election Day.
ALEX: **When** is it?
TONY: It's **on** the **first** Tuesday **in** November.
DINO: Not always.
TONY: Yes, it is.
DINO: No, it's not.
ALEX: Then **what day** is Election Day?
DINO: Election Day is **on** the **first** Tuesday after the **first** Monday **in** November. This year it's not **on** the **first** Tuesday **in** November.
TONY: OK, OK. You're such a genius.

AFTER YOU READ

Answer the questions.

1. When was Election Day in the United States in 2005? Circle it on the calendar.
2. In what month is Election Day in other countries?

NOVEMBER 2005

SUNDAY	MONDAY	TUESDAY	WEDNESDAY	THURSDAY	FRIDAY	SATURDAY
		1	2	3	4	5
6	7	8	9	10	11	12
13	14	15	16	17	18	19
20	21	22	23	24	25	26
27	28	29	30			

Grammar Presentation

QUESTIONS WITH *WHEN* AND *WHAT* + NOUN; PREPOSITIONS OF TIME; ORDINAL NUMBERS

When			Answers
When	Verb		
When	is	Independence Day in the United States?	It's on July 4th. On July 4th. July 4th.

***What* + Noun**			Answers
What	Noun		
What	**day**	is his graduation?	It's on Monday. On Monday. Monday.
What	**time**	does it start?	It's at 2:00. At 2:00. 2:00.

(continued)

Prepositions of Time	
Her graduation is	**in** December. **in** (the) winter. **in** 2007. **in** the morning. **in** the afternoon. **in** the evening.
Is your birthday	**on** Wednesday? **on** December 25th?
The party is	**at** 7:30. **at** night.

Ordinal Numbers		
1st = first	12th = twelfth	32nd = thirty-second
2nd = second	13th = thirteenth	40th = fortieth
3rd = third	14th = fourteenth	43rd = forty-third
4th = fourth	15th = fifteenth	50th = fiftieth
5th = fifth	16th = sixteenth	60th = sixtieth
6th = sixth	17th = seventeenth	70th = seventieth
7th = seventh	18th = eighteenth	80th = eightieth
8th = eighth	19th = nineteenth	90th = ninetieth
9th = ninth	20th = twentieth	100th = hundredth
10th = tenth	21st = twenty-first	101st = one hundred and first
11th = eleventh	30th = thirtieth	

GRAMMAR NOTES	EXAMPLES
1. Use ***when*** or ***what*** **+ a noun** for questions about **time**.	**Q: When** is your party? **A:** It's on Tuesday. **Q: What day** is your party? **A:** It's on Tuesday. **Q: What time** is your party? **A:** It's at 8:00.

2. We usually use **prepositions** when we answer questions about time.	
in + month, seasons, years	• It's **in January**. • Her graduation was **in 2003**.
in + the morning, the afternoon, the evening	• My son is at camp **in the afternoon**.
on + days of the week	• It's **on Mondays** and **Wednesdays**.
on + the date	• It's **on January 4**.
at + the exact time ***at + night***	• It's **at ten o'clock** in the morning and at eleven o'clock **at night**.

3. There are two kinds of numbers: **cardinal**—***one, two, three*** **ordinal**—***first, second, third***	
Use **cardinal numbers** to tell **how many** people, places, or things.	• She has **three classes** on Thursday.
Use **ordinal numbers** to number things in a **sequence**. The spelled form is used.	• Her **first class** is English. Her **second class** is math. Her **third class** is history. NOT: Her ~~1st~~ class is English.
Use **ordinal numbers** for streets and floors of buildings.	• Her apartment is on **Seventy-seventh Street**. It's on the **second floor**.
USAGE NOTE: For dates with the month and day, we usually use the cardinal number in writing. We always use the ordinal number in speaking.	• Writing: The conference is on **November 25**. Speaking: "His birthday is on **November 25th**."

Reference Notes

See Appendix 3, page A-3 for lists of cardinal and ordinal numbers, and for lists of the days, months, and seasons.

See Appendix 4, page A-4 for information about telling time.

Focused Practice

1 DISCOVER THE GRAMMAR

Look at Karen's calendar. Then circle the correct day, date, time, and/or time of day of each event on the chart.

SEPTEMBER

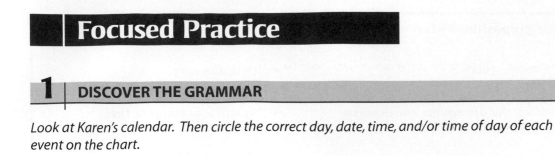

SUNDAY	MONDAY	TUESDAY	WEDNESDAY	THURSDAY	FRIDAY	SATURDAY
		1 yoga 6:00 P.M.	2	3	4 dentist 10:00 A.M.	5
6 Mary/ airport 10 P.M.	7 Labor Day	8 yoga 6:00 P.M.	9	10	11	12
13	14	15 yoga 6:00 P.M.	16	17	18	19
20	21	22 yoga 6:00 P.M.	23	24	25	26
27	28	29 yoga 6:00 P.M.	30			

Event	Day	Date	Time	Time of Day
Her yoga class is	Mondays on Tuesdays Wednesdays		5:00 at 5:30 6:00	in the morning. in the afternoon. in the evening.
She has a dentist's appointment	Wednesday on Thursday Friday	2 September 3 4	9:00 at 10:00 11:00	in the morning. in the afternoon. in the evening.
Mary's plane arrives	Friday on Saturday Sunday	4 September 5 6	6:30 at 7:30 10:00	in the afternoon. in the evening. at night.
Labor Day is	Monday on Tuesday Wednesday	September 7		

2 CHINESE NEW YEAR *Grammar Notes 2–3*

Complete the conversation. Choose from the words in parentheses.

KIM: What's your favorite holiday?

MEI: Chinese New Year. I really love the holiday.

KIM: When is it?

MEI: ___In___ (1. In / On) January or February. It's on a different day every year. ___in___ (2. In / On) 2004 it was ___on___ (3. in / on) Thursday, January 22. That was the ___first___ (4. one / first) day of the Year of the Monkey. ___in___ (5. In / On) 2005, the Year of the Rooster, it was ___on___ (6. on / in) February 9.

KIM: Why does the Chinese New Year fall on different days?

MEI: It's based on a lunar calendar. There are ___29___ (7. 29 / 29th) or ___30___ (8. 30 / 30th) days in a lunar month. But 2001 was a special year.

KIM: Oh, yeah. Why?

MEI: It was a leap year.

KIM: Is that the same as a Western leap year?

MEI: No. In a Western calendar, every ___four___ (9. four / fourth) years you add an extra day in February. In a Chinese leap year, you add an extra month.

KIM: So if you're born in that month, you don't get old as fast!

Year of the Monkey

Year of the Rooster

3 | DAN'S PARTY—CARDINAL AND ORDINAL NUMBERS *Grammar Note 3*

Complete the conversation. Choose from the words in parentheses.

KAORI: When's Dan's Halloween party?

RUSS: Two (1. (Two / Second)) weeks from today—on October thirty-first (2. (thirty-one / thirty-first)).

KAORI: Where does he live again?

RUSS: On Four (3. (Four / Fourth)) Street.

KAORI: Oh, yeah—the red building. What floor does he live on?

RUSS: The third (4. (three / third)) floor.

KAORI: I love Dan's Halloween parties.

RUSS: I know. I remember his first (5. (one / first)) party two years ago. It really was a lot of fun.

KAORI: His second (6. (two / second)) party was great too.

4 | NATIONAL HOLIDAYS *Grammar Notes 1–3*

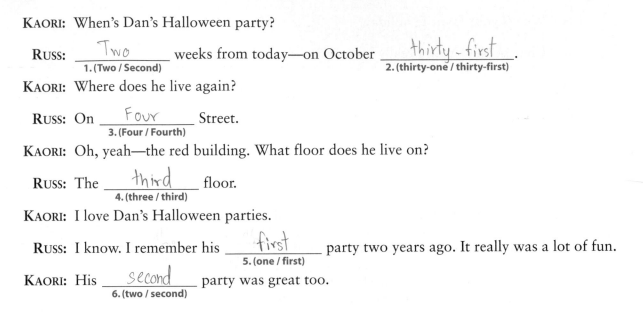

Write questions. Then look at the flags and dates and answer the questions.

1. is / When / Australia's national holiday

   Q: *When is Australia's national holiday?*

   A: *It's on January 26.*

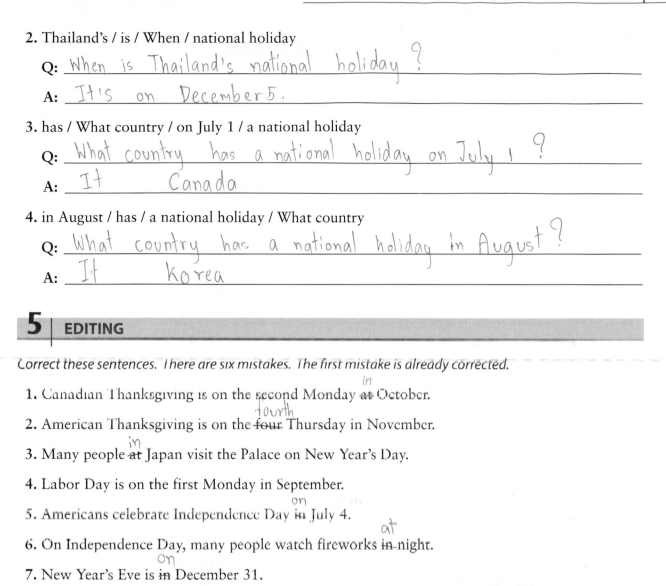

2. Thailand's / is / When / national holiday

Q: When is Thailand's national holiday?

A: It's on December 5.

3. has / What country / on July 1 / a national holiday

Q: What country has a national holiday on July 1?

A: It Canada

4. in August / has / a national holiday / What country

Q: What country has a national holiday in August?

A: It Korea

5 EDITING

Correct these sentences. There are six mistakes. The first mistake is already corrected.

1. Canadian Thanksgiving is on the second Monday ~~at~~ in October.
2. American Thanksgiving is on the ~~four~~ fourth Thursday in November.
3. Many people ~~at~~ in Japan visit the Palace on New Year's Day.
4. Labor Day is on the first Monday in September.
5. Americans celebrate Independence Day ~~in~~ on July 4.
6. On Independence Day, many people watch fireworks ~~in~~ at night.
7. New Year's Eve is ~~in~~ on December 31.

Communication Practice

6 LISTENING

Victor and Lisa are going to a party. They are confused. Listen to their conversation. Then listen again and complete the sentences.

1. John and Maria live ________________ Avenue between ________________ and ________________ Avenue.
2. Their apartment is ________________ floor.
3. John and Alice live ________________ Street between ________________ and ________________ Avenue.
4. John and Alice's apartment is ________________ floor.

7 | INFORMATION GAP: HOLIDAYS AROUND THE WORLD

Work in pairs. Student A, look at the chart on this page. Ask your partner questions to complete your chart.

Student B, look at the Information Gap on page 140 and follow the instructions there.

Examples: What country has a national holiday on _______________? (date)
What month is _______________'s national holiday?
What's the date of _______________'s national holiday?
What country has a national holiday in _______________? (month)
When is _______________'s national holiday?

NATIONAL HOLIDAYS AROUND THE WORLD

COUNTRY		MONTH	DAY	COUNTRY		MONTH	DAY
Argentina			25	Haiti		January	
Brazil		September		Italy		June	2
		April	16	Japan		December	22
Dominican Republic		February	27	Lebanon		November	22
Ecuador		August		Turkey		October	29
Greece			25	United States of America		July	4
Your country's national holiday:							

8 SCHOOL HOLIDAYS

Work in small groups. Look at a school calendar. What are your school's holidays? When are they?

9 WRITING

Write about your favorite holiday.

What is the name of the holiday? When is it? How long is it? What do you do? What do you wear? Why do you like this holiday?

Example

I'm from Changmai, Thailand. My favorite holiday is the Songkran Festival. It's the Thai New Year festival. This important Buddhist holiday usually falls in April and lasts for four days.

On the first day we clean our homes. That evening we put on our best clothes. On the second day we cook. On the third day we bring food to the temples and we begin throwing water on family and friends.

On the last day of the Songkran Festival we honor our grandparents and other older people by gently putting water on them and wishing them good luck and a happy future. Then we go outside and throw water on everyone. Water throwing is the best part of the holiday. The weather is very hot and the cold water feels great. Come to Changmai for the Songkran Festival. Bring a water gun, join the fun, and say, "Sawadee Pee Mai"—Happy New Year!

10 ON THE INTERNET

Find out more about one of your school holidays. Tell your classmates about that day.

Example: Labor Day is on the first Monday in September. It's a holiday for workers. People celebrate it in the United States, Canada, and a few other countries. Many people celebrate the whole weekend. They have picnics and barbeques with friends and family. For many people, it marks the end of the summer. The holiday is over a hundred years old.

UNIT 12 Possessive Nouns and Possessive Adjectives; Questions with *Whose*

Grammar in Context

BEFORE YOU READ

Look at these sentences. Answer the questions.

My name is Michelle Young.

1. Whose handwriting is neat?
a. Michelle's **b.** Rick's

2. Whose handwriting is difficult to read?
a. Michelle's **b.** Rick's

A teacher has three papers without names. Read this conversation.

WHOSE COMPOSITION IS THIS?

TEACHER: **Whose** composition is this?

BORIS: Is it a good paper?

TEACHER: It's excellent.

BORIS: It's **my** composition.

YOLANDA: No, that's not **your** handwriting. It's **Kim's** composition. **Her** name is right there. She's absent today.

TEACHER: Thanks, Yolanda. **Whose** paper is *this*?

BORIS: Is it a good paper?

TEACHER: It's OK.

BORIS: Then it's **my** composition.

JUAN: It's not **your** composition. It's **my** composition. See, **my** name is on the back.

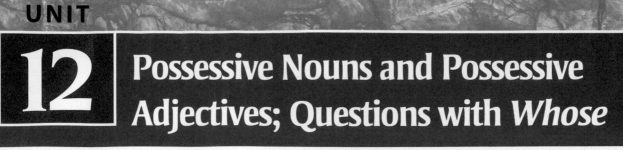

TEACHER: OK, Juan. Here, Boris. *This* is **your** composition.
BORIS: Is it a good paper?
TEACHER: It needs some work.
BORIS: I don't think it's **my** composition.
TEACHER: Uh . . . I think it is. I have a grade for everyone else.

AFTER YOU READ

Write **Kim, Juan,** and **Boris** on their compositions.

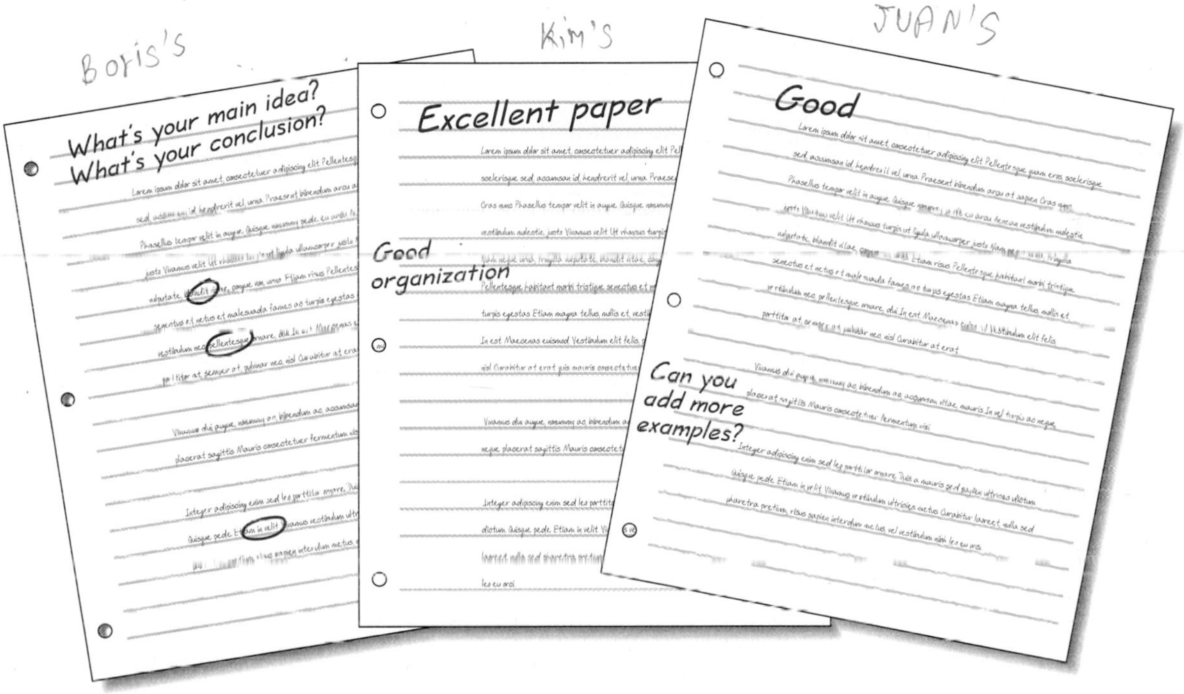

Grammar Presentation

POSSESSIVE NOUNS AND POSSESSIVE ADJECTIVES; QUESTIONS WITH *WHOSE*

Possessive Nouns	
Singular Nouns	**Plural Nouns**
John's last name is Tamez. **Russ's** last name is Stram.	The **girls'** gym is on this floor.
My **mother's** name is Rita. The **woman's** name is Carmen.	My **parents'** car is in the garage. The **women's** restroom is on the first floor.

(continued)

Possessive Adjectives		
Subject Pronouns	**Possessive Adjectives**	**Example Sentences**
I	**My**	I am a student. **My** name is Antonio.
You	**Your**	You are next to me. **Your** seat is here.
He	**His**	He is a professor. **His** subject is computers.
She	**Her**	She's my boss. **Her** name is Ms. Alvarado.
It	**Its**	It's my sister's dog. **Its** name is Lucky.
We	**Our**	We are businessmen. **Our** business is in the United States and Asia.
You	**Your**	You are students. **Your** class is in room 405.
They	**Their**	They are musicians. **Their** band is great.

Questions with *Whose*	
Questions	**Answers**
Whose hair is long?	Carmen**'s**. Carmen**'s** is. Carmen**'s** hair is long.
Whose eyes are green?	Svetlana**'s**. Svetlana**'s** are. Svetlana**'s** eyes are green.
Whose homework is this?	Yoko**'s**. It's Yoko**'s**. It's Yoko**'s** homework.
Whose books are these?	Ken**'s**. They're Ken**'s**. They're Ken**'s** books.

GRAMMAR NOTES	EXAMPLES
1. Possessive nouns and **possessive adjectives** show belonging.	• **Kim's car** (the car belongs to Kim) • **her car** (the car belongs to her)
2. Add an **apostrophe (') +** *s* to a **singular noun** to show possession.	• That's **Juan's** composition.
Add an **apostrophe (')** to a **plural noun** ending in *s* to show possession.	• My **grandparents'** home is next to my **parents'** home.
Add an **apostrophe (') +** *s* to an **irregular plural noun** to show possession.	• The **women's** restroom is on the first floor.

3. **Possessive adjectives** replace **possessive nouns**. Possessive adjectives agree with the possessive noun they replace.	• ~~**My father's**~~ His sisters are in Tokyo and Osaka. • ~~**My mother's**~~ Her brother is in Kyoto.
4. A **noun** always follows a possessive noun or a possessive adjective.	• Bekir's **book** is new. • His **book** is new.
▶ **BE CAREFUL!** A noun + apostrophe + *s* does not always mean possession.	
Anna's sometimes means *Anna* ***is***.	• **Anna's** late. (Anna **is** late.)
Do not confuse ***its*** and ***it's***. **its** = possessive adjective; ***it's*** = ***it is***	• This is my turtle. **Its** name is Tubby. • **It's** a hot day.
5. Use ***whose*** for questions about possessions.	• **Whose** notebook is this?
▶ **BE CAREFUL!** ***Who's*** is the short form of *who is*. It sounds like *whose*.	• **Who's** absent? • **Whose** name is not on the list?

Reference Note

See Appendix 10, page A-11 for more rules about **possessive nouns**.
See Appendix 9, page A-10 for more about irregular plural nouns.

Focused Practice

1 DISCOVER THE GRAMMAR

Read about Kyoko's family.

My father is a pharmacist. My father's father is a pharmacist too.

My mother is a teacher. My father's mother is a teacher too.

My brother is an actor. My brother's wife is an actor too.

Look at Kyoko's family tree. Whose occupations do you know? Write their occupations on the line next to their photos.

2 | FAMILY RELATIONSHIPS — *Grammar Notes 1–2*

Complete the sentences. Choose from the words in parentheses.

1. My __mother's__ mother is my __grandmother__.
   a. (mother / mother's) **b. (grandmother / grandmother's)**
2. My __father's__ mother is my __grandmother__, too.
   a. (father / father's) **b. (grandmother / grandmothers)**
3. My __brother's__ __son__ is my nephew.
   a. (brother / brother's) **b. (son / sons)**
4. My __brother's__ daughters are my __nieces__.
   a. (brother / brother's) **b. (niece / nieces)**
5. My husband's __brothers__ are my brothers-in-law.
   (brother / brothers)
6. My grandmother's daughter is my __aunt__ or my __mother__.
   a. (aunt / aunts) **b. (mother / mother's)**
7. My __grandfather's__ son is my __uncle__ or my father.
   a. (grandfathers / grandfather's) **b. (uncle / uncles)**
8. My father's __daughter__ is my __sister__ or __me__.
   a. (daughter / daughter's) **b. (sister / sisters)** **c. (me / my)**

3 | *MY, YOUR, HIS, HER, OUR, THEIR* — *Grammar Notes 1, 3*

Complete the sentences. Use a possessive adjective.

1. My sister studies in Toronto. __Her__ school is on Victoria Street.
2. She goes to Edgewood University. She likes __her__ classes.
3. Carlos's parents work at the United Nations. __Their__ jobs are interesting. His mother is a translator and his father is an interpreter.
4. Right now my brother is in Peru, __his__ wife is in Belize, and __their__ children are in the United States.
5. Does your brother like __his__ job?
6. Their rabbit's name is Biddy. __Its__ fur is soft.
7. Do you use __your__ calculator every day in math class?
8. Does your grandmother like __her__ new apartment? Is she happy there?

4 | WH- QUESTIONS

Grammar Note 5

Complete the questions. Use **where's, who's, whose, what's,** *and* **when's.**

1. Q: What's his last name? A: It's Kwon.
2. Q: Where's the dictionary? A: It's in my book bag.
3. Q: Whose homework is missing? A: Sandra's.
4. Q: Where's your seat? A: I'm next to the window.
5. Q: When's your birthday? A: It's next month.
6. Q: Whose last name begins with *s*? A: My name. It's Suzuki.
7. Q: Who's his father? A: His father is Joe Pieroni.
8. Q: What's this book about? A: It's about the Yucatan in Mexico.
9. Q: Whose test is this? A: It's Jason's. I know his handwriting.

5 | USEFUL QUESTIONS AND STATEMENTS

Grammar Notes 1–5

Complete the conversations. Choose from the words in parentheses.

1. **A:** Excuse me, is this your (a. you / your) seat?
   B: No. It's Leila's (b. Leila / Leila's) seat.
2. **A:** Excuse me. your (a. You / Your) dictionary was on the floor. Here.
   B: Thanks a lot.
3. **A:** Their (a. They / Their) class was canceled.
   B: Why?
   A: Their (b. They / Their) teacher was sick.
4. **A:** Is that her (a. she / her) scarf?
   B: No. It's my (b. I / my) scarf.
5. **A:** Whose (a. Who's / Whose) book is this?
   B: It belongs to the teacher.
6. **A:** Who's (a. Who's / Whose) absent today?
   B: Nobody. Everyone is here.
7. **A:** Where's the women's (a. womens / women's) locker room?
   B: It's down the hall.

8. **A:** Where's the ____men's____ room?
   a. (men's / mens')

   B: It's next to the water fountain.

9. **A:** Is that ____his____ seat?
   a. (he / his)

   B: No. ____It's____ the teacher's seat.
   b. (Its / It's)

   A: Oh.

10. **A:** Is your ____father's____ car in the garage?
    a. (fathers / father's)

    B: No. It's on the street.

6 | A NEW STUDENT — *Grammar Notes 1–4*

Read an article about a new student at the International Language Institute in Miami. Complete the sentences with a subject pronoun or a possessive adjective.

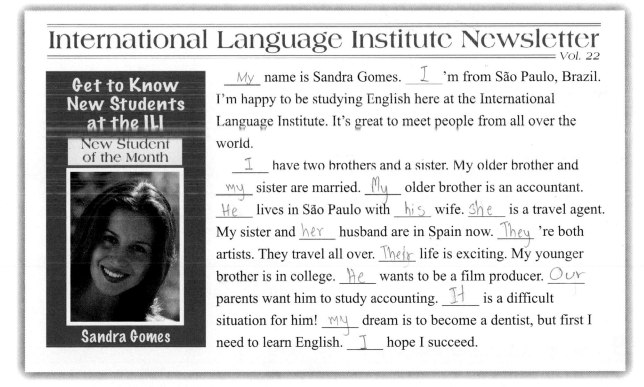

International Language Institute Newsletter

Vol. 22

Get to Know
New Students
at the ILI
New Student
of the Month
Sandra Gomes

____My____ name is Sandra Gomes. ____I____'m from São Paulo, Brazil. I'm happy to be studying English here at the International Language Institute. It's great to meet people from all over the world.

____I____ have two brothers and a sister. My older brother and ____my____ sister are married. ____My____ older brother is an accountant. ____He____ lives in São Paulo with ____his____ wife. ____She____ is a travel agent. My sister and ____her____ husband are in Spain now. ____They____'re both artists. They travel all over. ____Their____ life is exciting. My younger brother is in college. ____He____ wants to be a film producer. ____Our____ parents want him to study accounting. ____It____ is a difficult situation for him! ____My____ dream is to become a dentist, but first I need to learn English. ____I____ hope I succeed.

7 | EDITING

Read these conversations. There are seven mistakes. The first mistake is already corrected.

1. **A:** Is that ~~you~~ *your* dictionary?

   B: No. It's his dictionary.

   A: Who's?

   B: Dans.

2. **A:** Is Maria sister here?

   B: No, she's not.

   A: Is Maria here?

   B: No, but his brother is.

   A: Where is Maria?

   B: I think she's with his sister. Their at the movies.

Communication Practice

8 | LISTENING

Listen to these sentences. Circle the correct word.

1. Maria	Maria's	Marias	4. partner	partner's	partners
2. Maria	Maria's	Marias	5. partner	partner's	partners
3. Maria	Maria's	Marias	6. partner	partner's	partners

9 | GAME: WHOSE BROTHER IS THIS?

Bring in photos of family members. Write how the person is related to you on the back of the photo (for example, my sister, my mother, my aunt). The teacher collects the photos and gives each student a photo. Students ask questions about the photos.

Example: ANYA: Whose *sister* is this?
PABLO: I think it's Juan's.
JUAN: You're right. She's my sister.

Now Juan asks a question.

10 | FIND SOMEONE WHOSE . . . / FIND SOMEONE WHO'S . . .

Complete the questions. Use **whose** *or* **who's**. *Then ask your classmates these questions. Write their answers.*

Example: YOU: What month is your birthday?
ERIK: It's in February.

1. Whose birthday is in February? Erik's.
2. ________ good in art? ________________.
3. ________ name means something? ________________.
4. ________ a good athlete? ________________.
5. ________ eyes aren't brown? ________________.
6. ________ a good cook? ________________.
7. ________ first name has more than eight letters? ________________.
8. ________ birthday is in the summer? ________________.
9. ________ a good dancer? ________________.
10. ________ handwriting is beautiful? ________________.

11 | WRITING

Draw a family tree of your family like the tree on page 116. Then work in small groups. Tell your group about different people in your family.

Example: Roberto Gomes is my mother's brother. He's my favorite uncle. He's a businessman. He's in London now. He's an intelligent man with a good sense of humor.

Now write about yourself and your family.

Example: I'm from Recife in Brazil. I live with my parents and my younger brother. My older brother is married. He is a pilot and his wife is a pilot too. My mother worries about them, but she is proud of them. I want to be a pilot one day, but it's my secret for now.

12 | ON THE INTERNET

Exchange e-mail addresses with a classmate. Then send your classmate an e-mail message. Ask your classmate six questions about his or her family.

Examples: Where does your family live? How many people are there in your family? What are their names? What are their favorite free time activities?

UNIT

13 This / That / These / Those; Questions with *Or*

Grammar in Context

BEFORE YOU READ

Complete the sentences. Compare your answers with a partner's.

Do you like to hike or bike? I prefer to bike.

Do you like to camp or stay at a hotel? I prefer to hotel.

Do you like to travel with friends or alone? I prefer to frieds.

Read this conversation about a trip to a national park.

BRYCE CANYON NATIONAL PARK

MARIA: So how was your trip, Guillermo?

GUILLERMO: Great. I was in Bryce Canyon National Park.

MARIA: Is **that** in Utah **or** Colorado?

GUILLERMO: It's in Utah. I have over 200 pictures. **These** are my best photos.

MARIA: What are **those**?

Guillermo: They're called *hoodoos*. They're rock formations. **This** is me in front of a hoodoo.

Maria: **That**'s an amazing photo.

Guillermo: Thanks. **This** is Fairyland Canyon. It's near the entrance to the park. **These** hoodoos come in different shapes, sizes, and colors. Some have names, like the Wall of Windows.

Maria: Look at you! Is it really you on **that** horse?

Guillermo: Yes. I was on a horseback trip in the canyons. It was great. Listen, I want to send a photo to a friend in Chile. Do you like **this** picture **or that** one?

Maria: **This** one, the picture of you on a horse.

Guillermo: I think you're right. I'll send it to Roberto.

Maria: When's your next trip?

Guillermo: The first week in September. I'm thinking of the Canadian Rockies. Would you like to come?

Maria: You bet!*

Guillermo: That's great.

AFTER YOU READ

Circle the correct answer.

1. Is this national park in California or Utah?
   a. California b. Utah
2. Are these rock formations called hoodoos or voodoos?
   a. hoodoos b. voodoos
3. Are the rocks different colors or the same color?
   a. different colors b. the same color
4. Does Bryce Canyon National Park have horseback riding or horse racing?
   a. horseback riding b. horse racing

Grammar Presentation

THIS / THAT / THESE / THOSE

Singular		
This / That	Verb	
This	is	a good photo.
That	was	in Bryce.

Plural		
These / Those	Verb	
These	are	new photos.
Those	are	from my last trip.

(continued)

**You bet*: Sure

Singular			
This / That	Noun	Verb	
This	**photo**	is	clear.
That	**photo**	has	nice colors.

Plural			
These / Those	Noun	Verb	
These	**horses**	are	tired.
Those	**horses**	are	rested.

QUESTIONS WITH *OR* AND ANSWERS

Questions with *or*	Answers
Are you hungry **or** thirsty?	I'm thirsty.
Do you usually walk **or** drive?	I usually drive.

GRAMMAR NOTES

GRAMMAR NOTES	EXAMPLES
1. Use ***this***, ***that***, ***these***, and ***those*** to identify persons or things.	• Trips are fun. (all trips) • **This** trip is fun. (the trip I'm taking now)
2. Use ***this*** or ***that*** to talk about a singular noun. *This* refers to a person or thing **near you**. *That* refers to a person or thing **far from you**.	• **This** is my bag. (singular noun) • **That**'s your bag by the door. (singular noun)
3. Use ***these*** or ***those*** to talk about plural nouns. *These* refers to people or things **near you**. *Those* refers to people or things **far away**.	• **These** souvenirs are expensive. (plural noun) • **Those** t-shirts in the store window are on sale. (plural noun)
4. ***This*** and ***These*** can refer to events in the **present** and near future. *That* and *those* can refer to events in the **past**.	• **This** vacation is very expensive. • People travel a lot **these** days. • **That** vacation was a lot of fun. • In **those** times, people traveled less.
5. ***This***, ***that***, ***these***, and ***those*** can be **pronouns** or **adjectives**. When *this, that, these,* and *those* are **adjectives**, a noun always follows.	• **This** (pronoun) is my suitcase. • **This** (adjective) suitcase (noun) is red.
6. In speaking we use ***that's*** to **respond** to something a person says.	**A:** I'm going to Italy. **B: That's** great!

7. Questions with ***or*** ask for **a choice**.	**Q:** Do you like hiking **or** bike riding? **A:** I like hiking.
▶ **Be careful!** Do not answer a choice question with *yes* or *no*.	Not: **Q:** Do you like hiking or bike riding? **A:** ~~Yes.~~

Pronunciation Notes

The vowel sound in *this* is short. The lips are relaxed. /ɪ/
The vowel sound in *these* is long. The lips are not relaxed. The lips are stretched. /i/
Questions with *or* use rising intonation for the first choice, and falling intonation for the second choice.

Q: Do you like this photo or that photo?

Focused Practice

1 | DISCOVER THE GRAMMAR

*Read the conversations. Then circle **a**, **b**, or **c**.*

1. Guillermo: Who's that man over there?
   Hugo: He's a park ranger.
   a. Guillermo is asking about one park ranger. The ranger is near Guillermo.
   b. Guillermo is asking about park rangers. The rangers are not near Guillermo.
   (c.) Guillermo is asking about one park ranger. The ranger is not near Guillermo.

2. Guillermo: Are those snakes dangerous?
   Park Ranger: No, they're not.
   a. Guillermo is asking about a snake. The snake is not near Guillermo.
   (b.) Guillermo is asking about snakes. The snakes are not near Guillermo.
   c. Guillermo is asking about snakes. The snakes are near Guillermo.

3. Guillermo: Is this a pine tree?
   Park Ranger: Yes, it is.
   (a.) Guillermo is asking about a tree. The tree is near Guillermo.
   b. Guillermo is asking about a tree. The tree is not near Guillermo.
   c. Guillermo is asking about trees. The trees are near Guillermo.

4. Park Ranger: Is this your first trip to a national park?
   Guillermo: Yes, it is.
   a. The park ranger is asking about Guillermo's trip. The trip was last year.
   b. The park ranger is asking about a national park. The park is not far.
   (c.) The park ranger is asking about Guillermo's trip. It's the trip he's taking now.

2 | THIS ISN'T MY BACKPACK

Grammar Notes 1–4

Maria is unpacking her backpack. Complete the conversation with **this, that, these,** *and* **those**.

GUILLERMO: Is something wrong?

MARIA: Yes. these (1.) aren't my jeans and this (2.) isn't my sweatshirt.

GUILLERMO: Is that (3.) your backpack?

MARIA: Uh-oh. It's the right color and shape, but it's not my bag.

[cell phone rings]

MARIA: Hello?

SYLVIA: Is this (4.) Maria Hernandez?

MARIA: Yes.

SYLVIA: I'm Sylvia Green. I'm sorry. I think I have your backpack.

MARIA: Is it green with a black pocket? Is there a pair of pink pants inside?

SYLVIA: Yes to both.

MARIA: That (5.) 's my bag. And those (6.) are my pants. Where are you?

SYLVIA: I'm at the Lake Louise Tent Campgrounds.

MARIA: That's great. I am too. Let's meet in fifteen minutes at the entrance.

SYLVIA: See you in fifteen minutes. Thanks.

3 | CHOICE QUESTIONS

Grammar Note 7

Change the two questions to one question with **or**. *Then answer the question.*

1. Is Jasper in Canada? Is Jasper in the United States?

   A: *Is Jasper in Canada or the United States?*

   B: *It's in Canada.* It's in the province of Alberta.

2. Is that a snake? Is that a stick?

   A: Is that a snake or stick?

   B: Don't worry. It's a stick.

3. Is that campground open all year round? Is that campground open only in the summer?

 A: It that campground open all year round or only in the summer ?

 B: It's open only in the summer . You can't reach it in the winter.

4. It this trail easy? Is this trail difficult?

 A: It this trail easy or difficult ?

 B: ______ It's for advanced hikers.

5. Do they speak English? Do they speak French?

 A: Do they speak English or French ?

 B: They 're speak French . They're from Haiti.

4 | PRONUNCIATION

Listen and circle the word you hear in each sentence.

1. This	These	4. this	these	6. This	These
2. This	These	5. this	these	7. This	These
3. this	these				

5 | EDITING

Correct these conversations. There are four mistakes. The first mistake is already corrected.

1. A: ~~This~~ These are my friends Tom and Marco.

 B: Nice to meet you.

2. A: Do you have a night flight or a morning flight?

 B: ~~Yes~~ A morning flight. I leave at 9 A.M.

3. A: Is ~~these~~ this your flashlight?

 B: Yes, it is. Thanks.

4. A: Are ~~these~~ those men on the mountain OK?

 B: I think so. But it's hard to see them from here.

Communication Practice

6 | LISTENING

Maria is packing for a camping trip. Look at the list. Listen and check (✓) what she takes.

____ 1. boots

____ 2. a sweatshirt

____ 3. guide books

____ 4. a guide book

____ 5. an umbrella

____ 6. batteries

____ 7. heavy pants

7 | A NEW LANGUAGE

Learn a few words in a new language from a classmate. Work in small groups. Your new language "teacher" points to objects in the room. He or she teaches you vocabulary in a language he or she knows. Use **this, that, these,** *or* **those.**

Examples: In English, these are *keys*. In Spanish, they're *llaves*.
In English, that's *a window*. In Japanese, it's a 窓 or まど (pronounced "mado").
In English, those are *chairs*. In Russian, they're стул (pronounced "stool ya").

8 | WRITING

A *Bring in a picture of a famous tourist site. Tell the class about the site.*

Example: This is a picture of the Great Wall. This wall is in China.

Hang the pictures up in the class. A student thinks of one of the places. The class asks choice questions. The class guesses the place.

Example: Is it in South America or Asia?
It's in Asia.
Is it in China or Thailand?
It's in China.
Is it a building or a wall?
It's a wall.
Is it the Great Wall?
Yes, it is.

B *Write about one of the places.*

Example: This is a picture of the Galapagos Islands. These islands are part of Ecuador. Giant turtles live there. These turtles have unusual bodies. They are different from turtles in other parts of the world. Their bodies help them live on the Galapagos Islands. For example, their mouths are curved. This helps them eat cactus. Their feet are not smooth. This helps them walk on rough surfaces. Tourists come to the Galapagos Islands to see different kinds of animals and plants. The first famous visitor to the Galapagos Islands was Charles Darwin.

9 | ON THE INTERNET

Download pictures and get information about one of these national parks in Canada: Banff, Jasper, Kluane, Kootenay, Nahanni, Wood Buffalo, or Yoho. Tell your class about the park.

Where is it?

What is special in this park?

UNIT 14

One / Ones / It

Grammar in Context

BEFORE YOU READ

You get three gifts: a sweatshirt, a CD of your favorite singer's music, and a gift card. Which one do you like best? Why?

Read these conversations of a shopper and two salespeople.

A Gift

SALESPERSON: Can I help you?

SHOPPER: Yes, thanks. I want a red sweatshirt.

SALESPERSON: What size?

SHOPPER: Large. It's for a friend.

SALESPERSON: Here's **one**. It's cute. It says, "Don't worry. Be happy."

SHOPPER: No. I don't think so. Not for her.

SALESPERSON: How about these sweatshirts? **This one** has pockets and **that one** has a hood. The **ones** with hoods are on sale.

SHOPPER: Hmm. I can't decide. Maybe a CD is a better idea.

(at the music store)

2ND SALESPERSON: Need any help?

SHOPPER: Thanks. I want to get a CD for a friend.

2ND SALESPERSON: What kind of music does your friend like?

SHOPPER: R & B I think.

2ND SALESPERSON: Here's **one**. **It**'s Beyoncé's latest.

SHOPPER: I think she has **it**.

2ND SALESPERSON: Well, why don't you get her a gift card? Here. This card is for $25.00. Your friend can buy any CD in the store.

SHOPPER: Will she think I'm lazy?

2ND SALESPERSON: Are you kidding? The gift card is our most popular gift this year.

SHOPPER: OK. I'll take **one**.

AFTER YOU READ

Change these false statements to true ones.

1. The salesperson shows the woman a sweatshirt. It's a ~~green~~ *red* sweatshirt, size large.
2. The woman wants a gift. It's for her cousin.
3. The woman looks at a sweatshirt with pockets and one with a hole.
4. Gift cards are an unusual gift this year. The woman buys one.

Grammar Presentation

ONE

	A / An	Singular Count Noun or Noun Phrase	
I don't need	**a** **an**	**pen**. **original copy**.	I have **one**.

	Adjective	Singular Count Noun	
I need a	**gray**	**shirt.**	He needs a **blue one.**

This / That	*One*	
This **That**	**one**	is my book. is Marco's.

ONES

	Adjective	Plural Count Noun	
The	**gray**	**sweatshirts**	are twenty dollars.

The **gray ones** are twenty dollars.

IT

	The	Noun	*It*
Where's	**the**	**CD**?	**It**'s on the table.

	Possessive Adjective	Noun	*It*
Where's	**your**	**watch**?	**It**'s in the drawer.

	This/That	Noun	*It*
Where's	**that**	**book**?	**It**'s on my desk.

GRAMMAR NOTES	EXAMPLES
1. Use ***one*** in place of *a* or *an* plus a singular count noun.	**A:** Does he have a car? **B:** Yes, he has **one**. (*one* = a car)
2. Use ***one*** in place of a noun phrase.	**A:** I want a red sweatshirt. **B:** Here's **one**. (*one* = a red sweatshirt)
3. Use ***one*** or ***ones*** after an adjective in place of a singular or plural count noun.	**A:** He wants three shirts, two red **ones** and one black **one**. (*ones* = shirts, *one* = shirt)
4. Use ***one*** after *this* or *that*.	**A:** Do you like this watch? **B:** No. I don't like **this one**. I like **that one**. (*one* = watch)
▶ **BE CAREFUL!** Do not use ***ones*** after *these* or *those*.	**A:** Do you want these? **B:** No, I want **those**. NOT: No, I want those ~~ones~~.

5. Use ***it*** in place of *the* + a noun.	**A:** Where's **the card**? **B:** **It**'s on the floor. (*it* = the card)

6. Use ***it*** in place of a possessive pronoun or noun (*my, your, his, her, its, our, their,* or John's) plus a singular count noun.	**A:** Where's **your gift**? **B:** **It**'s in my book bag. (*it* = my gift)

7. Use ***it*** in place of *this* or *that* plus **a** singular count noun.	**A:** Where's **that gift**? **B:** **It**'s in the closet. (*it* = that gift)

Focused Practice

1 DISCOVER THE GRAMMAR

Rosa and Carmen are roommates. Read their conversation. Look at the underlined words. Circle what they refer to.

ROSA: What's up?

CARMEN: Maria's party is tonight. I have a blouse, but I need a long black skirt.

ROSA: I have one (1.). Here. You can borrow it. — **1. a.** a blouse **(b.)** a long black skirt

CARMEN: Are you sure?

ROSA: Of course. And here are three belts— a silver belt and two black ones (2.). — **2. a.** a silver belt **b.** belts

Choose one (3.). — **3. a.** belts **b.** a belt

CARMEN: This one (4.) is nice. — **4. a.** belt **b.** belts

Is it OK if I borrow it (5.)? — **5. a.** Rosa's belt **b.** a belt

ROSA: Of course. And here's my silver necklace. It (6.) matches the belt. — **6. a.** a silver necklace **b.** Rosa's silver necklace

CARMEN: Thanks a lot.

ROSA: No problem. Have a great time.

CARMEN: Thanks.

2 SHORT CONVERSATIONS

Grammar Notes 1–4

Complete the conversations. Use **one** *or* **ones**.

1. **A:** I need a birthday card for her.

   B: Here. I have an extra ________.

2. **A:** I have two new belts. This ________ is for you.

   B: Thanks.

3. **A:** How many TVs do they have?

   B: They have two old ________, and a new ________.

4. **A:** Where do the glasses go?

   B: The blue ________ go on the top shelf and the green ________ go here.

3 HOW TO GET RID OF IT?

Grammar Notes 1–7

Complete the sentences. Use **it** *or* **one**.

A man gets a gift of a new umbrella. He decides to throw away his old ______ (1.). He puts the old ______ (2.) in the wastebasket. A friend recognizes ______ (3.) and returns ______ (4.). Then the man leaves the old umbrella on the train. The train conductor returns ______ (5.) the next day. The man tries hard to throw away his umbrella, but ______ (6.) always comes back. He says to his wife, "I really don't need this old umbrella. I have a beautiful new ______ (7.)." She agrees. Finally he lends ______ (8.) to a friend. He never sees ______ (9.) again.

4 QUESTIONS

Grammar Notes 1–7

Replace the underlined words with ***one***, ***ones***, *or* ***it***.

1. I need a gift for Tom. Do you have a ~~gift~~ *one*?
2. That ring is beautiful. Where is that ring from?
3. I have two sweaters. Which sweater looks better with this skirt?
4. I like your scarf. Is your scarf handmade?
5. These are the old magazines. Where are the new magazines?
6. My dictionary is on the second shelf. I always put my dictionary next to my grammar book.
7. I see a lot of green apples. Do you have any red apples?
8. This gift is for Bill. Is that gift for Sam?

5 | EDITING

Correct these sentences. There are seven mistakes. The first mistake is already corrected.

1. She has two red sweaters and a blue ~~ones~~ one.
2. These apples are delicious. Try one. But first wash one.
3. We have two gift cards. It is in your desk and one is on the counter.
4. These ones are new. Those ones are old.
5. Do you need silver earrings or gold one?
6. I don't want a new leather jacket. I have it.

Communication Practice

6 | LISTENING

Listen to the conversation. Complete the chart. What kind of gifts does she want to get for her friends and relatives?

1. cousins	2. friends	3. brother	4. grandmother	5. father	6. mother

7 | TALK ABOUT GIFTS

Work in pairs. Talk about gifts. Tell which ones you like to get and which ones you like to give.

handmade gifts	big gifts	small gifts	________________
expensive gifts	practical gifts	funny gifts	________________

Example: A: I like to get handmade gifts. I think they're the best.

8 | WRITING

Write about a special gift you gave or one you received.

9 | ON THE INTERNET

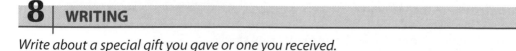

You want to buy a gift for a friend. Look at the store's online catalog. Choose two gifts (a watch, a CD player, etc.). Download pictures and descriptions. Bring the pictures and descriptions to class. Then work in small groups. Ask your group: "Which one do you like?"

Example: A: Look at these watches. Which one do you like?
B: I like this one. It's beautiful, but it's very expensive.

PART

IV

From **Grammar** to **Writing**

Punctuation I: The Apostrophe, The Comma, The Period, The Question Mark

1 *Read this e-mail. Then circle all the punctuation marks.*

Subject: Juan's Surprise Party

Dear Hector,

Are you free on the 16th? I hope so.

Ray and I want to invite you to a surprise party for Juan on November 16th, at 9:00 P.M. It's his 21st birthday. The party is at Ali and Ted's apartment.

Hope to see you there.

Ron

Study these rules of punctuation.

The Apostrophe (')	
1. Use an apostrophe to show possession and to write contractions.	• **Carol's** book is here. • We **aren't** late.

The Comma (,)	
2. Rules for commas vary. Here are some places where commas are almost always used:	
a. in a list of more than two things	• He is wearing **a shirt, a sweater,** and **a jacket**.
b. after the name of a person you are writing to	• Dear **John,**
c. after *yes* or *no* in a sentence	• **Yes,** I am. • **No,** I'm not.
d. when you use *and* to connect two sentences.	• His house is huge**, and** his car is expensive.

The Period (.)

3. a. Use a period at the end of a statement.

b. Use a period after abbreviations.

- We are English language **students**.
- The party is on **Nov.** 16th.

The Question Mark (?)

4. Use a question mark at the end of a question.

- Are you planning a **party?**
- Where are you **going?**

2 *Add punctuation marks to this note.*

Dear Uncle John

Bob and I want to invite you to a party for my parents 25th wedding anniversary Its on Sunday Dec 11th

The party is at our home at 23 Main St Its at three o'clock I hope you can make it

Emily

3 *Invite a friend to a party. Include the following information:*

Who is the party for?
Who is giving the party?
What is the occasion?
When is the party?
Where is the party?

PART

IV

Review Test

I

Read each conversation. Circle the letter of the underlined word or group of words that is not correct.

1. A: Who's [A] Mr. Vogel? — A B C D
   B: Mr. Vogel is [B] Ana [C] teacher [D].

2. A: Do you like [A] red grapes? — A B C D
   B: I like [B] green grapes, but I don't like [C] red one [D].

3. A: When [A] is your first [B] class? — A B C D
   B: It's at [C] two on the afternoon [D].

4. A: Where's [A] the library? — A B C D
   B: It's near [B] the elevator in the [C] third floor [D].

5. A: How much are the ties? — A B C D
   B: This [A] one [B] in my hand costs [C] $50. That [D] ties over there cost $15.

6. A: Now he's [A] a [B] doctor. — A B C D
   B: This is [C] great [D].

II

Circle the correct word(s) to complete the sentences.

1. My classroom is on the two / second floor.
2. My one / first class is at 9:30.
3. My grandfather is seventy-five / seventy-fifth years old.
4. November is the eleven / eleventh month of the year.

III *Circle the correct word to complete the sentences.*

1. This / These is my dictionary.
2. That / Those books are for level 6.
3. Is this / that your bag in the corner?
4. That / Those rugs are from Cairo.
5. Are this / these papers important?

IV *Use **it**, **one**, or **ones** to complete the sentences.*

1. I have a green sweater and two white ________.
2. I have a green sweater. ________ is very warm.
3. He has a blue sweater and a gray ________.
4. I like that scarf. ________ has beautiful colors.
5. I have a new computer. ________ is very fast.
6. The old tools were very good. The new ________ are terrible.

V *Read the invitation. Use the words in the box to complete the questions and answers on the next page. Use some words more than once.*

at	Nuray's	what	where
Fiore's	on	when	whose

Birthday Party
When: November 25th
For: Nuray
Place: 350 East 77th Street Apt. 2A
Time: 9:00 PM
RSVP: Fiore at 917-980-8768

1. Q: What is on November 25th? A: A birthday party for Nuray.
2. Q: Whose birthday party is on November 25th? A: Nuray's birthday party.
3. Q: Where is the party? A: It's at 350 East 77th Street, Apt. 2A.
4. Q: When is the party? A: It's on November 25th.
5. Q: What time is the party? A: It's at 9:00 P.M.
6. Q: Whose phone number is 917-980-8768? A: Fiore's.

VI *Write questions about the underlined word.*

1. A: When is uncle Mike's birthday?
   B: Uncle Mike's birthday is on March 15th.
2. A: Where is Scott?
   B: Scott is in the park.
3. A: What is his aunt's last name?
   B: His aunt's last name is Macabe.
4. A: Who is in the living room?
   B: Ilona is in the living room.
5. A: Whose car is in the garage?
   B: Rick's car is in the garage.

VII *Cross out the underlined words. Use* **His, Her, Its,** *or* **Their.**

1. Mary's (Her) uncle is a professor.
2. The Browns' (Their) car is big.
3. Tom's (His) sister is a history teacher.
4. This is my bird. My bird's (Its) name is Lucky.
5. The students' (Their) tests are on the teacher's desk.

► *To check your answers, go to the Answer Key on page RT-2.*

INFORMATION GAP FOR STUDENT B

Unit 11, Exercise 7

Student B, answer your partner's questions. Then ask your partner questions to complete your chart.

Examples: What country has a national holiday on _______________? (date)
What month is _______________'s national holiday?
What's the date of _______________'s national holiday?
What country has a national holiday in _______________? (month)
When is _______________'s national holiday?

NATIONAL HOLIDAYS AROUND THE WORLD

COUNTRY		MONTH	DAY	COUNTRY		MONTH	DAY
Argentina			**25**	**Haiti**		**January**	**1**
Brazil		**September**	**7**			**June**	**2**
Denmark		**April**	**16**	**Japan**		**December**	
		**February**	**27**	**Lebanon**			**22**
Ecuador		**August**	**10**			**October**	**29**
Greece			**25**	**United States of America**		**July**	**4**

Your country's national holiday:

PART V

Present Progressive; Imperatives; *Can/Could*; Suggestions: *Let's*, *Why Don't We*

UNIT 15 The Present Progressive: Affirmative and Negative Statements

Grammar in Context

BEFORE YOU READ

Look at the pictures below. When do you think events 2.–7. are happening? Check your answers on the bottom of the page.

2. a. 1893	**3. a.** 1939	**4. a.** 1960	**5. a.** 1981	**6. a.** 1992	**7. a.** 1989
b. 1929	**b.** 1959	**b.** 1974	**b.** 1991	**b.** 2002	**b.** 2003

Read about these events.

1. Marcus and Julius **are playing** with yo-yos. It's 100 BC.

2. It's the Chicago World's Fair. Ted and Rose are **riding** the first Ferris wheel. It's the height of a 25-story building.

3. Sue and Ralph Miller **are watching** TV. The Millers are the first on their street to own a color TV.

4. The Suzukis **are visiting** Mexico. They**'re flying** to Cozumel. This year jets **are flying** to Cozumel for the first time.

5. Luis is at a video arcade. He**'s playing** Pac Man. He loves this new game.

6. Berta **is sending** her photo to her boyfriend. She **isn't sending** it by mail. She**'s using** her phone.

7. Yumi **is getting** food from a vending machine. She **isn't using** coins. She **is using** her cell phone to buy the food.

8. Roberto and Marco **are playing** with yo-yos. Yo-yos are over 2,000 years old. It's 2006.

2. a 3. b 4. b 5. a 6. b 7. b

AFTER YOU READ

Match the words on the left and the right to complete the sentences.

e 1. They're playing — a. by jet.

d 2. She's using — b. a Ferris wheel.

c 3. They're visiting — c. Mexico.

b 4. He's riding — d. a camera phone.

f 5. She's buying something — e. with yo-yos.

a 6. They're flying — f. from a vending machine.

Grammar Presentation

PRESENT PROGRESSIVE

Affirmative Statements		
Subject	***Be***	**Base Form of Verb + *-ing***
I	**am**	**eating.**
You	**are**	
He	**is**	
She		
It		
We	**are**	
You		
They		

Negative Statements			
Subject	***Be***	***Not***	**Base Form of Verb + *-ing***
I	**am**	**not**	**flying.**
You	**are**		
He	**is**		
She			
It			
We	**are**		
You			
They			

GRAMMAR NOTES

1. Use the **present progressive** (also called the present continuous) to talk about an **action** that is or is not **happening now**.

Now

Past ———————X———————▶ **Future**

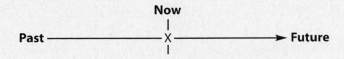

USAGE NOTE: We often use the time expressions ***now***, ***right now***, and ***at the moment*** with the present progressive.

▶ **BE CAREFUL!** We don't usually use non-action verbs in the present progressive.

EXAMPLES

- I **am sending** a fax.
- Their machine **is not working**.

- The machine **isn't working** ***now***.
- ***Right now*** she**'s resting**.
- ***At the moment*** he**'s talking** on the phone.

NOT: The textbook ~~is costing~~ $80.

(continued)

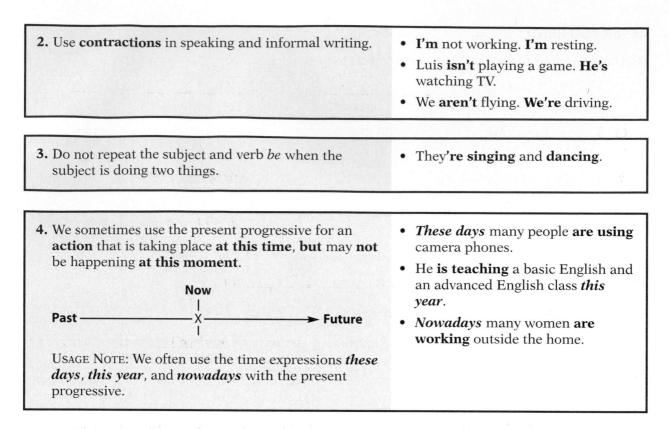

2. Use **contractions** in speaking and informal writing.	• **I'm** not working. **I'm** resting. • Luis **isn't** playing a game. **He's** watching TV. • We **aren't** flying. **We're** driving.

3. Do not repeat the subject and verb *be* when the subject is doing two things.	• They**'re singing** and **dancing**.

4. We sometimes use the present progressive for an **action** that is taking place **at this time, but** may **not** be happening **at this moment**. 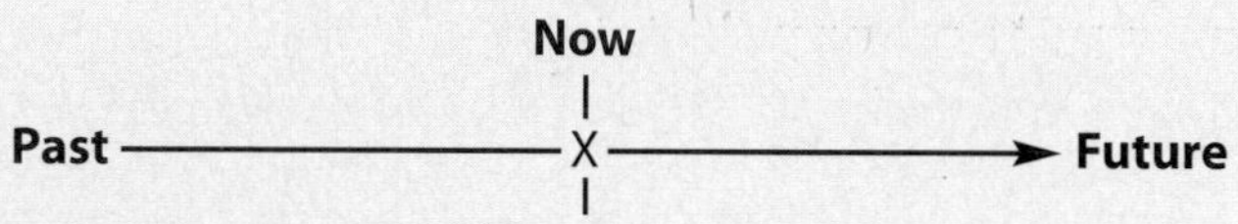 USAGE NOTE: We often use the time expressions ***these days***, ***this year***, and ***nowadays*** with the present progressive.	• ***These days*** many people **are using** camera phones. • He **is teaching** a basic English and an advanced English class ***this year***. • ***Nowadays*** many women **are working** outside the home.

Reference Notes

See Unit 27, page 266 for a discussion of non-action verbs.
See Appendix 15, page A-16 for spelling rules for the present progressive.

Focused Practice

1 DISCOVER THE GRAMMAR

A *Look at Grammar in Context on page 142. There are eight verbs in the present progressive. Write each verb in its base form and* **-ing** *form.*

1. play playing
2. ride riding
3. watch watching
4. fly flying
5. send sending
6. get getting
7. use using
8. visit visiting

B *Write the two negative statements about the events.*

She isn't sending it by mail.

She isn't using coins.

2 ON A PLANE *Grammar Note 1*

Complete the sentences in the affirmative or negative of the present progressive. Choose from the verbs in Exercise 1, Discover the Grammar.

1. The Herraras are going to Chile. They ___are visiting___ friends in Santiago, Chile.
2. Their plane ___is flying___ at a speed of 1,000 kilometers per hour.
3. It was cold on the plane before. Now it ___is getting___ warmer.
4. Mr. Herrara ___is playing___ video games.
5. Mr. Herrera (not) ___isn't watching___ the movie. His son ___is watching___ the movie.
6. In the movie a man ___is riding___ a horse named "Seabiscuit."
7. Mrs. Herrara ___is using___ her BlackBerry®.
8. She ___is sending___ a message to her friends in Chile. She (not) ___isn't sending___ a fax.

3 WHAT'S MARIA DOING NOW? *Grammar Notes 1–3*

Write about Maria. Use the words given and use the present progressive.

1. It's 7:00 A.M.

   Maria / exercise / watch the news on TV

   Maria is exercising and watching the news on TV.

2. It's 8:00 A.M.

   She / get on the train

   She is getting on the train.

3. It's 8:15 A.M. Maria is on the train.

   Now / she / check e-mail / eat a roll / drink a cup of coffee

   Now she is drinking a cup of coffee, eatting a roll and checking e-mail.

4. It's 6:00 P.M. Maria is on the train.

   a. She / go home

   She is going home.

   b. She / talk to friends on her cellphone

   She is talking to friends on her cellphone.

(continued)

5. It's 7:00 P.M.

Maria / eat dinner / watch a video

Maria is eatting dinner and watching a video.

6. It's 9:30 P.M. Maria is meditating.

a. She / not talk

She is not talking.

b. She / not think

She is not thinking.

c. She / not watch TV or videos

She is not watching TV or videos.

d. She / relax

She is relaxing.

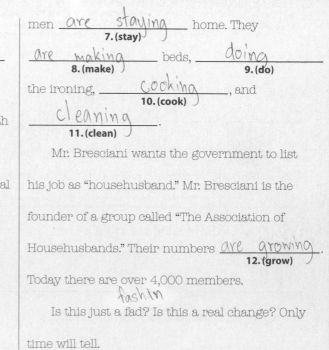

7. It's 11:00 P.M.

She / sleep / dream

She is sleeping dream.

4 | IS ITALY CHANGING?

Grammar Notes 1–4

Complete this news article. Use the present progressive of the verb in parentheses.

Is Italy *Changing?*

It's 8:00 in the evening in a small Tuscan town in Italy. Dr. Bresciani is returning (1. return) home from work. Her husband Francisco is preparing (2. prepare) a delicious salad to go with the chicken marsala.

In traditional Italy, Francisco is not your usual husband. Mr. Bresciani shops, cooks, and cleans. Mr. Bresciani says, "Italy is changing (3. change). Italians are marrying (4. marry) later. Nowadays women are not staying (5. stay/not) home. They are working (6. work) outside the home. More men are staying (7. stay) home. They are making (8. make) beds, doing (9. do) the ironing, cooking (10. cook), and cleaning (11. clean).

Mr. Bresciani wants the government to list his job as "househusband." Mr. Bresciani is the founder of a group called "The Association of Househusbands." Their numbers are growing (12. grow). Today there are over 4,000 members.

Is this just a fad (fashin)? Is this a real change? Only time will tell.

5 | EDITING

Correct this postcard. There are thirteen mistakes. The first mistake is already corrected.

Dear Eun Young,

It was great to hear from you.

'm
I ^ sitting on a park bench in Prospect Park and waiting for Sung Hyun. It's a beautiful day. An older man is takes pictures. Two boys is running and is laughing. Some women doing tai chi. A young woman is talks on her cell phone. A father is push his baby in a stroller. The baby holding a bottle. He isn't drinks from the bottle. He playing with it.

I hope your work is going well. Sung Hyun is works hard and I studying hard. We're plan a vacation in Hawaii next summer. I hope you can join us.

Fondly,

Bo Jeong

To:

Ms Eun Young Kim

2543 Palm Blvd. Apt. E4

Los Angeles, CA 90069

Communication Practice

6 | LISTENING

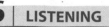

Listen to a telephone conversation. Then listen again and mark the statements **T** *(true) or* **F** *(false).*

___T___ 1. The mother is calling from a train.

___F___ 2. The mother is calling from a plane.

___T___ 3. The father isn't watching TV.

___F___ 4. The father isn't cooking.

___F___ 5. Emily is doing her homework.

___T___ 6. Emily is helping her father.

___F___ 7. The mother isn't hungry.

___T___ 8. The mother is looking forward to dinner.

___T___ 9. They are preparing lasagna.

7 | INFORMATION GAP: ON THE PLANE

Student B, turn to page 186. Follow the directions on that page.

Student A, look at the picture of people on a plane. First tell Student B about one of the people in your picture. Then Student B will tell you about that person in his or her picture. Use the present progressive. Find five differences.

Example: A: In my picture, the man in 14A is playing a video game.

8 | WRITING

Look at people in a school cafeteria, a park, a mall, or on a train or a bus. Write about four people.

- Where are you? What time is it?
- What are the people doing?
- What are they wearing?

Example: I'm in our school cafeteria. It's 12:30 P.M. Two girls are paying for their food. One girl is very tall. The other is not. The tall girl is wearing black pants and a black t-shirt. The shorter girl is wearing jeans and a red sweater. They're carrying a lot of books. The tall girl isn't smiling. She's carrying a tray with a cup of yogurt and a salad. The shorter girl is carrying a tray with a sandwich, a salad, an apple, and cookies. She's talking a lot. The tall girl is listening. She isn't saying a word. I think they're in the same class. I don't think they're close friends.

9 | ON THE INTERNET

E-mail a friend. Tell where you are. Tell what's happening around you.

Example:

Hi Ricardo,

I'm writing to you from the computer lab at school. Five students are in the lab with me. Ali ison my right. He is Instant Messaging a friend. Ranya is on my left. She is playing games. Boris is next to Ranya. He is doing research. Another student is writing a paper. An older man is not using his computer. He's talking to someone on the phone.

What are you doing? Something fun? I hope so.

Well, I'll see you tomorrow.

Igor

UNIT

16 The Present Progressive: *Yes/No* and *Wh-* Questions

Grammar in Context

BEFORE YOU READ

Check (✓) the kinds of TV shows you like.

comedies	☐	news	☐	sports	☐	reality shows	☐
movies	☐	music television (MTV)	☐	talk shows	☐	documentaries	☐
quiz shows	☐	cartoons	☐	soap operas	☐	cooking shows	☐

What's your favorite TV show? ____________________

Abby has a cold. Her husband, Greg, is calling to see how she is. Read their conversation.

I'M WATCHING A FUNNY SHOW

ABBY: Hello.

GREG: Hi, Abby. **How're you feeling?** Any better?

ABBY: Uh-huh. I'm not coughing as much.

GREG: Good. **Are you reading?**

ABBY: No. I'm watching TV.

GREG: **What are you watching?**

ABBY: An old *I Love Lucy* show.

GREG: **What's Lucy doing?**

ABBY: She and Ethel are working.

GREG: **Where are they working?**

ABBY: In a chocolate factory.

GREG: **What's happening now?**

ABBY: Lucy isn't working fast enough. So she's eating some chocolates and putting some in her pockets. It's really funny.

GREG: Lucy is good medicine. **Are you taping the show for me?**

ABBY: Why? You're not a Lucy fan.

GREG: No, but I'm catching your cold.

ABBY: Oh no. I'll call you later. Bye.

GREG: Bye, honey.

AFTER YOU READ

Match the questions and the answers.

__c__ 1. Is Abby reading?

__b__ 2. Is Greg watching TV?

__g__ 3. Who's watching TV?

__f__ 4. What's Abby watching?

__e__ 5. Who's catching a cold?

__d__ 6. Where's Lucy working?

__a__ 7. Is Abby enjoying the show?

a. Yes, she is.

b. No, he's not.

c. No, she's not. She's watching TV.

d. At a chocolate factory.

e. Greg is.

f. The *I Love Lucy* show.

g. Abby is.

Grammar Presentation

PRESENT PROGRESSIVE: *YES/NO* QUESTIONS AND *WH-* QUESTIONS

Yes/No Questions		
Be	Subject	Base Form of Verb + *-ing*
Am	I	**working**?
Are	you	
Is	he she it	
Are	we you they	

Short Answers					
Affirmative			Negative		
Yes,	you	**are**.	No,	you**'re**	**not**.
	I	**am**.		I**'m**	
	he she it	**is**.		he**'s** she**'s** it**'s**	
	you we they	**are**.		you**'re** we**'re** they**'re**	

Wh- Questions			
Wh- Word	*Be*	Subject	Base Form of Verb + *-ing*
Why	are	you	staying home?
What	are	you	watching?
Who	is	he	meeting?
Where	are	they	going?

Answers
I'm sick.
The *I Love Lucy* show.
His teacher. He's meeting his teacher.
To the movies. They're going to the movies.

Wh- Questions about the Subject		
Wh- Word	*Be*	Base Form of Verb + *ing*
Who	is	reading?
What	is	happening?

Answers
My friend (is).
They're making candy.

GRAMMAR NOTES	EXAMPLES
1. Use the **present progressive** to ask about **something that is happening now**. Reverse the subject and *be* when asking a ***yes/no* question**.	statement • He is working. *yes/no* question • Is he working?
2. Most ***wh-* questions** in the present progressive use the same word order as *yes/no* questions. Use *whom* only for formal English.	• Where **is he working**? • What **are they doing**? • Who **are you meeting**? • **Whom** is the president meeting?
3. ***Who*** and ***What*** **questions about the subject** use statement word order.	statement • Lucy is working. *wh-* question • Who is working? statement • Nothing is happening. *wh-* question • What is happening?

Focused Practice

1 DISCOVER THE GRAMMAR

Read the conversation on page 151 again.

1. Write the two complete *yes/no* questions.
   Are you reading? and Are you taping the show for me?
2. Write the *wh-* question about the subject. What's happening now?
3. Write the three other *wh-* questions in the chart below.

Wh- **Word**	***Be***	**Subject**	**Base Form of Verb + *-ing***
How	*are*	*you*	*feeling?*
What	are	you	watching
What	is	Lucy	doing
Where	are	they	working

2 | YES/NO QUESTIONS

Grammar Note 1

Write yes/no questions in the present progressive. Use the words in parentheses. Then match your questions with the answers below.

b 1. (you / watch / TV) *Are you watching TV?*

a 2. (he / look at / the TV Guide?) Is he looking at the TV Guide?

e 3. (they / enjoy / the talk show) Are they enjoying the talk show?

c 4. (we / paying a lot for cable TV) Are we paying a lot for cable TV?

d 5. (the movie / start now) Is the movie start now?

a. Yes. He's checking the time of the ball game tonight.

b. Yes, I am. I'm watching the news.

c. Yes, we are. It's expensive.

d. No, it isn't. It's too early.

e. Yes, they are. They watch that show every week.

3 | QUESTIONS

Grammar Notes 1–3

A *Abby and Greg are talking on the telephone. Complete their conversation. Use the words in parentheses and the present progressive.*

GREG: Hello.

ABBY: Hi, Greg. *How are you feeling* ? Are you feeling any better ?
1. (How / you / feel) 2. (you / feel / any better)

GREG: No, I'm not.

ABBY: Are you taking the medicine ?
3. (you / take / the medicine)

GREG: No.

ABBY: Well, take it. It's good for you.

GREG: Where are you calling from ?
4. (Where / you / call from)

ABBY: I'm on Fifth Avenue and, listen to this. Renée Zellweger is walking ahead of me.

GREG: No kidding! What street are you walking on ?
5. (What street / you / walk on)

ABBY: I'm on Fifth Avenue between 55th and 56th Street.

GREG: What's she wearing ?
6. (What / she / wear)

ABBY: She's wearing a pink suit. She looks great.

GREG: Is she talking to anyone ?
7. (she / talk / to anyone)

ABBY: She's talking to a man and three women. She's giving them her autograph.

What are you doing? Are you watching TV?
8. (What / you / do) 9. (you / watch / TV)

GREG: I'm looking at Renée Zellweger too. I'm watching the movie *Chicago*.

ABBY: That was a good movie. What's happening?
10. (What / happen)

GREG: Renée Zellweger and Catherine Zeta-Jones are dancing.

ABBY: Oh. I remember that part. Well, feel better! I'll be home after my class. Bye, hon.

GREG: Bye-bye.

B *Listen and check your work.*

4 COMMON TWO-WORD VERBS

Grammar Notes 1–2

Complete the questions. Use the words in the box and the present progressive.

listen to	look at	look for	wait for

1. A: What are you watching?
   B: Nothing now. I 'm waiting for the game to come on. My favorite team is playing.
2. A: What 's she looking at?
   B: She's looking at the mail.
3. A: Are you looking for your glasses?
   B: Yes, I am. Why? Do you see them?
4. A: What are they listening to?
   B: Mozart's opera *The Magic Flute*.

5 EDITING

Correct this conversation. There are eight mistakes. The first mistake is already corrected.

A: Are you ~~listen~~ listening to the radio?

B: No, I am not. I'm watching TV.

A: What are you watching?

B: I'm watching a cooking show.

A: Oh. What is happening?

(continued)

B: The chef is preparing dinner for six.

A: What he's making?

B: Spinach lasagna and salad.

A: What's he use?

B: Spinach, cheese, tomato sauce, and mushrooms.

A: He making the tomato sauce?

B: No. It's from a can, but it looks good. I'm getting hungry.

Communication Practice

6 | LISTENING

Roberto is returning home. He meets his friend Cesar. Roberto is listening to a ball game. Write possible ways to complete the conversation. Then listen and write what you hear.

ROBERTO: Hey, Cesar. What are you listening to ?

CESAR: The ball game.

ROBERTO: Who 's playing ?

CESAR: The Red Sox and the Astros.

ROBERTO: Where are they playing ?

CESAR: In Fen way park .

ROBERTO: Who's winning ?

CESAR: It's a tie . It's the bottom of the ninth. Wait . . . Something's happening. Everyone's shouting.

ROBERTO: What 's happening ?

CESAR: It's a home run.

ROBERTO: Yes! That's terrific. The Red Sox won.

7 | INFORMATION GAP: SURFING THE CHANNELS

A *Work in pairs. Student B, turn to the Information Gap on page 186. Student A, look at the programs on channels 2 and 4. Write the* wh- *questions that you need to ask to complete the sentences. Ask your partner your questions. Answer your partner's questions about channels 5 and 7.*

1. A: *Where is the man lying*? B: *He's lying on the floor*.
2. A: Who isn't breathing? B: The man isn't breathing.
3. A: What are they doing? B: They are crying.
4. A: Who are they calling? B: The police.
5. A: What are big men wearing? B: Uniforms.
6. A: What are they doing? B: running.
7. A: What is a tall man carrying? B: A football.

- CHANNEL 2: A man is lying on the floor (1.). The man (2.) isn't breathing. The man's wife and housekeeper are crying (3.). A family friend is calling the police (4.).
- CHANNEL 4: Some big men are wearing uniforms (5.). They're running (6.) on a playing field. A tall man is carrying a football (7.).
- CHANNEL 5: A woman is sitting at a desk. She's wearing a suit. She is talking about the president's trip to Asia.
- CHANNEL 7: A young couple and an older couple are having dessert in an expensive restaurant. The older woman is smiling. She is throwing a pie in her husband's face.

B *Work with your partner. Match the type of show and the channel.*

Channel	Type of Show
____ 1. Channel 2	a. a comedy
____ 2. Channel 4	b. a news show
____ 3. Channel 5	c. a murder mystery
____ 4. Channel 7	d. a sports show

8 | WHAT ARE YOU WATCHING?

Work in pairs. Write a telephone conversation with your partner. Student A is watching TV when Student B calls. Student B, ask Student A questions about his or her show. Use the present progressive. Then write more sentences to continue the conversation.

A: Hello.

B: Hi, ______________________. This is ______________________. Are you busy?

A: Oh, hi, ______________________. I ______________________ (watch) TV.

B: What ______________________ (watch)?

A: ______________________

B: What's happening?

A: ______________________

9 | ON THE INTERNET

Search for TV shows you like. If you can, print one or two photos of the show. What's the name of the show? What kind of show is it? Who are the stars? What are they doing in the photos?

Example: I like the documentaries on *National Geographic Explorer.* The shows are always different. This summer I saw shows on race cars, elephants, and Afghanistan.

UNIT 17

The Imperative

Grammar in Context

BEFORE YOU READ

Do you like contests? What kind?

WIN A
PLASMA TV
Write why you love to watch TV.

Guess the number of pennies.
The winner gets a dollar for every penny.

Write a paragraph:
Clothes Make the Woman
Win a Day of Shopping at The Wrap

Parents and Children is a family magazine. Every month the magazine has a contest. It gives readers money for true stories about children. Read about a contest.*

Kids Are Funny! We're not kidding.

Send us your story and **win** a great prize.

Write a true story about your child, or about yourself as a child.

Don't write more than 100 words.

Include your name, address, and phone number with your story.

Don't send a return envelope. We do not return stories.

E-mail it to: PC.com (Click "kids")

or

Write to:

Parents and Children
480 Elk Street
Madison, Wisconsin 53704

*For more information, **visit** our website at PC.com*

AFTER YOU READ

Correct this contest information.

1. Send us a ~~sad~~ funny story.
2. Include your name, ~~e-mail~~ address, and phone number with the story.
3. Don't write more than ~~10~~ 100 words.
4. Visit our ~~office in Madison~~ website at PC.com for current information.
5. E-mail *~~Teachers~~ Parents and Children* at p~~&~~c.com.

Grammar Presentation

THE IMPERATIVE

Affirmative	
Base Form of Verb	
Write	to the magazine.

Negative		
Don't	**Base Form of Verb**	
Don't	**send**	money.

GRAMMAR NOTES / EXAMPLES

GRAMMAR NOTES	EXAMPLES
1. The **imperative** uses the **base form of the verb**.	• **Walk** three blocks and turn right.
2. Use the **imperative** to:	
a. Give directions and instructions.	• **Write** to the magazine.
b. Give orders.	• **Stand** there.
c. Give advice or suggestions.	• **Take** the train. **Don't take** the bus.
d. Give warnings.	• **Be** careful! It's hot.
e. Make polite requests.	• **Please call** before noon.
3. ***Don't*** comes before the base form for the negative imperative.	• **Don't call** us after 10:00 P.M. • **Don't be** late.
4. In an imperative statement, the subject is always *you*, but we don't say it or write it.	• **Ask** for directions. (You) ask for directions.
5. Use ***please*** to make orders, warnings, and requests more polite. *Please* can come at the beginning or the end of the sentence.	• **Please** stand there. • **Please** be careful. • **Please** call before noon. • Call before noon, **please**.

Focused Practice

1 DISCOVER THE GRAMMAR

Check the sentences that use the imperative.

__✓__ 1. Write to the magazine.

_____ 2. I'm writing to the magazine.

__✓__ 3. Win a trip to Florida.

__✓__ 4. Please visit us online.

_____ 5. They often win contests.

__✓__ 6. Don't send photos.

_____ 7. You write a funny story and you get $300.

__✓__ 8. Take the number 6 bus.

__✓__ 9. Be careful!

2 GREAT ADVICE! *Grammar Notes 1–5*

Every month FOG Magazine *gives prizes to people with great ideas. Read this month's "That's a Great Idea!" Complete the sentences. Use the verbs in the box.*

Don't shop	Enter	Please don't write	Send	Wash
Don't use	Make	Point	Shop	

THAT'S A GREAT IDEA!

• ***You want to remove a bandage. You don't want it to hurt.***

___Point___ (1.) a hair dryer at the bandage for a few seconds.

Ricardo Alvarez

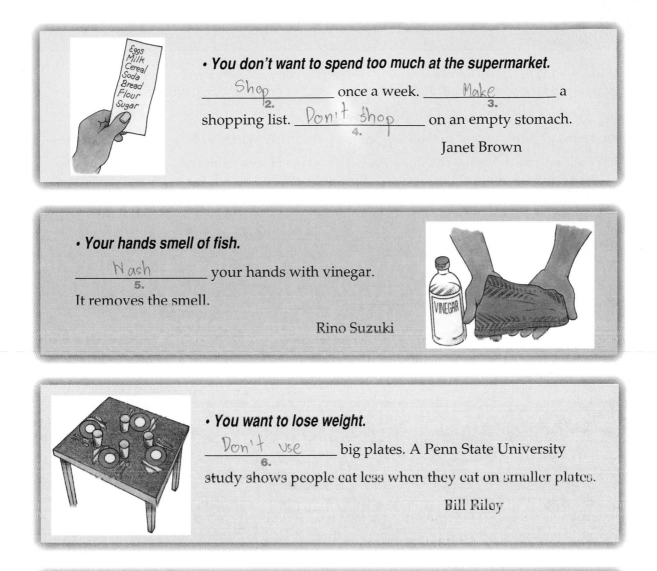

• You don't want to spend too much at the supermarket.

___Shop___ (2.) once a week. ___Make___ (3.) a shopping list. ___Don't shop___ (4.) on an empty stomach.

Janet Brown

• Your hands smell of fish.

___Wash___ (5.) your hands with vinegar.

It removes the smell.

Rino Suzuki

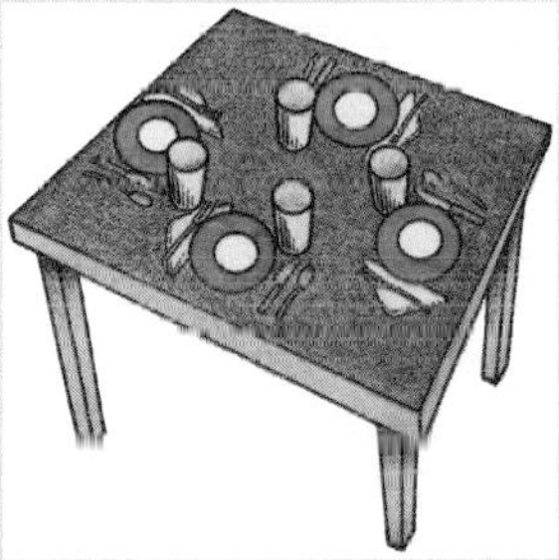

• You want to lose weight.

___Don't use___ (6.) big plates. A Penn State University study shows people eat less when they eat on smaller plates.

Bill Riley

___Enter___ (7.) our "That's a Great Idea!" contest. Keep your ideas short. ___Please don't write___ (8.) more than 50 words. ___Send___ (9.) your ideas to:

That's a Great Idea!,

FOG Magazine, 10 Thinktank Street, Gray Matter, NY 10606

Winners receive a prize.

3 | GIVING DIRECTIONS *Grammar Notes 1–4*

A *Miyuki is visiting her friend Carol in her apartment on the corner of 70th Street and 3rd Avenue. Read their conversation. Then look at the map. Put an **x** at the post office.*

CAROL: Miyuki, I think your idea is really great.

MIYUKI: Thanks, Carol. I want to mail it from the post office. Where's the nearest post office?

CAROL: Walk up Third Avenue to 72nd Street. That's two blocks from here. The post office is between Second and Third Avenue. Turn right at 72nd Street. It's in the middle of the block, on the north side of the street.

MIYUKI: Thanks.

CAROL: I need to go to the bank. The post office is on the way. We can walk together.

MIYUKI: Great.

B *Now write directions from Carol's home to the bank.*

___Walk___ up Third Avenue to ___72ND street___ Street. ___turn___ right. Walk ___two___ blocks. The bank is on the corner of the street.

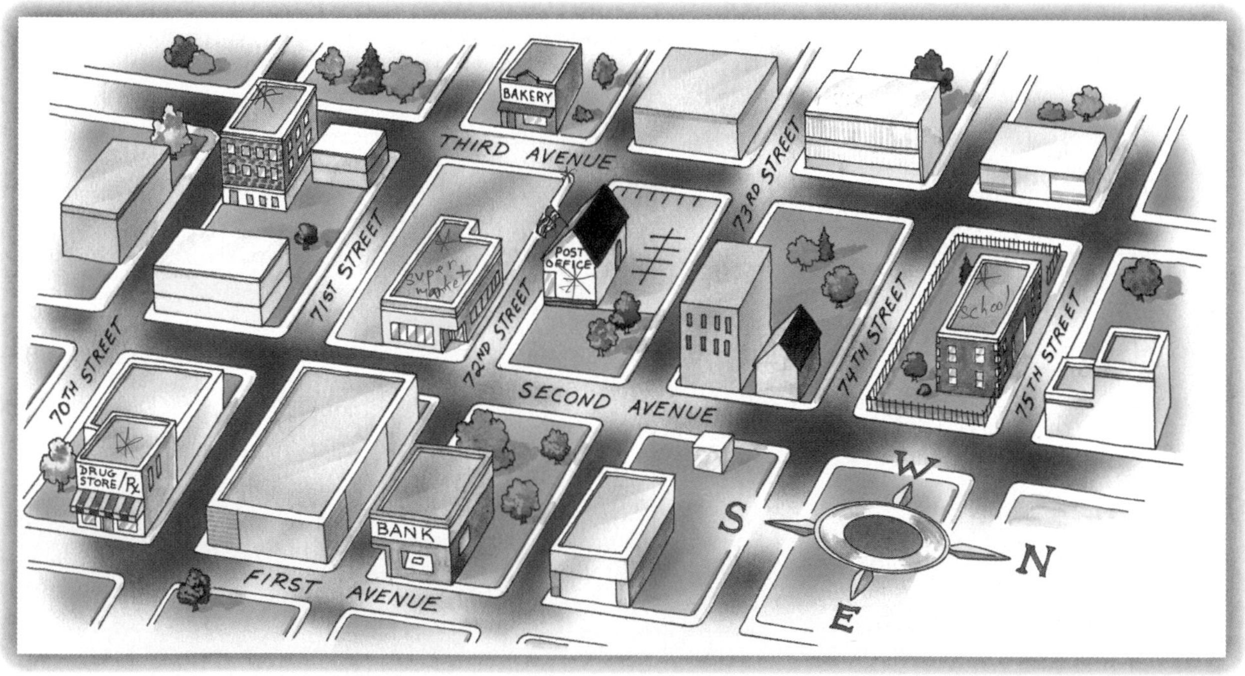

4 POLITE REQUESTS *Grammar Note 5*

Complete the requests. Choose from the words or phrases in parentheses.

1. ___Please mail___ this for me when you're at the post office.
   (Please mail / Please don't mail)
2. It's cold in here. Please ___don't open___ the window.
   (open / don't open)
3. I like to sleep late. ___Please don't call___ before 11:00 A.M.
   (Please call / Please don't call)
4. The concert starts at 8:00. ___Please come___ on time.
   (Please come / Please don't come)
5. We're baking this cake for Grandpa. ___Don't eat___ it, please.
   (Don't eat / Eat)
6. He doesn't understand how your camera works. ________ him how to use it.
   (Please show / Please don't show)
7. Those glasses break easily. ___Please don't touch___ them.
   (Please touch / Please don't touch)

5 CONTEST INFORMATION *Grammar Notes 1–2*

Complete the sentences with the correct phrasal (two-word) verbs.

Check out	Fill in	Pick up	Send in

JELLY BEAN CONTEST

1. ___Pick up___ an entry form at Cathy's Candy Store.
2. ___Fill in___ your name, address, and e-mail address.
3. ___Send in___ your entry before March 31.
4. ___Check out___ the winning entry at Cathycandy@fog.com

6 EDITING

Correct the sentences. There are five mistakes. Put a check (✓) next to each of the two correct sentences.

_✓_ 1. Win a vacation for two.

___ 2. Please ~~to~~ include your name and address.

___ 3. For information, visit~~s~~ our website at www.longtrip.com.

_✓_ 4. Enter here.

___ 5. [Don't] Write ~~not~~ more than 100 words. 2 way 2 say Or write no more than 100 words

___ 6. Don't send~~s~~ money.

___ 7. [Please] Send your entry ~~please~~ before the end of this month.

Communication Practice

7 | LISTENING

Listen to the phone messages on Penny and Steve's answering machine. Listen again and complete the chart.

Caller	Message for	Message	Caller's Number
Denise			

8 | AN AD

Prepare a short advertisement for your school. Write no more than 50 words. Hang your ad on the wall. The class selects the best ad.

Example: Come to FOG Language School. Have fun while you learn. Learn to speak, read, and write English. Register early and receive a discount.

9 | WRITING

Look at the map in Exercise 3.

A *Work in pairs. You and your partner are in front of Carol's building. Ask your partner how to get to one of the following places. Then switch roles.*

- the bakery
- the supermarket
- the school
- the drugstore

Example: **A:** How do I get to the nearest bakery?
B: Walk up Third Avenue. The bakery is between 71st and 72nd Streets. It's in the middle of the block.

B *Write directions from Carol's home to two places on the map. Read your directions aloud. The class names the places.*

Example: **A:** Walk up Third Avenue to 71st Street. Turn right. Walk to First Avenue. It's on the corner of 71st Street and First Avenue.
B: A drugstore?
A: Right.

10 | ON THE INTERNET

Look up contests on the Internet. Find sentences in the imperative. Read them to the class.

UNIT

18

Can / Could

Grammar in Context

BEFORE YOU READ

Do you or a friend have a parrot? If so, can it talk? What language does it speak?

Read about an amazing parrot.

A Genius Parrot

Everyone knows parrots **can talk.** By "talk" we mean they **can repeat** words. Most parrots **can't** really **express** ideas.

N'kisi is different. N'kisi is an African Gray parrot. He **can say** almost 1,000 words. He **can use** basic grammar. He **can talk** about the present, past, and future. When he doesn't know a form, he **can invent** one. For example, he used the word "flied," not "flew," for the past of the verb "fly."

N'kisi lives in New York City with his owner, Aimee Morgana. He **couldn't talk** much at first. At first he **could** only **say** a few words. But Aimee was a great teacher and N'kisi was a good student. Now N'kisi talks to anyone near him.

Donald Broom, a professor of Veterinary Medicine at the University of Cambridge, is not surprised. He says that parrots **can think** at high levels. In that way, they are like apes and chimpanzees.

Les Rance of the Parrot Society says, "Most African Grays are intelligent. They **can learn** to do easy puzzles. They **can say** 'good night' when you turn the lights off at night. They **can say** 'good-bye' when you put a coat on. But N'kisi **can do** many more things. N'kisi is an amazing bird. He's not just smart. He's a genius."

AFTER YOU READ

Mark these statements **T** *(true),* **F** *(false), or* **?** *(it doesn't say).*

_____ **1.** N'kisi can say more than 1,100 words.

_____ **2.** N'kisi can't use basic grammar.

_____ **3.** N'kisi can talk about the past and the future.

_____ **4.** N'kisi can understand Italian.

_____ **5.** Parrots can't think at high levels.

_____ **6.** N'kisi could only say a few words at first.

Grammar Presentation

CAN/CAN'T FOR ABILITY AND POSSIBILITY; *COULD* FOR PAST ABILITY

Affirmative and Negative Statements		
Subject	***Can / Could***	**Base Form of Verb**
I You He She It We You They	**can** **can't** **could** **couldn't**	**speak** Spanish.

(not) able to
(no) ability } can (can't)

can
can't } present

could
couldn't } past

Yes/No Questions		
Can/Could	**Subject**	**Base Form of Verb**
Can	you	**understand**?
Could	you	**understand**?

Answers
Yes, we can understand. No, we can't understand.
Yes, we could understand. No, we couldn't understand.

GRAMMAR NOTES	EXAMPLES
1. ***Can*** expresses **ability** or **possibility**. It comes before the verb. The verb is always in the **base form**.	• He **can say** 950 words. • We **can travel** by bus or train.
2. The **negative** of ***can*** is ***can't***. NOTE: ***Cannot*** is also a correct form of the negative.	• I **can't** understand you. • I **cannot** understand you.
3. Reverse the subject and *can* for *yes/no* questions.	**Q: Can he** speak about the past? **A:** Yes, he can. OR No, he can't.

4. ***Could*** expresses **past ability**. The **negative** of *could* is ***couldn't***. ***Could not*** is also correct.	• I **could** run fast in high school. • I **couldn't** drive five years ago. • I **could not** drive five years ago.

5. Reverse the subject and *could* for *yes/no* questions.	**Q: Could you** speak English last year? **A:** Yes, I could. OR No, I couldn't.

Pronunciation Note

When *can* is followed by a base form verb, we usually pronounce it /kən/ or /kn/ and stress the base form verb: We can **dánce**. In sentences with *can't* followed by a base form verb, we stress both *can't* and the base form verb: We **cán't dánce**.

Focused Practice

1 DISCOVER THE GRAMMAR

A *Read the sentences in column A. Underline* **can, can't**, *or* **couldn't** + base **form** verbs. *Circle negative statements.*

B *Match the sentences in column A with the possible reasons in column B.*

	A	B
e	**1.** N'kisi can talk about the past.	**a.** He's very strong.
b	**2.** We can't understand her.	**b.** She speaks too fast.
f	**3.** I'm sorry. I can't help you now.	**c.** He was too short.
g	**4.** I can't hear you.	**d.** They have colds.
a	**5.** He can lift 50 kilos (110 pounds).	**e.** He's a smart bird.
d	**6.** They can't smell the roses.	**f.** I'm busy.
c	**7.** The boy couldn't reach the button.	**g.** It's very noisy here.

2 | CAN AND CAN'T — *Grammar Notes 1–2*

Complete the sentences. Use **can** *or* **can't** *and the verb in parentheses.*

1. Most African Gray parrots ___can learn___ (learn) to speak. They are very intelligent birds.
2. I ___can't see___ (see) the sign. We are too far away.
3. My dog ___can't sit___ (sit), but he ___can bring___ (bring) me my shoe. I'm trying to teach him to get things.
4. We ___can walk___ (walk) to our school. It's near our home.
5. They ___can speak___ (speak) two languages, Spanish and Italian. They're learning English now.
6. My uncle ___can't drive___ (drive). He wants to take driving lessons.
7. He ___can't open___ (open) the door. His arms are full.

3 | N'KISI WANTS A CAR — *Grammar Note 3*

N'kisi and Aimee were in a car. After the ride this is what N'kisi said. This is a real conversation. Read the conversation. Then write yes/no *questions and answer the questions.*

N'KISI: Wanna [I want to] go in a car right now.

AIMEE: I'm sorry. We can't right now—maybe we can go later.

N'KISI: Why can't I go in a car now?

AIMEE: Because we don't have one.

N'KISI: Let's get a car.

AIMEE: No, N'kisi, we can't get a car now.

N'KISI: I want a car.

1. Q: ___Can N'kisi talk?___ (N'kisi / talk) A: ___Yes, he can.___
2. Q: ___Can he ask questions?___ (he / ask questions) A: ___Yes, he can___
3. Q: ___Can he make suggestions?___ (he / make suggestions) A: ___Yes, he can___
4. Q: ___Can Aimee and N'kisi get a car now?___ (Aimee and N'kisi / get a car now) A: ___No, they can't___
5. Q: ___Can you believe this conversation?___ (you / believe this conversation) A: ___No, I can't___

4 PAST ABILITIES

Grammar Notes 4–5

*Complete the sentences with **could** or **couldn't** and the verbs in parentheses.*

1. My cat was not a good hunter. He couldn't catch (a. catch) any mice. Could your cat catch (b. catch) mice?
2. Michael was a smart gorilla. He could use (a. use) sign language. He could make (b. make) 600 different gestures.
3. My dog Charlie was a good watchdog, but he couldn't do (do) any tricks.
4. He was a child genius. He couldn't understand (understand) college physics when he was 10 years old.
5. I couldn't speak (speak) English well a few months ago. But now I can.
6. Long ago he was on the all-star tennis team. He could play (play) tennis very well.
7. She could lift (lift) incredible weights in high school. She was on a weight-lifting team.

5 EDITING

*Read the sentences. There are six mistakes. The first mistake is already corrected. Add **can** to fix one mistake.*

A: Can you ~~coming~~ come to my party? It's next Saturday night.

B: Yes, thanks. How can I get to your home?

A: You can ~~to~~ take the train and a taxi.

B: Can you meet me at the train station?

A: I'm sorry I can't. I ~~no~~ can't drive. Maybe Bob can ~~meets~~ meet you. He has a car and he can ~~to~~ drive.

Communication Practice

6 LISTENING

Listen and repeat the sentences. Listen again and complete the sentences. Then listen a third time and mark the stress.

1. My friend can séw, but he cán't cóok.
2. My dog can sit, but it can't beg.
3. Kelly can lift 100 kilos, but Nitza can't.
4. José can play tennis. He can play basketball, too.
5. Elena can read English newspapers, but she can't understand spoken English well.

7 | FIND SOMEONE WHO CAN . . .

A *Walk around the class. Ask your classmates questions with* **can** *or* **could**. *Ask about now and about five years ago. If they answer* **yes**, *write their names in the box.*

Example: VICTOR: Can you play an instrument?
CAROLINA: Yes, I can. I can play the guitar.
VICTOR: Could you play the guitar five years ago?
CAROLINA: No, I couldn't.

	Now	Five years ago
1. play an instrument	*Carolina*	
2. design a web page	wroong can	wroong couldn't
3. fix a car	Frasana can't	Frasana couldn't
4. fly a plane	Mandy can't	Mandy couldn't
5. write with both hands	Diana can	Diana could
6. ~~snowboard~~ swim	lasida can	lasida could
7. ~~windsurf~~ cook	watch can Abdu windsurf can	watch could Abdu windsurf couldn't

B *Report to your class.*

Example: Erna can play the piano and design a web page. Five years ago she could play the piano, but she couldn't design a web page.

8 | GAME: WHAT CAN YOUR GROUP DO?

Work in small groups. When your group can do one of the following, raise your hand. The first group to do a task wins.

1. Can you say "I love you" in more than five languages?
2. Can you name the colors of the flags of eight countries?
3. Can you name the capitals of ten countries?

9 WRITING

Write about an interesting pet. What kind of animal is it? What does it look like? Where does it live? Does it have a name? What is it? What can it do? What can't it do?

Example: I have a beautiful green parakeet. His name is Chichi. He is two years old. He lives in a cage in the living room. Sometimes he flies around the room. Chichi can sing very beautifully. Chichi couldn't do anything when he was a baby. But now he can sit on my finger and eat from my hand. He can't speak, but I'm happy about that. I tell him all my secrets and he doesn't tell anyone. That's a wonderful quality. I love my Chichi.

10 ON THE INTERNET

Find out more about animals who can use or understand language. Search for Koko the gorilla (California, USA) or Rico the border collie (Germany), or learn more about African Grey parrots like N'kisi. Report to the class.

UNIT

19 Suggestions: *Let's, Why don't we . . . ?, Why don't you . . . ?*; Responses

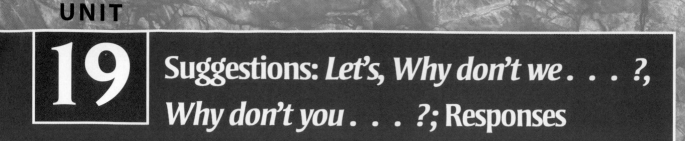

Grammar in Context

BEFORE YOU READ

What kind of sports do you like to do?
What kind of sports do you like to watch?

- soccer or football
- rock climbing
- snorkeling or scuba diving
- other sport

Four friends are on vacation in Maui. Read their conversation.

RODICA: The weather is perfect. **Let's spend** the afternoon at the beach.

ARDA: Yeah. **Let's go** snorkeling again.

PAUL: **Why don't we try** scuba diving?

RODICA: Scuba diving? That's not so easy. You need to take lessons. And the tank is heavy.

SHIRA: I have a better idea. **Let's go** Snuba® diving.

ARDA: Snuba diving? What's that?

SHIRA: It's something new. I read a brochure about it. It combines scuba diving and snorkeling. It's pretty safe. They say anyone over eight years old can do it. So, what do you think? Want to try it? Are you game?

RODICA: Sure. Why not? It sounds like fun.

SHIRA: OK. **Why don't we get** a disposable underwater camera? I want pictures of the fish.

RODICA: Me too. Shira, **why don't you get** the camera? Arda and I can get information about Snuba diving at the front desk.

SHIRA: OK. Then **let's meet** back here.

RODICA: Great.

AFTER YOU READ

Change the sentences to match the information in the conversation above.

The weather is bad. Five friends decide to go snorkeling. They also decide to buy phones. They want to take pictures of themselves. Arda and Rodica get information at the hotel pool.

Grammar Presentation

SUGGESTIONS

Affirmative		
Let's	Base Form of Verb	
Let's	**go**	to the beach.

Negative			
Let's	*Not*	Base Form of Verb	
Let's	**not**	**go**	to the beach.

Suggestions for a Group		
Why Don't We	Base Form of Verb	
Why don't we	**go**	on a bike tour?

Suggestions for Another Person		
Why Don't You	Base Form of Verb	
Why don't you	**get**	the cameras?

RESPONSES

Agree
OK.
That's a good idea. (Good idea.)
That sounds good to me. (Sounds good to me.)
Sounds like a plan.

Disagree
No, I don't feel like it.
Why don't we . . . instead.
Sorry, not today.
I can't. I . . .

GRAMMAR NOTES	EXAMPLES
1. Use ***Let's*** or ***Let's not*** + **the base form** for suggestions that include you and another person.	• **Let's go.** • **Let's not eat** there.
2. Use ***Why don't we*** and the base form for suggestions that include you and another person.	• **Why don't we** go to the pool?
Use ***Why don't you*** to make a suggestion or give advice to another person.	• **Why don't you** look on the Internet?
Remember to put a question mark (**?**) at the end of sentences with *Why don't we* and *Why don't you*.	• **Why don't we** meet in the lobby**?** • **Why don't you** call home**?**
3. To **agree** to a suggestion we sometimes use, ***OK***, ***That's a good idea***., or ***That sounds good to me***.	**A:** Let's meet at eight o'clock. **B:** **OK.** OR **That's a good idea.**
To **reject** a suggestion we usually **give a reason** and **make another suggestion**.	**A:** Let's meet at eight o'clock. **B:** **That's too early. Why don't we meet at eight-thirty?**

Focused Practice

1 DISCOVER THE GRAMMAR

A *Read the statements. Underline the suggestions.*

B *Unscramble the conversation. Write the conversation on the lines below.*

- OK. The prices there are better.
- Let's get some souvenirs.
- That's true, but the prices are high. Why don't we go to the market?
- That's a good idea. Why don't we go to the gift shop? They have some beautiful things.

A: ______________________________

B: ______________________________

A: ______________________________

B: ______________________________

2 LET'S AND LET'S NOT

Grammar Note 1

Complete the sentences. Use **Let's** *or* **Let's not** *and the verb in parentheses.*

1. We're out of film. ___Let's get___ (get) some at the gift shop.
2. The taxis here are expensive. ________________ (take) a bus.
3. The food there was terrible. ________________ (go) back.
4. It's cold today. ________________ (go) swimming in the ocean.
5. The store isn't far. ________________ (walk) there.
6. Snuba diving was fun. ________________ (do) it again.
7. This is our last day here. ________________ (sleep) late. Let's get up early and see the volcanoes.

3 CONVERSATIONS

Grammar Notes 1–2

Complete the conversations. Use the sentences below.

> **a.** Why don't we meet at the pool?
> **b.** Let's walk to the beach.
> **c.** Why don't we try that new Lebanese restaurant?
> **d.** Why don't you call the front desk and complain?
> **e.** Let's not go to the market for souvenirs.
> **f.** Let's ask the receptionist.

1. SHIRA: Let's go to Luigi's Restaurant.
   RODICA: Again? ________________________________
2. ARDA: Let's meet in the gift shop in about 15 minutes.
   SHIRA: It's so nice outside. ________________________________
3. ARDA: ________________________________ Then we can go for a swim.
   SHIRA: It's far. Why don't we drive?
4. RODICA: It's too crowded at the market. ________________________________
   ARDA: OK. We can buy souvenirs at the shopping mall.
5. ARDA: Is there a fitness room at the hotel?
   SHIRA: I don't know. ________________________________
6. RODICA: The TV in my room doesn't work.
   ARDA: ________________________________

4 | MAKE A SUGGESTION

Grammar Notes 1–3

Complete the suggestions. Use the phrasal (two-word) verbs in the box. Then circle the letter of the correct response.

check out	find out	pick up	sit down	turn on

1. **A:** Let's ________________ some sandwiches. We can eat them in the park.
   B: **a.** Sounds like a plan.
   b. Yes.

2. **A:** Let's ________________ over there. There are two empty seats.
   B: **a.** I don't feel like it. Why don't we go for a swim or play ball?
   b. No, we aren't.

3. **A:** Why don't we ________________ about a tour for this afternoon?
   B: **a.** Because I'm busy.
   b. I'm sorry, I can't. I have a scuba diving lesson at 2:00.

4. **A:** Why don't you ________________ the TV? We can hear the news.
   B: **a.** Good idea.
   b. Yes, I can.

5. **A:** Why don't we ________________ the menu at that fish restaurant? It looks nice.
   B: **a.** Because I don't like fish.
   b. Sorry. I don't like fish.

5 | EDITING

Correct these conversations. There are five mistakes. The first mistake is already corrected.

1. **A:** Let's ^get something to eat.
   B: I'm not hungry now. How about in an hour?

2. **A:** Why don't we go to the movies?
   B: Yes.

3. **A:** Why do not we help them?
   B: OK.

4. **A:** Let's us go snuba diving.
   B: That's a good idea.

5. **A:** Why don't we meet for dinner at 6:00?
   B: That's a little early. Let's at 6:30.

Communication Practice

6 | LISTENING

Rodica, Arda, and Shira are talking about their plans for the afternoon. Listen. Then listen again and check the things they decide to do.

_____ 1. go whale watching
_____ 2. go bike riding
_____ 3. go windsurfing
_____ 4. take photos
_____ 5. go surfing
_____ 6. take a boat ride
_____ 7. go to the market
_____ 8. buy handmade baskets

7 | ROLE PLAY

Work in pairs (A and B). Student A makes a suggestion. Student B agrees or makes another suggestion and gives a reason why. Continue until you both agree. Take turns.

Example: **A:** Let's have pizza.
B: I'm tired of pizza. Why don't we have Chinese food?
A: That's a good idea.

1. Let's have pizza.
2. Let's take a break.
3. Let's play tennis.
4. Let's go Snuba diving.
5. Let's visit Hawaii.
6. Let's study grammar tonight.

8 SOUVENIRS

Work in pairs. You and your partner are on vacation in Hawaii. You each want to buy souvenirs for five people. Give each other suggestions. Use **Why don't you** *for suggestions.*

Example: A: I want to get souvenirs for my parents, my brother, my best friend, and a coworker.
B: Why don't you buy a basket for your mother?
A: That's a good idea. What about my brother? Any ideas for him?

9 ON THE INTERNET

A *Find out places you can do one of the following sports:*

- parasailing
- bungee jumping
- surfing
- water skiing
- horseback riding
- ice skating

B *Work in pairs. Have a conversation with your partner. Make a suggestion to do one of the above sports.*

Example: A: Let's go parasailing.
B: Where can we go?
A: I read about a place in South Africa.
B: Really?
A: Uh-huh. It's near Johannesburg. It's . . .

PART V

From **Grammar** to **Writing**

Subjects and Verbs

1 *What's wrong with these sentences?*

A	**B**
1. He a handsome man.	**1.** Am wearing blue pants.
2. She a red skirt.	**2.** Are tired?
3. I from Argentina.	**3.** Is a cool day.

All sentences in A are missing a verb. All sentences in B are missing a subject.

Study the information about subjects and verbs.

Every sentence needs a subject and verb.	
The **subject** is a noun or pronoun. It tells who or what the sentence is about.	• **John** is running. • **They** are watching TV.
The **verb** tells the action or links the subject with the rest of the sentence.	• It **is raining**. • He **is** a doctor.

2 *Correct this paragraph. Then underline the subject and circle the verb in each sentence.*

I in Central Park. It a sunny day in September. Is crowded. Some children soccer. They're laughing and shouting. Some people are running. Three older women on a bench. Are watching the runners and soccer players. A young man and woman are holding hands. Are smiling. Are in love. Central Park a wonderful place to be, especially on a beautiful September day.

3 *Imagine you are in one of these places. Write a paragraph about the people you see.*

1. You are on a busy street.

2. You are in an airport or train station.

3. You are in a park.

PART V

Review Test

I

Read each conversation. Circle the letter of the underlined word or group of words that is not correct.

1. A: What you're (A) doing (B)?
   B: We're (C) watching (D) the news on TV.
   A B C D

2. A: She's studying (A) Portuguese.
   B: No (B), she's no studying (C) Portuguese. She's (D) studying Italian.
   A B C D

3. A: Aunt Jessica is (A) in the hospital (B).
   B: Let's (C) to send (D) her flowers.
   A B C D

4. A: They're (A) playing (B) basketball.
   B: Why (C) you don't (D) join them?
   A B C D

5. A: How's his English?
   B: Good. Last year he couldn't (A) understand (B) anything. Now he cans (C) understand and speak (D) well.
   A B C D

6. A: Those cookies (A) are for the party. Please (B) not to (C) eat them.
   B: OK (D). They look delicious.
   A B C D

7. A: How can I (A) get (B) to the bank?
   B: Walk (C) two blocks to Second Street. Turns (D) left.
   A B C D

II *Read each dialogue. Circle the letter of the correct response.*

1. **A:** Let's have lunch now.
   B: _____
   a. It's too early. Why don't we wait until noon?
   b. Yes, you're right.

2. **A:** Why don't you call home?
   B: _____
   a. OK.
   b. Let's call home.

3. **A:** Let's rent a movie.
   B: _____
   a. No, we don't.
   b. That sounds like a good idea.

4. **A:** Are they waiting for us?
   B: _____
   a. No, they aren't.
   b. Yes, we are.

5. **A:** What's he doing?
   B: _____
   a. He's playing.
   b. He can play.

6. **A:** Can you hear me?
   B: _____ Please speak louder.
   a. No, we can't.
   b. No, I couldn't.

7. **A:** Did you enjoy the play?
   B: No, I didn't. _____
   a. I can't see the stage.
   b. I couldn't see the stage.

III *Read each situation. Write one affirmative statement and one negative statement in the imperative. Use the phrases in the box.*

forget your scarf	read the directions	start before 10:00	~~stop~~
take the highway	use the side streets	~~walk~~	wear your jacket

1. The traffic light is red.
   a. Stop.
   b. Don't walk.

2. You have a test at 10:00.
   a. ______________________
   b. ______________________

3. There are many cars on the highway.

a. ____________________

b. ____________________

4. It's cold outside.

a. ____________________

b. ____________________

IV *Complete the paragraph. Use the affirmative or negative present progressive of each verb in parentheses.*

Jen and Jon are at the library, but they ____________ (1. study). Jen ____________ (2. write) a letter to her grandmother. Jon ____________ (3. look) at a magazine. Their textbooks are open, but they ____________ (4. read) them. They ____________ (5. relax). They ____________ (6. take) a break.

V *Correct the mistake in each conversation.*

1. A: Is it's raining outside?

   B: Yes, it is. I'm not leaving.

2. A: Are they play soccer?

   B: No, they're playing baseball.

3. A: How is his English?

   B: He speaks well now, but last year he can't speak at all.

4. A: Why don't we to take a walk?

   B: OK.

5. A: Please you are quiet.

   B: Sorry.

▶ *To check your answers, go to the Answer Key on page RT-2.*

INFORMATION GAP: STUDENT B

Unit 15, Exercise 7

Student B, look at the picture of people on a plane. First, tell Student A about one of the people in your picture. Then Student A will tell you about that person in his or her picture. Use the present progressive. Find five differences.

Example: B: In my picture, the man in 14A is watching a movie.

INFORMATION GAP FOR STUDENT B

Unit 16, Exercise 7

A *Student B, look at the programs on channels 5 and 7. Write the wh- questions that you need to ask to complete the sentences. Answer your partner's questions about channels 2 and 4. Ask your partner your questions.*

1. **B:** Who's sitting at a desk? **A:** A woman is sitting at a desk.
2. **B:** What is she wearing? **A:** She's wearing a suit.
3. **B:** What's she talking about? **A:** The president's trip to Asia.
4. **B:** Where are they having dessert? **A:** An expensive restaurant.
5. **B:** Who's smiling? **A:** The old woman.
6. **B:** Who's throwing a pie? **A:** The old woman.

- CHANNEL 2: A man is lying on the floor. The man isn't breathing. The man's wife and housekeeper are crying. A family friend is calling the police.
- CHANNEL 4: Some big men are wearing uniforms. They're running on a playing field. A tall man is carrying a football.
- CHANNEL 5: A woman (1.) is sitting at a desk. She's wearing a suit (2.). She is talking about the president's trip to Asia (3.).
- CHANNEL 7: A young couple and an older couple are having dessert in an expensive restaurant (4.). The old woman (5.) is smiling. she (6.) is throwing a pie in her husband's face.

PART VI

The Simple Past

UNIT

20 The Simple Past: Regular Verbs—Affirmative and Negative Statements

Grammar in Context

BEFORE YOU READ

Look at the chart. Are you from one of these countries? Have you visited any of these countries? Which ones? Which cities did you visit? When?

Example: I'm from Mexico. I was in Canada in 1999. I visited Montreal and Quebec. I was in the United States last summer. I visited San Francisco and Los Angeles.

Most Popular Tourist Places

	Country	2003 (arrivals in millions)	Percent change from 2002
1.	France	75.0	−2.6
2.	Spain	52.3	+0.3
3.	United States	40.4	−3.6
4.	Italy	39.6	−0.5
5.	China	33.0	−10.3
6.	United Kingdom	24.8	+2.6
7.	Austria	19.1	+2.6
8.	Mexico	18.7	−4.9
9.	Germany	18.4	+2.4
10.	Canada	17.5	−12.7

Read the postcard. What city did Karen and Gene visit? The answer is at the bottom of the page.

Dear Dahlia and Jon,

They say everyone loves this city. Now we know why.

Yesterday morning we **watched** foot-volley on Ipanema Beach. It was unbelievable! The players were great. They **didn't miss** the ball. In the afternoon we **visited** Sugarloaf. The view from the top was out of this world. Then in the evening we **enjoyed** a delicious meal at a churrascaria (barbecued meat restaurant).

Our flight here was the only bad part of the trip. We **didn't land** until 11:30 at night, and the flight was very bumpy. But the people at our hotel were helpful and our room is beautiful.

Our body language is still better than our Portuguese, but we are trying.

Ciao!
Karen and Gene

To: Dahlia and Jon Lamb
2909 Northport Trail
Charleston, SC 29401
USA

AFTER YOU READ

Change these false statements to true ones.

1. Dahlia and Jon visited Rio de Janeiro.
2. Karen and Gene played foot-volley on Ipanema Beach.
3. Karen and Gene enjoyed a meal at an Italian restaurant.
4. Karen and Gene's plane arrived in the evening.
5. The people at the hotel were unhelpful.
6. Karen and Gene speak Portuguese well.

They visited Rio de Janeiro.

Grammar Presentation

THE SIMPLE PAST: REGULAR VERBS—AFFIRMATIVE AND NEGATIVE STATEMENTS

Affirmative Statements	
Subject	**Base Form of Verb**
I You He She It We You They	walk**ed**. arrive**d**. stud**ied**.

Negative Statements		
Subject	***Did Not***	**Base Form of Verb**
I You He She It We You They	**did not** **didn't**	**walk**. **arrive**. **study**.

Common Past Time Markers		
Yesterday	***Ago***	***Last***
yesterday **yesterday** morning **yesterday** afternoon **yesterday** evening	two days **ago** a week **ago** a month **ago** a year **ago** a couple of days **ago**	**last** night **last** Monday **last** week **last** summer **last** year

GRAMMAR NOTES

EXAMPLES

1. Use the **simple past** to tell about **things that are finished**.

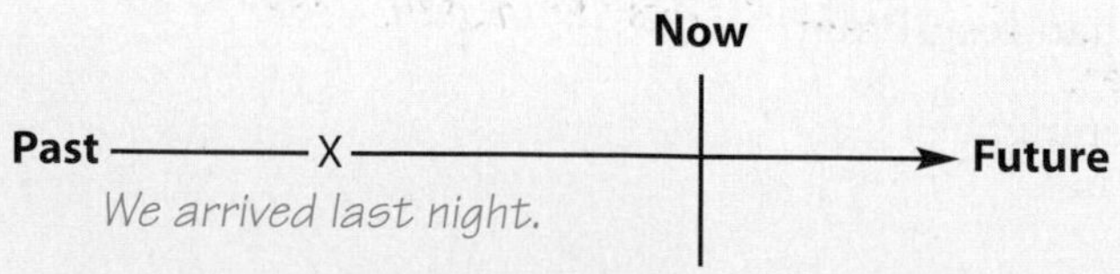

- We **arrived** last night.

2. There are three endings for the regular simple past: ***-d***, ***-ed***, and ***-ied***.

*arrive – arrive**d***

*land – land**ed***

*try – tr**ied***

- I **arrived** late.
- We **landed** in Caracas.
- He **tried** to change his flight.

Regular simple past verbs end in three sounds: **/d/**, **/t/**, or **/ɪd/**.

- /d/ – He arrived late.
- /t/ – They worked at a hotel.
- /ɪd/ – We waited a long time.

3. In the simple past, the **verb form** is the **same for all persons**.	• **I visited** Seoul. • **She visited** Mexico City. • **They visited** Madrid.

4. For **negative statements** in the simple past, use ***did not*** **+ the base form of the verb**. Use the contraction ***didn't*** for negative statements in speaking or informal writing.	• We **did not stay** at a hotel. • They **did not see** the art museum. • We **didn't stay** at a hotel.

5. Time markers usually come at the beginning or at the end of a sentence.	• **Yesterday morning** I studied. • I studied **yesterday morning**.

6. ***Today, this morning, this afternoon,*** and ***this evening*** can be past time markers if they mean "before now."	• I studied grammar **today**. *(It is now 9:00 P.M. I studied grammar in the afternoon.)* • **This morning** I listened to the news. *(It is now the afternoon.)*

Reference Note

See Appendix 17, page A-18 for complete spelling and pronunciation rules for the simple past.

Focused Practice

1 DISCOVER THE GRAMMAR

Read the sentences. Underline the verbs in the simple past. Write the base form of the verb next to each sentence. Circle six more time markers.

1. We arrived in San Francisco last Wednesday. *arrive*
2. We visited the Fairmont Hotel on Thursday. visit
3. Yesterday afternoon we walked around Fisherman's Wharf. walk
4. High school friends invited us for dinner last night. invit
5. Dan baked a delicious cake yesterday morning. bake
6. Sheila carried it to the dining room. carry
7. Sheila dropped it and I cried out, "Oh no!" drop cry
8. After dinner we walked around Chinatown. walk
9. We talked about politics. talk
10. This morning I called and thanked them for a great evening. call thank

2 SPELLING AND PRONUNCIATION *Grammar Note 2*

A *Complete the sentences. Use the simple past of the verbs in the box. Then follow the directions for Part B below.*

arrive	borrow	cook	hug	joke	~~miss~~	visit	walk	want	watch

	/t/	/d/	/ɪd/
1. I'm sorry I'm late. I ___missed___ my train.	☑	☐	☐
2. The plane ___arrived___ on time.	☐	☐	☐
3. Last night she ___visited___ the art museum.	☐	☐	☐
4. He ___cooked___ a delicious meal for us.	☐	☐	☐
5. I'm tired. I ___walked___ up a lot of hills in San Francisco this morning.	☐	☐	☐
6. We ___wanted___ to take a tour of Alcatraz in the afternoon but the tour was filled.	☐	☐	☐
7. We ___borrowed___ a guidebook from our friends.	☐	☐	☐
8. Two nights ago they ___watched___ a parade.	☐	☐	☐
9. The comedian ___joked___ about the politicians.	☐	☐	☐
10. Everyone ___huged___ and kissed us when we left.	☐	☐	☐

B 🎧 *Now listen to the sentences. Then listen again and check (✓) the final sound of each verb. (See Appendix 17 on page A-18 for pronunciation rules for the regular simple past.)*

3 NEGATIVE STATEMENTS *Grammar Note 4*

Read the first sentence of each item. Underline the verb in the sentence. Complete the second sentence with the negative form of that verb.

1. He stayed with friends. He ___didn't stay___ at a hotel.
2. They arrived at nine at night. They ___didn't arrive___ at nine in the morning.
3. I wanted a nonsmoking room. I ___didn't want___ a smoking room.
4. It rained in the morning. It ___didn't rain___ in the afternoon.
5. She only invited you. She ___didn't invite___ your whole family.
6. He helped you. He ___didn't help___ me.
7. I wanted an egg. I ___didn't want___ an egg roll.

4 | TRAVEL LOG *Grammar Notes 1–4*

Complete the travel log with the affirmative or negative of the verbs in parentheses. (Two sentences are negative.) Use the simple past.

Carlos and I rented (1. rent) a car last Wednesday morning. We arrived (2. arrive) here in San Francisco Wednesday night. We shared (3. share) the driving so it was easy. The weather was fine. I like San Francisco. It's a colorful city.

On Thursday it rained (4. rain), but the weather didn't stop (5. stop) us from sight-seeing. We carried (6. carry) umbrellas and walked (7. walk) around Fisherman's Wharf and Chinatown. Friday we visited (8. visit) the University of California at Berkeley. Carlos's father attended (9. attend) Berkeley in the sixties. I think it's an interesting place. Berkeley students are very open.

Friday night Carlos's cousin called (10. call) and invited (11. invite) us to his home in Long Beach, but we didn't want (12. want) to drive so far. We promised (13. promise) to see him on our next trip to California. I hope we get back there soon. All in all, it was a great trip.

5 | THEY TRAVEL A LOT *Grammar Note 5*

Complete the conversations. Use **last, ago,** *or* **yesterday**.

1. BEN: Were you away?

SAMUEL: Yes, I was in Mexico City last (a.) week.

BEN: Oh. I was there a couple of months ago (b.). When did you get back?

SAMUEL: Yesterday (c.) afternoon. Ian called me last (d.) night. He wants us to meet for lunch.

BEN: Good. I'll call him today.

2. STEVE: Where is Demetrios?

ALLY: I don't know. He's always on the road [traveled]. He was in Montreal last (a.) weekend. He was in Prague last (b.) month. And two months ago (c.) he visited his family in Greece.

STEVE: OK, but where is he now?

6 | SIMPLE PAST AND SIMPLE PRESENT

Grammar Notes 1–6

Complete the conversations. Use the words in parentheses. Use the simple past and the simple present in each conversation.

1. **A:** When do you usually travel?

   B: We usually travel (usually / travel) in the summer, but last summer we traveled (travel) in the fall.

2. **A:** Does John like guided tours?

   B: No. He doesn't like (like / not) most guided tours, but he liked (like) the one yesterday in San Francisco.

3. **A:** When does that restaurant open?

   B: It usually opens (usually / open) at 7:00 A.M., but it didn't open (open / not) until 7:30 yesterday.

4. **A:** Do you usually travel on business?

   B: I rerely travel (rarely / travel) on business, but last month I traveled (travel) twice on business.

5. **A:** When do you start work?

   B: I usually start (usually / start) at 9:00, but I started (start) at 8:00 yesterday because I was very busy.

6. **A:** Does the baby always nap in the afternoon?

   B: She usually naps (usually / nap) in the afternoon, but this afternoon she didn't nap (nap / not). She played (play) in her crib.

7 EDITING

Correct the postcard message. There are six mistakes. The first mistake is already corrected.

Dear Ilene,

Paris is magical at night! It's 10 p.m. and I'm writing to you from a café. We arrived here two days ~~before~~ ago. Paul's friend Pierre picks us up. We toured the city during the day and at night we did walked along the Seine River. Today we dining in Montmartre and we visited the Louvre Museum. I not like the Mona Lisa, but maybe I understood it not. Now we're at the Eiffel Tower and it looks just like it does in the photo.

We hope all is well with you. Don't work too hard.

Love,

Michelle and Paul

To:

Ilene Carson
85 Maple Street
Plymouth, DE 19905
USA

Communication Practice

8 LISTENING

Listen to the conversation. Check (✓) all of the true statements. Change the false statements to true ones.

_____ 1. She didn't stay with friends.

_____ 2. She stayed at a traditional *ryokan*.

_____ 3. She rented a car.

_____ 4. She didn't use public transportation.

_____ 5. She practiced Japanese.

_____ 6. She didn't visit the different parts of Osaka.

_____ 7. She learned how to use chopsticks.

_____ 8. She didn't enjoy the trip.

9 | WHAT I DID LAST WEEKEND

Work in small groups. Tell your group what you did and didn't do last weekend. Then add information to the activities you did.

Example: Last weekend I watched TV. On Friday night, I watched Hitchcock's movie *The Birds*. It was scary. On Sunday, I watched football with some friends.

1. I watched TV.
2. I played a sport.
3. I played a computer game.
4. I listened to music.
5. I used the Internet.
6. I visited friends or relatives.
7. I e-mailed a friend or relative.
8. I worked.

10 | GUESS THE SITUATION

Work in pairs. Read these lines. Describe the situation. Use the verbs in the box. (There are different possibilities.) Write down your answers. Tell your answers to the class.

arrived late	asked for	delivered	dialed	didn't return	returned

Example: "Here's the money. Please keep the change."

Someone delivered a pizza to a man. The man said, "Here's the money. Please keep the change."

1. "Here's the money. Please keep the change."
   Norman delivered thai food to Joe. Norman said "Here's the money. Please keep the chang."
2. "Sorry, wrong number."
   Someone asked for a woman. The woman said "Sorry, wrong number."
3. "Walk two blocks and turn right."
   Someone asked me for direction. I said "walk two blocks and turn right."
4. "We missed the first 10 minutes."
   John and JC arrived late at class. They said "We missed the first 10 minutes."
5. "I'm getting angry. That's the third time I left a message for him to call back."
   Jane called Mike, but he didn't return her calls. Jane said "I'm getting angry. That's the third time I left a message for him to call back
6. "Here. And thanks again for letting me use it."
   My friend borrowed my car and she returned it to me. She said "Here. And thanks again for letting me use it."

11 WRITING

Write about a city you know. Pretend you were there last week and write an e-mail message to a classmate. Use at least five of the verbs in the word box in your message.

arrive	rent	stay at	visit	want
enjoy	shop	tour	walk around	watch

Example

Hola, Jack!

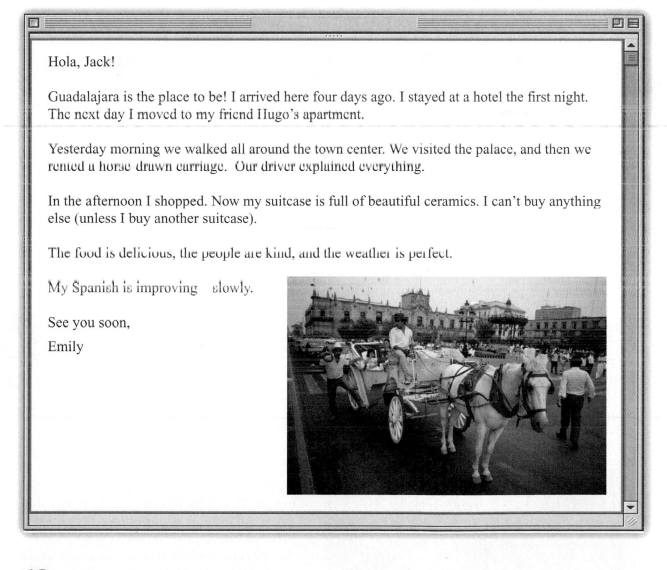

Guadalajara is the place to be! I arrived here four days ago. I stayed at a hotel the first night. The next day I moved to my friend Hugo's apartment.

Yesterday morning we walked all around the town center. We visited the palace, and then we rented a horse drawn carriage. Our driver explained everything.

In the afternoon I shopped. Now my suitcase is full of beautiful ceramics. I can't buy anything else (unless I buy another suitcase).

The food is delicious, the people are kind, and the weather is perfect.

My Spanish is improving slowly.

See you soon,

Emily

12 ON THE INTERNET

Find out about places to see in a city you want to visit. Pretend you were there last week and write a postcard or e-mail message to a classmate.

UNIT

21 The Simple Past: Irregular Verbs—Affirmative and Negative Statements

Grammar in Context

BEFORE YOU READ

	Yes	No
I heard many folktales as a child.	☑	☐

What does the saying "You never know what will happen" mean?

Read this Chinese folktale.

YOU NEVER KNOW WHAT WILL HAPPEN

A long time ago there lived a poor Chinese peasant. One day a beautiful horse appeared on his farm. When the peasant's friends **saw** the horse they **said**, "How lucky you are!"

The peasant answered, "You never know what will happen."

Two days later the horse **ran** away. The peasant's friends **came** and **said**, "What a terrible thing. How unlucky you are! The fine horse **ran** away." The peasant **didn't get** excited. He simply **said**, "You never know what will happen."

Exactly one week later the horse returned. And it **brought** three other horses. When the peasant's friends **saw** the horses they **said**, "Oh. You are so lucky. Now you have four horses to help you." The peasant looked at them and once again **said**, "You never know what will happen."

The next morning the peasant's oldest son **was** in the field. Suddenly one of the horses **ran** into him, and the boy **fell** to the ground. He **was** badly hurt. He **lost** the use of his leg. Indeed, this **was** terrible, and many people **came** to the peasant and

expressed their sadness for his son's misfortune. But again the peasant simply **said**, "You never know what will happen."

A month after the accident, soldiers **rode** into the village. They shouted, "There is a problem along the border! We are taking every healthy young man to fight." The soldiers **took** all the other young men, but they **didn't take** the peasant's son. All the other young men **fought** in the border war, and they all died. But the peasant's son lived a long and happy life. As his father **said**, you never know what will happen.

AFTER YOU READ

Number these events in the order they occurred (1 to 8).

___3___ The horse came back with three other horses.

___1___ A horse appeared on a peasant's land.

___4___ One of the four horses ran into the peasant's son; the son was hurt.

___5___ Soldiers rode into the village and took all the healthy young men to fight.

___8___ The peasant's son lived a long and happy life.

___7___ All the other young men died.

___2___ The horse ran away.

___6___ The soldiers didn't take the peasant's son.

Grammar Presentation

THE SIMPLE PAST: IRREGULAR VERBS—AFFIRMATIVE AND NEGATIVE STATEMENTS

Affirmative Statements		
Subject	**Verb**	
I You He She It We You They	**bought** **rode** **saw**	the horses.

Negative Statements			
Subject	***Did not / Didn't***	**Base Form of Verb**	
I You He She It We You They	**did not** **didn't**	**buy** **ride** **see**	the horses.

Affirmative of *Be*		
Subject	***Was / Were***	
He	**was**	lucky.
They	**were**	unlucky.

Negative of *Be*		
Subject	***Was / Were***	
I	**wasn't**	home.
We	**weren't**	at the library.

GRAMMAR NOTES

EXAMPLES

1. Many common verbs are irregular. **Irregular past verbs** do not add *-ed*. They often look different from the base form.

BASE FORM	PAST
see	*saw*
go	*went*
come	*came*
bring	*brought*
eat	*ate*

- We **saw** a beautiful horse.
- They **went** to work.
- She **came** late.
- He **brought** a friend to school.
- He **ate** a big lunch.

2. For **negative statements** in the past, use ***did not* + the base form of the verb** (except for the verb *be*).

- They **did not see** him.
- She **did not eat** lunch.

The short form of *did not* is ***didn't***. Use *didn't* for speaking and informal writing.

- They **didn't** see him.
- She **didn't** eat lunch.

▶ **BE CAREFUL!** Do not use the simple past form after *didn't*.

NOT: They didn't ~~saw~~ him.
They didn't ~~ate~~ lunch.

3. The **past tense of *be*** is ***was*** or ***were***. The **negative** of *was* is ***was not***, and the negative of *were* is ***were not***. Use ***wasn't*** and ***weren't*** for speaking and informal writing.	• I **was** at the library last night. • They **were not** home this morning. • It **wasn't** late. • They **weren't** in Mexico City.

4. We use *was* or *were* + *born* to tell when or where people were born.	• I **was born** in Nicaragua. • She **was born** in Lima. • They **were born** in 1989.

Reference Notes

See Appendix 7, page A-7 for a list of irregular past forms.
See Unit 3, page 24 for a discussion of the past of *be*.
See Unit 20, page 190, and Unit 22, page 208 for more about the simple past.

Focused Practice

1 DISCOVER THE GRAMMAR

Circle the verbs in the past. Then write the verb and the base form of that verb in the chart below.

I have two brothers. My older brother was a great student. He brought home prizes and won awards. My younger brother disliked school. He never did well. My parents worried about him. Then in his second year of high school, he had a great chemistry teacher. He became interested in chemistry. He began to study hard. He's now a chemistry professor at a university. So, you never know what will happen.

Past	Base Form
was	*be*
brought	*bring*
won	win
disliked	dislike
worried	worry
had	have
became	become
did	do
began	begin

2 | RAGS TO RICHES

Grammar Notes 1–4

Complete the sentences with the affirmative or negative of the verbs in parentheses.

John Tu is the cofounder and head of Kingston Technology. He is a billionaire today, but he ______ (1. be / not) always rich. Tu ______ (2. be) born in China. His family ______ (3. move) to Taiwan when he ______ (4. be) a young boy. Tu ______ (5. like / not) school and he ______ (6. do / not) well. He ______ (7. feel) different from the other students. He ______ (8. fit / not) in.

Tu ______ (9. want) to go to the university in Taiwan, but his grades ______ (10. be) too low. He ______ (11. go) to Germany and ______ (12. study) there. Later he ______ (13. move) to the United States. He ______ (14. open) a gift shop in Arizona and ______ (15. buy) some real estate. He ______ (16. make) money in real estate and ______ (17. use) the money to start a computer business. In 1987, Tu ______ (18. lose) a lot of money but he ______ (19. give / not) up. He and his partner ______ (20. rebuild) their business into a bigger company with over 500 employees. Today, John Tu has a two-billion-dollar business.

3 | YOU NEVER KNOW WHAT WILL HAPPEN

Grammar Notes 1–4

Complete the sentences of each paragraph. Use the simple past of the words in the box. Use each word once.

be	be/not	become	begin	have/not	love	name	study

She ______ (1.) born in 1965 in England. Her parents ______ (2.) her Joanne Kathleen. She ______ (3.) writing at the age of five. She wasn't interested in sports and she ______ (4.) any athletic ability, but she always ______ (5.) to read. She ______ (6.) French at the university and ______ (7.) a bilingual secretary. But she ______ (8.) very good at it.

end	have	move	start	teach

At 26 she ___moved___ (9.) to Portugal. She became an English teacher and ___tought___ (10.) English as a foreign language. At this time she first ___started___ (11.) working on a story about a boy with special powers named Harry. She met a journalist in Portugal. They married and ___had___ (12.) a daughter in 1993. Unfortunately, the marriage ___ended___ (13.) in divorce.

have/not	move	sell	want

She ___moved___ (14.) to Scotland to be near a sister. She really ___wanted___ (15.) to finish her book. In Scotland life was hard because she ___didn't have___ (16.) much money. After many attempts (try), she finally ___sold___ (17.) her book for about $4,000.

become	give	write

Several months later, an American company became interested in her writing and ___gave___ (18.) her money to write full-time. Soon her book ___became___ (19.) a best-seller. She ___wrote___ (20.) several more Harry Potter books. Today, J. K. Rowling is rich and famous.

So you never know what will happen.

4 | A MISTAKE

Grammar Notes 1–3

Complete the sentences with the affirmative or negative of the verbs in parentheses. Three of the sentences are in the negative.

My grandfather, Ben Brown, ___took___ (1. take) a cruise. At dinner the first night, a Frenchman ___sat___ (2. sit) across from my grandfather. Before the man ___sat___ (3. sit) down, he ___looked___ (4. look) at my grandfather and said, "Bon appétit." My grandfather only spoke English. He ___didn't speak___ (5. speak) French. He ___didn't understand___ (6. understand) the Frenchman. My grandfather ___stood___ (7. stand) up and said, "Ben Brown." The same thing ___happened___ (8. happen) the next two nights.

(continued)

My grandfather met (9. meet) a Canadian and said (10. say) to the man, "There's a Frenchman at my dinner table. Every night he introduces himself." The Canadian spoke both French and English. He asked my grandfather some more questions. Soon he understood (11. understand) my grandfather's mistake. He explained (12. explain) the misunderstanding to my grandfather. So then my grandfather knew (13. know) that "Bon appétit" was not the man's name, but was French for "Enjoy your meal."

The next night my grandfather came (14. come) to dinner after the Frenchman. This time my grandfather didn't say (15. say) "Ben Brown." Instead my grandfather smiled (16. smile) and with a perfect French accent said, "Bon appétit." The Frenchman stood (17. stand) and replied, with a perfect American accent, "Ben Brown."

5 | EDITING

Correct these sentences. There are nine mistakes. The first mistake is already corrected.

My grandfather ^was born in Peru. He had an older brother and sister. Their dad (my great grandfather) ~~were~~ was a dreamer. The family ~~have not~~ didn't have much money. When he was 13, my grandfather's mother ~~did~~ died and his dad remarried. My grandfather ~~no~~ didn't like his stepmother. He move moved in with his sister and her husband. All three ~~leave~~ left for America. They ~~did~~ start ed a small business. They worked hard and the business ~~growed~~ grew. Today my sister and I are running the business.

Communication Practice

6 | LISTENING

Listen to Paul's story. Complete the sentences.

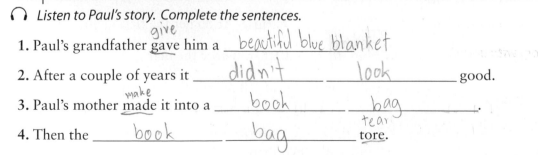

1. Paul's grandfather gave (give) him a beautiful blue blanket
2. After a couple of years it didn't look good.
3. Paul's mother made (make) it into a book bag.
4. Then the book bag tore (tear).

5. His mother made it into a ___pencil___ ___case___.
6. Paul ___lost___ the ___case___.
7. He felt ___terrible___.
8. His friends said, "___forget___ ___about___ ___it___."
9. Paul didn't ___forget___ about it. He ___wrote___ about it instead.
10. Many years later Paul's ___son___ found the story.

7 | A MEMORY GAME

Sit in a circle. Take notes. The first student tells one thing he or she did last weekend. The next student tells what the first one did and then what he or she did. Continue until every student speaks.

Example: ANN: I went to the movies.
JOE: Ann went to the movies, and I read a book.

8 | HOW WAS YOUR DAY?

Work in small groups. Tell about a wonderful day and a terrible day. Use **First**, **Then**, *and* **After that**.

Examples: I had a wonderful day. First, I saw my grandmother. Then, I went to the park. After that, I rented a video.

Yesterday I had a terrible day. First, I got to school late. Then, I broke my glasses. After that, I lost my keys.

9 | WRITING

Write your autobiography. The year is now 2066. Where and when were you born? Where did you go to school? What did you do in your free time? What did you become? Why? Where did you live? Did you marry? Did you have children? Did you travel? Did you become rich or famous? Did you make a difference in the world? Were you happy?

or

Write a family story with a surprise ending.

10 | ON THE INTERNET

Find a short folktale or fable on the Internet that you didn't know before. Tell it to the class.

UNIT

22 The Simple Past: *Yes/No* and *Wh-* Questions

Grammar in Context

BEFORE YOU READ

Do you know the name J. R. R. Tolkien?

Have you seen The Lord of the Rings *movies?*

Have you read The Lord of the Rings *books?*

What do you know about the author?

Read these questions and answers about J.R.R. Tolkien.

Q: Where was Tolkien **born**? **When was** Tolkien **born**?

A: Tolkien's family was English, but J.R.R. Tolkien was born in South Africa in 1892. His father was there on business.

Q: We know him as J.R.R. Tolkien. **What did** his family **call** him?

A: His family and friends called him Ronald. The initials J.R.R. stand for John Ronald Reuel.

Q: Did he **grow up** in South Africa? If not, **where did** he **grow up**?

A: He didn't grow up in South Africa. When he was four, his mother took him and his younger brother back to England. He grew up in the countryside of England, in a place called Sarehole.

Q: What did he **like** to do as a child?

A: He was always good at languages and he liked to invent new languages with his two young cousins.

Q: What did he **study**? **Where did** he **study**?

A: He studied Old and Middle English (the languages in England from 500 to 1500) at Exeter College, Oxford.

Q: Did he **marry**? **Did** he **have** any children?

A: Yes, he did. He married his childhood sweetheart, Edith Bratt. They had four children.

Q: When did he **discover** his gift for storytelling?

A: He discovered his gift when he told his children his stories. They all loved his stories.

Q: Did he **write** full-time?

A: No, he didn't. First he worked on the *New English Dictionary.* Then in 1920 he started teaching, first at the University of Leeds, and later at Oxford. He was a lively and imaginative teacher. He wrote *The Hobbit* in the 1930s.

Q: How long did it **take** Tolkien to write *The Lord of the Rings*?

A: *The Lord of the Rings* novels took 12 years to complete. They did not come out until Tolkien was near retirement.

Q: Did Tolkien **expect** *The Lord of the Rings* to be so popular?

A: No, he didn't. He was very surprised.

Q: When did he **die**?

A: He died in 1973, at the age of 81.

AFTER YOU READ

Circle the letter of the correct answer.

1. Did Tolkien live in South Africa for many years?
   a. Yes, he did. **b.** No, he didn't.

2. Did Tolkien have any brothers or sisters?
   a. Yes, he did. **b.** No, he didn't.

3. Did Tolkien's family and friends call him "John"?
   a. Yes, they did. **b.** No, they didn't.

4. Where did he grow up?
   a. in London **b.** in Sarehole

5. Did Tolkien write full-time?
   a. Yes, he did. **b.** No, he didn't.

6. Who first enjoyed his stories?
   a. his children **b.** his students

Grammar Presentation

THE SIMPLE PAST: *YES/NO* AND *WH-* QUESTIONS AND ANSWERS

Yes/No Questions		
Did	Subject	Base Form of Verb
Did	I you he she it we you they	**start**?

Affirmative Short Answers		
Yes,	you I he she it you we they	**did**.

Negative Short Answers		
No,	you I he she it you we they	**didn't**.

Wh- Questions			
Wh- Word	*Did*	Subject	Base Form of Verb
What	**did**	I	**ask**?
Where		you	**go**?
When		he	**write**?
Why		we	**leave**?
Who(m)		you	**call**?
How long		they	**stay**?

Answers
You asked about his name.
I went to the library. (To the library.)
He wrote at night, after work. (At night, after work.)
We went someplace else.
I called my friend. (My friend.)
They stayed for an hour. (For an hour.) (An hour.)

Wh- Questions about the Subject		
Wh- Word	Past Form of Verb	
Who	**wrote**	*The Hobbit*?
What	**happened**?	

Answers
J. R. R. Tolkien wrote it. (J. R. R. Tolkien.)
It became a big success.

GRAMMAR NOTES

EXAMPLES

1. ***Yes/No* questions** in the **simple past** have the same form (***Did* + subject + base form**) for regular and irregular verbs.

   The verb ***be*** is the one exception.

- regular verb
Did you **want** that book?
- irregular verb
Did you **write** your report?
- **Were** you good at writing?

2. Most ***wh-* questions in the past** begin with the **question word** followed by ***did* + the subject + the base form** of the verb.	• **What did** he **write**? • **Why did** he **write**? • **Where did** he **write**? • **Who did** he **work** for?
3. *Wh-* questions in the past **do not use *did*** when the **question is about the subject**.	subject • Tolkien wrote *The Hobbit.* **Q: Who** wrote *The Hobbit*? **A:** Tolkien. NOT: **Q:** Who ~~did write~~ *The Hobbit*?
4. We usually give **short answers** to *yes/no* and *wh-* questions, but we can also give **long answers**.	**Q:** Did you work yesterday? **A:** Yes. OR Yes, I did. OR Yes, I worked yesterday.

Pronunciation Note

Yes / No questions use rising intonation. *Wh* questions use falling intonation.

Did you hear the story? What did you think about it?

Focused Practice

1 DISCOVER THE GRAMMAR

A *Read questions 1–6 in Exercise B below. Underline the base form verbs.*

1. Which questions are *yes/no* questions? 1, 4, 6, 6
2. Which one is a *wh-* question about the subject? ______

B *Match the questions and answers.*

a. I read *The Hobbit.*	d. Yes, I saw it three times.
b. J. R. R. Tolkien.	e. No, I didn't. I got it at the library.
c. I read most of it.	f. Yes, I did. I finished it last night.

1. A: Did you finish your book report?
   B: Yes, I did. I finished it last night.
2. A: What did you read?
   B: I read The Hobbit.

(continued)

3. **A:** Who wrote it? write

   B: J.R.R. Tolkien.

4. **A:** Did you buy the book?

   B: No, I didn't I got it at library.

5. **A:** Did you see the movie?

   B: Yes, I saw it three times.

6. **A:** Did you read the whole book?

   B: Yes, I read most of it

2 | YES/NO QUESTIONS

Grammar Note 1

Write **yes/no** *questions. Use the verb from the first sentence.*

1. I read all his books. Did you read them too?
2. We enjoyed the movie. Did you enjoy it too?
3. It had a good storyline. Did it have a lot of action?
4. I didn't understand everything. Did she understand everything?
5. We didn't like the ending. Did he like the ending?
6. I expected a different ending. Did you expect a different ending? get, something happen.
7. We saw a review online. Did they see the review online?

3 | SHORT ANSWERS

Grammar Note 4

Write affirmative or negative short answers.

1. **A:** Did you finish your homework?

   B: Yes, I did. I finished it before dinner.

2. **A:** Did they go to the movies?

   B: No, they didn't. They stayed home and watched TV.

3. **A:** Did I call too late?

   B: No, you didn't. I'm usually up at this hour.

4. **A:** Did we get any mail?

   B: Yes, we did. We got some bills and a letter from your uncle.

5. **A:** Did the package arrive?

   B: Yes, It did. It came in the early mail.

6. **A:** Did you buy the DVD?

   B: No, I didn't. I plan to buy it next weekend.

7. **A:** Did you rent any DVDs?

   B: Yes, I did. I rented a comedy and a romance.

4 INTERVIEW WITH AN AUTHOR *Grammar Notes 1–4*

*Sherryl Woods is a best-selling romance and mystery writer. Her books are available in over 20 countries. She has written more than 100 books. Read an interview **(I)** with Sherryl Woods **(SW)**. Complete the questions.*

INTERVIEWER: When did yor write your first book?
1. (When / you / write)

SHERRYL WOODS: In 1980. It came out in 1982.

I: Did you always want to be a writer?
2. (you / always / want)

SW: No, I didn't. For many years I wanted to be a graphic artist.

I: Were you always good at writing?
3. (be / you)

SW: Well, my first-grade teacher wrote, "Sherryl is good at everything except making up stories."

I: Did you like your first-grade teacher?
4. (you / like)

SW: I can't remember.

I: When did you start to write?
5. (When / you / start)

SW: After I graduated from college, I became a journalist.

I: How long did you work as a journalist?
6. (How long / you / work)

SW: I worked for newspapers for fourteen years.

I: Why did you start writing romance novels?
7. (Why / you / start)

SW: Romances were new in the '80s. I read one and said, "I can do this too."

I: Who helped you the most?
8. (Who / help / you)

SW: My agent did. She was there for me from the beginning.

I: How did you feel when your books became popular?
9. (How / you / feel)

SW: It was exciting. I remember the first time I saw someone with my book. I said, "That's my book." The woman looked at me and said, "No, it's not. It's mine." I said, "No, no, no. It's my book. I wrote it."

5 | EDITING

John Steinbeck was a great American writer. Correct these questions and answers about him. There are 11 mistakes. The first mistake is already corrected.

Q: When ^was John Steinbeck ~~was~~ born?

A: He born in 1902.

Q: Where he was born?

A: He was born in Salinas, California.

Q: Where did he studied writing?

A: He studied writing at Stanford University.

Q: He graduate from Stanford?

A: No, he didn't.

Q: Does he marry?

A: Yes, he did. He married in 1930.

Q: When he published *Tortilla Flat*?

A: In 1936.

Q: What year did he published *The Grapes of Wrath*?

A: In 1938. It was his best book.

Q: What were it about?

A: It was about a family who lost their farm and became fruit pickers in California.

Q: Did he won many prizes?

A: Yes, he did. He won a Pulitzer Prize, a Nobel Prize in Literature, and the U.S. Medal of Freedom.

Q: When did he died?

A: He died in New York in 1968.

Communication Practice

6 | LISTENING

Ali is asking Berrin about his grandparents. Listen to their conversation. Mark the statements **T** *(true) or* **F** *(false).*

T 1. Berrin's grandfather had a large farm.

F 2. Berrin went to the farm every winter.

F 3. Berrin's father had seven sisters and brothers.

F 4. Berrin's grandmother never helped on the farm.

T 5. Berrin's grandmother wrote poetry.

F 6. Berrin's grandparents met at a wedding.

7 | WHAT WAS HE/SHE LIKE?

Work in pairs. Ask your partner about one of his or her grandparents.

Examples: Which of your grandparents do you know best? Where did he/she grow up? What did he/she do? Did he/she live with your family?

8 | WRITING

A *Work in small groups. Complete the chart with names of famous people from the past.*

Artists	Writers	Musicians	Scientists	Actors	Athletes
Andy Warhol	John steinbeck	Elvis	Newton	charlie – chapen	
Davinci	J.R.R Tolkien	Mozar	Galileo		
Miquel Angel		Betowen			
		B.I.G			

B *Write 12 questions about one of the people from Exercise A. Use the words in parentheses.*

1. *Where was Andy Warhol born?*
(Where / he or she / born?)
2. When did Johnsteimbeck born?
(When / he or she / born?)
3. Where did J.R.R Tolkein grow up?
(Where / he or she / grow up?)
4. What did Chari Chapen do in his free time?
(What / he or she / do in his or her free time?)
5. Did Chari Chapen have a happy childhood?
(he or she / have / a happy childhood?)
6. Did Chari Chapen traval?
(he or she / travel?)
7. Did he work hard?
(he or she / work hard?)
8. Did Chari Chapen make alot of monney?
(he or she/ make a lot of money?)
9. Did Chari Chapen have a children?
(YOUR QUESTION)
10. Where was Chari Chapen born?
(YOUR QUESTION)
11. When did Chari Chapen die?
(YOUR QUESTION)
12. What did Chari Chapen do in his job?
(YOUR QUESTION)

9 | ON THE INTERNET

Look on the Internet for information about the person you chose in Exercise 8. Try to answer your questions from Exercise 8B. Read your questions and answers to the class. Do not say the name of the person. Let your classmates guess the person.

Example: Where was he born? He was born in Pittsburgh, Pennsylvania.

PART VI

From **Grammar** to **Writing**
Punctuation II: The Exclamation Point (!), The Hyphen (-), Quotation Marks (" . . . ")

1 *What's wrong with these sentences?*

1. You're kidding
2. She's twenty one years old
3. He said I love you
4. He worked for many years before he became rich.

Study this information about punctuation.

The Exclamation Point (!)	
Use the exclamation point after **strong, emotional statements.** (Don't use it too often.)	• What a surprise! • You're kidding! • How wonderful!

The Hyphen (-)	
a. Use a hyphen in **compound numbers** from twenty-one to ninety-nine.	• There were **twenty-two** students in the class.
b. Use a hyphen **at the end of a line** when dividing a word. Words must be divided by syllables. (Check your dictionary if you are unsure.)	• We visited them at the **begin-ning** of the year.

Quotation Marks (" . . . ")	
Use quotation marks **before** and **after the exact words** of a speaker. Use a comma before the quote.	• She said, "I just love your new sweater."

2 *Add the correct punctuation to the sentences in Exercise 1.*

3 *Read the story. Circle the exclamation marks and hyphens. Add quotation marks where necessary.*

Whose Baby Is It?

Solomon was a king. He lived about 3,000 years ago. Everyone came to Solomon because he was very wise.

One day two women approached King Solomon. One carried a baby. The woman said, We live nearby and had our babies three days apart. Her baby died in the night, and she changed it for mine. This baby is really mine.

The other woman said, No! That woman is lying. That's my baby.

The two women started arguing. They continued until King Solomon shout-ed, Stop!

He then turned to his guard and said, Take your sword and chop the baby in two. Give one part to this woman and the other to that one. The guard pull-ed out his sword. As he was about to harm the baby, the first woman screamed, No! Don't do it. Give her the baby. Just don't kill the baby.

King Solomon then said, Now I know the real mother. Give the baby to the woman who has just spoken.

4 *Work in small groups.*

1. Think about these questions. Take notes.

   What was your favorite story as a child?

   When did you first hear it? Who told it to you? Why did you like it?
2. Tell your story to your group.
3. Write your story. When you are finished, read your story twice. First pay attention to the story. Next pay attention to the grammar and punctuation.
4. Rewrite your story. Hang it on the wall. Go around and read the stories of your classmates.

PART VI

Review Test

I *Read each conversation. Circle the letter of the underlined word or group of words that is not correct.*

1. A: You didn't (A) finished (B) your dinner.
   B: That's because it (C) wasn't (D) good.
   A B C D

2. A: Who(m) (A) you did (B) call?
   B: I called (C) John. I wanted (D) Susan's phone number.
   A B C D

3. A: When did (A) they visit (B) Hawaii?
   B: They visit (C) Hawaii last fall. They were (D) there for a week.
   A B C D

4. A: How long (A) did it took (B) you to get to work?
   B: It took (C) me over an hour. Traffic was (D) very heavy.
   A B C D

5. A: Did (A) she drank (B) a glass of milk?
   B: Yes. She drank (C) it with some cookies. Then she did (D) her homework.
   A B C D

6. A: Where did (A) you see (B) them?
   B: I did (C) saw (D) them during the Thanksgiving vacation.
   A B C D

II *Read each question. Circle the letter of the correct answer.*

1. When did you get up?
   a. At eight-thirty.
   b. Yes, I did.
   c. Because it was early.
2. Who visited us last week?
   a. They do.
   b. They were.
   c. They did.
3. Where did they go yesterday?
   a. To the movies.
   b. At noon.
   c. With their friends.
4. Did they have a good breakfast?
   a. Yes, they do.
   b. Yes, they had.
   c. Yes, they did.
5. How long did they stay?
   a. By bus.
   b. A few hours.
   c. An hour ago.
6. Did she have a good vacation last summer?
   a. No, she hasn't.
   b. No, she didn't.
   c. No, she wasn't.
7. Who did you stay with?
   a. My relatives.
   b. John did.
   c. On Saturday.
8. Did it rain last night?
   a. No, it doesn't.
   b. No, it didn't.
   c. No, it don't.

III *Complete this popular story about George Washington. Use the past of each verb in parentheses.*

George Washington was the first president of the United States. He ______________ (1. live) in a beautiful home in Virginia. His mother ______________ (2. have) a special garden with a beautiful little cherry tree. Everyone ______________ (3. love) that cherry tree. One day George ______________ (4. get) a hatchet as a present. He ______________ (5. decide) to try the hatchet. He ______________ (6. go) to the cherry tree and ______________ (7. chop) it down. As soon as he ______________ (8. see) the tree fall on the ground, he ______________ (9. feel) terrible. He ______________ (10. walk) sadly back to the house and ______________ (11. go) to his room. He ______________ (12. play, not) that afternoon. He ______________ (13. eat, not) that evening. That night George's father said, "Someone ______________ (14. chop) down our cherry tree." George ______________ (15. decide) to tell his father the truth. He ______________ (16. walk) toward his father and said, "I ______________ (17. do) it. I ______________ (18. chop) it down with my new hatchet. I cannot tell a lie."

"Thank you for telling the truth," his father ______________ (19. say).

IV *Complete the conversations. Use the simple present, present progressive, or simple past form of each verb in parentheses.*

1. A: Why ______________ you ______________ so late?
   a. (arrive)

   B: I ______________ to set my alarm clock last night.
   b. (forget)

2. A: There aren't any grapes. Who ______________ them all?
   a. (eat)

   B: I don't know. I ______________ them. I ______________ grapes.
   b. (eat, not) c. (like, not)

3. A: I ______________ a beautiful gift in the mail last week.
   a. (get)

   B: Who ______________ it? Uncle Sam?
   b. (send)

4. A: What ______________ his answering machine ______________?
   a. (say)

   B: It says, "I'm sorry I ______________ your call. Please leave your name and a short message. Thank you. Have a nice day."
   b. (miss)

5. A: Let's study together.

   B: Gee, I'm not in the mood to study. I ______________ all day yesterday. What ______________ you ______________ yesterday?
   a. (study) b. (do)

   A: I ______________ tennis.
   c. (play)

6. A: Where are the kids?

   B: Annie ______________ outside, and Dave ______________ homework.
   a. (play) b. (do)

   A: What about Annie's homework?

   B: She ______________ it last night.
   c. (do)

7. A: Where are the cookies?

   B: I ______________ them last night.
   a. (hide)

   A: Why ______________ you ______________ them?
   b. (hide)

   B: I ______________ to lose weight.
   c. (try)

   A: Well, I'm not. I ______________ those cookies.
   d. (want)

V *Circle the correct time marker to complete the sentences.*

1. A week ago / Every Monday I wash my clothes.
2. Did you see your friend this morning / now?
3. We visited them two weeks last / ago.
4. I spoke to the doctor last / ago Thursday.

▶ ***To check your answers, go to the Answer Key on page RT-3.***

APPENDICES

1 Map of the World

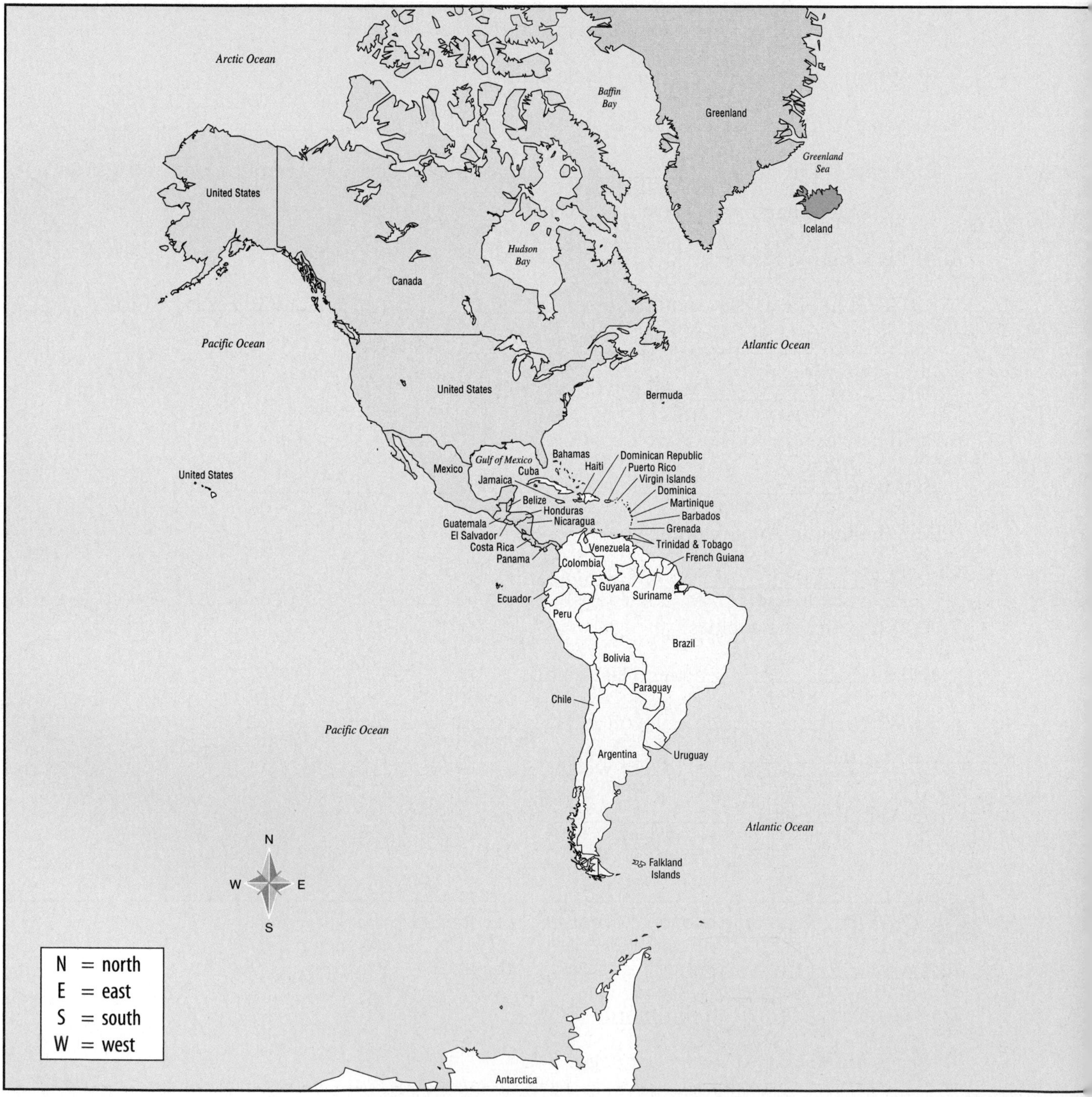

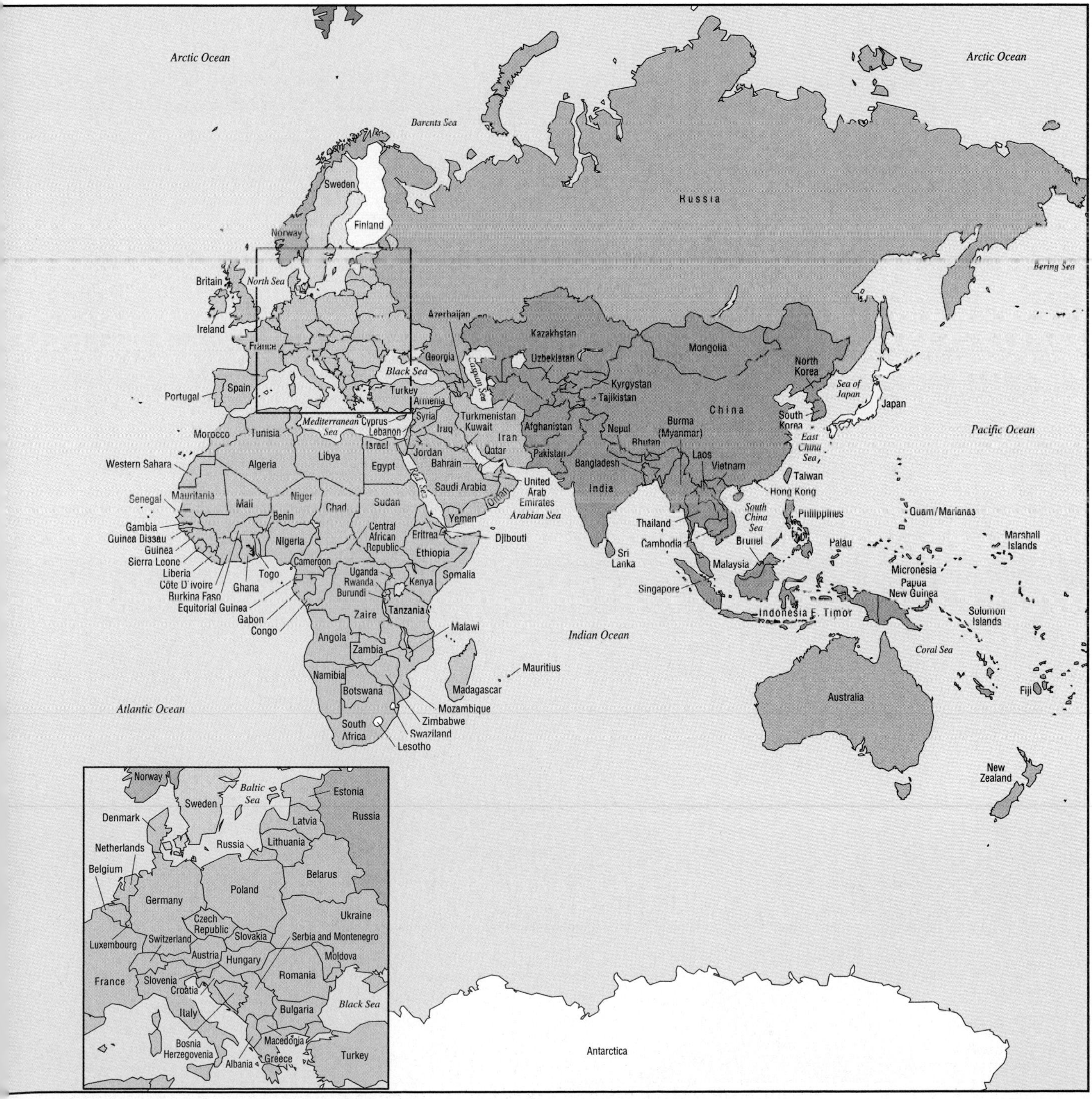

Arctic Ocean
Arctic Ocean
Barents Sea
Russia
Sweden
Finland
Norway
Bering Sea
Britain
North Sea
Ireland
France
Kazakhstan
Mongolia
Azerbaijan
Georgia
Uzbekistan
Caspian Sea
Black Sea
North Korea
Portugal
Spain
Turkey
Kyrgystan
Tajikistan
Sea of Japan
Japan
Armenia
China
South Korea
Morocco
Tunisia
Mediterranean Sea
Cyprus
Lebanon
Syria
Turkmenistan
Iraq
Kuwait
Iran
Afghanistan
Nepal
Burma (Myanmar)
Bhutan
East China Sea
Pacific Ocean
Israel
Western Sahara
Algeria
Libya
Egypt
Jordan
Bahrain
Qatar
Pakistan
Bangladesh
Laos
Vietnam
Taiwan
Red Sea
Saudi Arabia
United Arab Emirates
India
Hong Kong
Senegal
Mauritania
Mali
Niger
Chad
Sudan
Oman
Yemen
Arabian Sea
South China Sea
Philippines
Guam/Marianas
Gambia
Guinea Bissau
Guinea
Sierra Leone
Liberia
Côte D'ivoire
Burkina Faso
Equitorial Guinea
Gabon
Congo
Benin
Nigeria
Togo
Ghana
Cameroon
Central African Republic
Eritrea
Ethiopia
Djibouti
Somalia
Thailand
Cambodia
Brunei
Sri Lanka
Malaysia
Singapore
Palau
Marshall Islands
Micronesia
Papua New Guinea
Uganda
Rwanda
Burundi
Kenya
Zaire
Tanzania
Malawi
Indonesia
E. Timor
Solomon Islands
Angola
Zambia
Indian Ocean
Coral Sea
Namibia
Botswana
Mauritius
Madagascar
Mozambique
Zimbabwe
Swaziland
South Africa
Lesotho
Atlantic Ocean
Australia
Fiji
New Zealand
Antarctica
Norway
Baltic Sea
Estonia
Sweden
Denmark
Russia
Latvia
Netherlands
Russia
Lithuania
Belgium
Belarus
Poland
Germany
Ukraine
Czech Republic
Slovakia
Serbia and Montenegro
Luxembourg
Switzerland
Austria
Moldova
Hungary
France
Slovenia
Croatia
Romania
Bulgaria
Black Sea
Italy
Bosnia Herzegovenia
Macedonia
Greece
Albania
Turkey

2 Map of the United States and Canada

3 Numbers, Temperature, Months, Days, Seasons, Titles

Cardinal Numbers

1 = one	11 = eleven	21 = twenty-one
2 = two	12 = twelve	30 = thirty
3 = three	13 = thirteen	40 = forty
4 = four	14 = fourteen	50 = fifty
5 = five	15 = fifteen	60 = sixty
6 = six	16 = sixteen	70 = seventy
7 = seven	17 = seventeen	80 = eighty
8 = eight	18 = eighteen	90 = ninety
9 = nine	19 = nineteen	100 = one hundred
10 = ten	20 = twenty	200 = two hundred
		1,000 = one thousand
		1,000,000 = one million
		10,000,000 = ten million

Examples:

That building has **seventy-seven** floors.
There are **thirty** days in April.
There are **six** rows in the room.
She is **twelve** years old.
He has **four** children.

Ordinal Numbers

1st = first	11th = eleventh	21st = twenty-first
2nd = second	12th = twelfth	30th = thirtieth
3rd = third	13th = thirteenth	40th = fortieth
4th = fourth	14th = fourteenth	50th = fiftieth
5th = fifth	15th = fifteenth	60th = sixtieth
6th = sixth	16th = sixteenth	70th = seventieth
7th = seventh	17th = seventeenth	80th = eightieth
8th = eighth	18th = eighteenth	90th = ninetieth
9th = ninth	19th = nineteenth	100th = one hundredth
10th = tenth	20th = twentieth	200th = two hundredth
		1,000th = one thousandth
		1,000,000th = one millionth
		10,000,000th = ten millionth

Examples:

He works on the **seventy-seventh** floor.
It's April **thirtieth**.
He's in the **sixth** row.
It's her **twelfth** birthday.
Bob is his **first** child. Mary is his **second**. John is his **third**, and Sue is his **fourth**.

Temperature

We measure the temperature in degrees (°).

Changing from degrees Fahrenheit to degrees Celsius:

$$(F^\circ - 32) \times 5/9 = {}^\circ C$$

Changing from degrees Celsius to degrees Fahrenheit:

$$(9/5 \times {}^\circ C) + 32 = F^\circ$$

Days of the Week

Weekdays	Weekend
Monday	Saturday
Tuesday	Sunday
Wednesday	
Thursday	
Friday	

Months of the Year

Month	Abbreviation	Number of Days
January	Jan.	31
February	Feb.	28*
March	Mar.	31
April	Apr.	30
May	May	31
June	Jun.	30
July	Jul.	31
August	Aug.	31
September	Sept.	30
October	Oct.	31
November	Nov.	30
December	Dec.	31

*February has 29 days in a leap year, every four years.

THE SEASONS

Spring: March 21st–June 20th

Summer: June 21st–September 20th

Autumn or Fall: September 21st–December 20th

Winter: December 21st–March 20th

TITLES

Mr. (Mister) /mɪstər/	unmarried or married man
Ms. /mɪz/	unmarried or married woman
Miss /mɪs/	unmarried woman
Mrs. /mɪsɪz/	married woman
Dr. (Doctor) /daktər/	doctor (medical doctor or Ph.D.)

4 Time

It's one o'clock.
(It's 1:00.)

It's five after one.
(It's 1:05.)

It's one-ten.
It's ten after one.
(It's 1:10.)

It's one-fifteen.
It's a quarter after one.
(It's 1:15.)

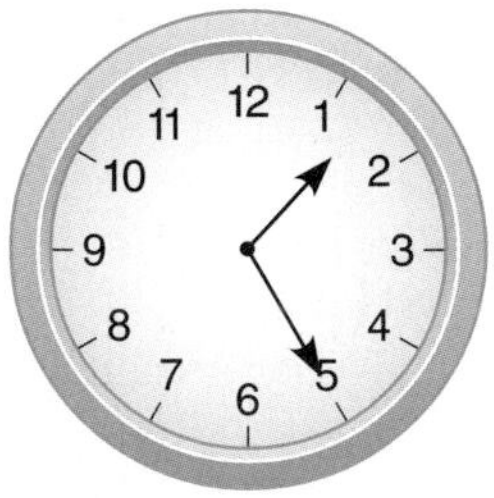

It's one twenty-five.
It's twenty-five after one.
(It's 1:25.)

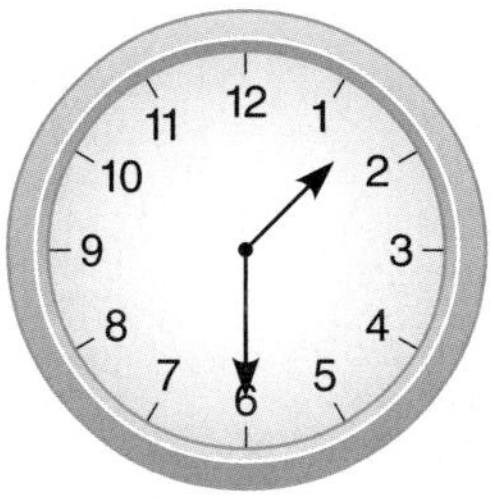

It's one-thirty.
It's half past one.
(It's 1:30.)

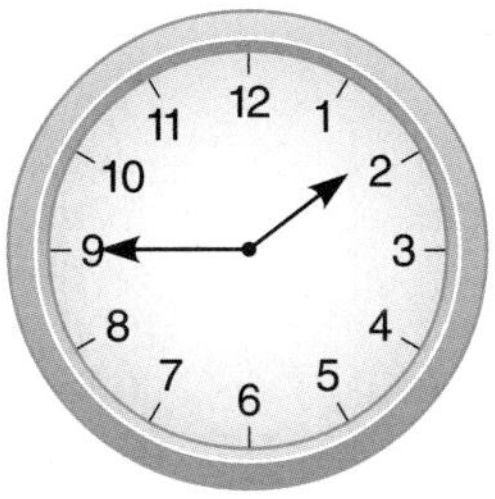

It's one forty-five.
It's a quarter to two.
(It's 1:45.)

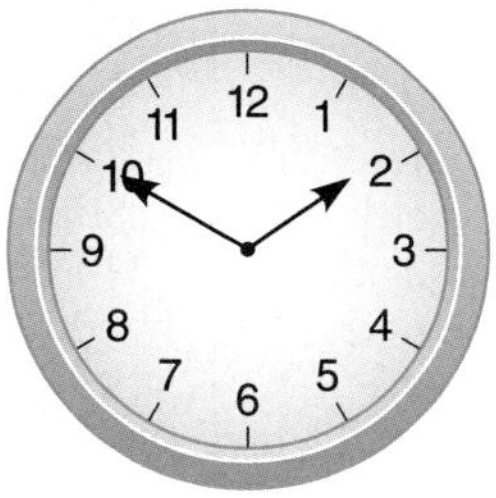

It's one-fifty.
It's ten to two.
(It's 1:50.)

TALKING ABOUT TIME

1. You can ask about time this way:	**A: What time is it?** **B:** It's one o'clock.
2. A.M. means before noon (the hours between midnight and noon).	It's 10:00 **a.m.**
P.M. means after noon (the hours between noon and midnight).	It's 10:00 **p.m.**
▶ **BE CAREFUL!** When people say 12:00 A.M., they mean midnight. When people say 12:00 P.M., they mean noon.	
3. We often write time with numbers.	It's one o'clock. = It's **1:00**. It's two-twenty. = It's **2:20**.

5 Parts of the Body; Medical Problems

1. face
2. hair
3. eye
4. ear
5. nose
6. mouth
7. tooth (teeth)
8. lip
9. chin
10. throat
11. neck
12. shoulder
13. arm
14. elbow
15. hand
16. finger
17. stomach
18. waist
19. hip
20. thigh
21. leg
22. knee
23. foot (feet)
24. ankle
25. toe
26. back

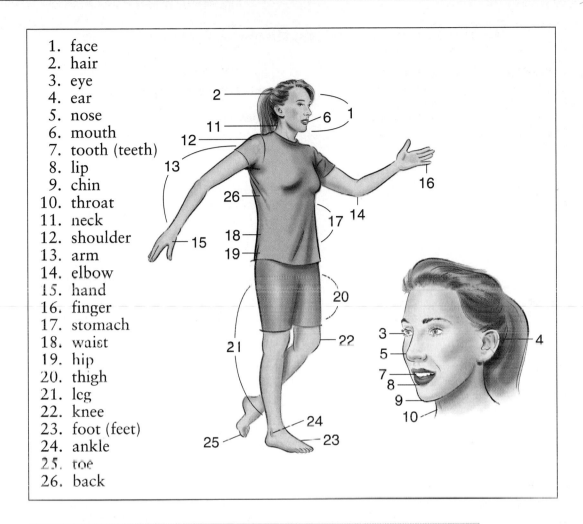

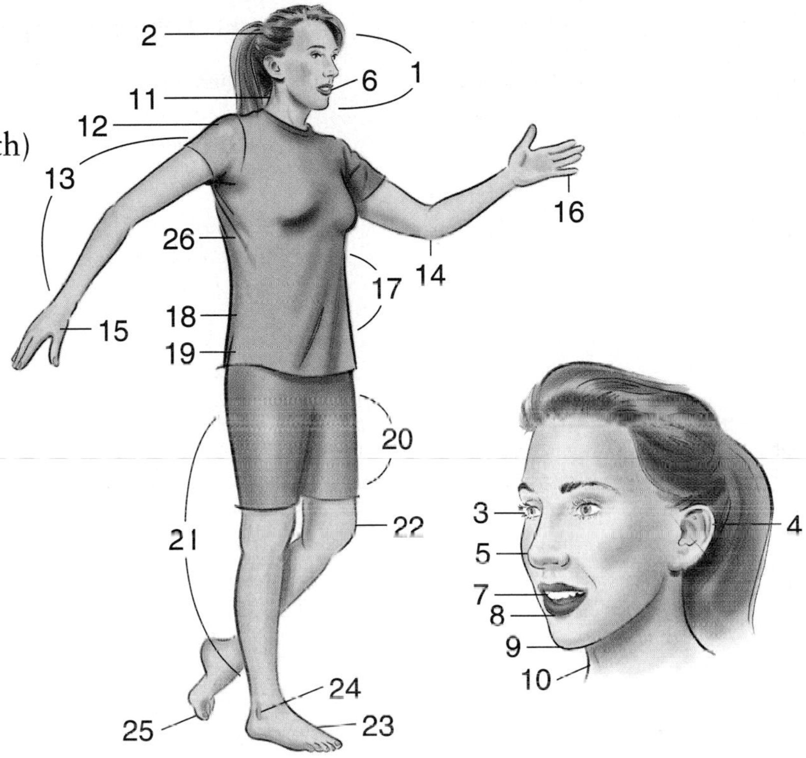

Medical Problems

I have a backache.
I have an earache.
I have a headache.
I have a sore throat.
I have a stomachache. (I'm nauseous; I have diarrhea; I'm constipated.)
I have a fever.
My nose is running.
I have a cough.
I have a pain in my back.
My neck hurts.

U.S. Holidays (Federal and Legal Holidays and Other Special Days)

January	
*New Year's Day	January 1st
*Martin Luther King, Jr.'s Birthday	January 15th (observed on the closest Monday)
February	
Valentine's Day	February 14th
*George Washington's Birthday	February 22nd (observed on the closest Monday)
March	
April	
April Fools' Day	April 1st
May	
Mother's Day	the second Sunday in May
*Memorial Day	May 30th (observed on the last Monday in May)
June	
Flag Day	June 14th
Father's Day	the third Sunday in June
July	
*Independence Day	July 4th
August	
September	
*Labor Day	the first Monday in September
October	
*Columbus Day	October 12th (observed on the closest Monday)
Halloween	October 31st
November	
Election Day	the first Tuesday after the first Monday in November
*Veterans' Day	November 11th
*Thanksgiving	the fourth Thursday in November
December	
*Christmas	December 25th
New Year's Eve	December 31st

*federal legal holidays

Canadian Holidays (Legal and Public Holidays)

January	
New Year's Day	January 1st
Sir John A. Macdonald's Birthday	January 11th
February	
Valentine's Day	February 14th
March	
†St. Patrick's Day	the Monday nearest March 17th
March or April	
†Good Friday	
†Easter Monday	
April	
April Fool's Day	April 1st
May	
Mother's Day	the second Sunday in May
Victoria Day	the Monday preceding May 25th
June	
Father's Day	the third Sunday in June
St. John the Baptist's Day	the Monday nearest June 24th (only in Quebec)
July	
Canada Day	July 1st
August	
Civic Holiday	the first Monday in August (celebrated in several provinces)
Discovery Day	the third Monday in August (only in the Yukon)
September	
Labor Day	the first Monday in September
October	
Thanksgiving Day	the second Monday in October
Halloween	October 31st
November	
Remembrance Day	November 11th
December	
Christmas Day	December 25th
Boxing Day	December 26th

†Many Americans in the United States observe these religious holidays too. However, these days are not official U.S. holidays.

7 Base Forms and Past Forms of Common Irregular Verbs

BASE FORM	PAST FORM
become	became
begin	began
bite	bit
blow	blew
break	broke
bring	brought
build	built
buy	bought
catch	caught
choose	chose
come	came
cost	cost
do	did
draw	drew
drink	drank
drive	drove
eat	ate
fall	fell
feed	fed
feel	felt
fight	fought
find	found
fly	flew
forget	forgot
get	got
give	gave
go	went
grow	grew
hang	hung
have	had
hear	heard
hide	hid
hit	hit
hold	held
hurt	hurt
keep	kept
know	knew
lead	led

BASE FORM	PAST FORM
leave	left
lend	lent
lose	lost
make	made
meet	met
pay	paid
put	put
quit	quit
read*	read*
ride	rode
ring	rang
run	ran
say	said
see	saw
sell	sold
send	sent
shake	shook
shoot	shot
shut	shut
sing	sang
sit	sat
sleep	slept
speak	spoke
spend	spent
stand	stood
steal	stole
swim	swam
take	took
teach	taught
tear	tore
tell	told
think	thought
throw	threw
understand	understood
wake	woke
wear	wore
win	won
write	wrote

*Pronounce the base form / rid /. Pronounce the past form / rɛd /.

THE PRESENT OF *BE*

Singular		
Subject	***Be***	
I	**am**	a student.
You	**are**	
He She	**is**	
It	**is**	in the United States.

Plural		
Subject	***Be***	
We You They	**are**	in the United States.

THE PAST OF *BE*

Singular			
Subject	***Be***		**Time Marker**
I	**was**	at a restaurant	last night.
You	**were**		
He She It	**was**		

Plural			
Subject	***Be***		**Time Marker**
We You They	**were**	at a restaurant	last night.

THE PRESENT PROGRESSIVE

Subject	*Be*	Base Form of Verb + *-ing*
I	**am**	working.
You	**are**	
He She It	**is**	
We You They	**are**	

THE SIMPLE PRESENT AND THE SIMPLE PAST

The Simple Present	
Subject	**Verb**
I You We They	**work.**
He She It	**works.**

The Simple Past	
Subject	**Base Form of Verb + *-ed / -d / -ied***
I You He She It We You They	**worked.** **arrived.** **cried.**

THE FUTURE

Will **for the Future**			
Subject	***Will***	**Base Form of Verb**	
I You He She It We You They	**will**	**work**	tomorrow.

Be Going to **for the Future**				
Subject	***Be***	***Going to***	**Base Form of Verb**	**Time Marker**
I	**am**	**going to**	**work**	tomorrow.
You	**are**			
He She	**is**			
You We They	**are**			
It	**is**	**going to**	**rain**	tomorrow.

SPELLING RULES

1. Add -s to form the plural of most nouns.	student chief picture	student**s** chief**s** picture**s**
2. Add ***-es*** to form the plural of nouns that end in ***ss, ch, sh,*** and ***x***. (This ending adds another syllable.)	class watch dish box	class**es** watch**es** dish**es** box**es**
3. Add ***-es*** to form the plural of nouns that end in o preceded by a consonant.	potato	potato**es**
EXCEPTION: Add ***-s*** to plural nouns ending in o that refer to music.	piano soprano	piano**s** soprano**s**
4. Add ***-s*** to form the plural of nouns that end in o preceded by a vowel.	radio	radio**s**
5. To form the plural of words that end in a consonant + ***y***, change the ***y*** to ***i*** and add ***-es***.	dictionary fly	dictionar**ies** fl**ies**
6. To form the plural of words that end in a vowel + ***y***, add ***-s***.	boy day	boy**s** day**s**
7. To form the plural of certain nouns that end in ***f*** or ***fe***, change the ***f*** to ***v*** and add ***-es***.	hal**f** loa**f** kni**fe** wi**fe**	hal**ves** loa**ves** kni**ves** wi**ves**
8. Some plural nouns are **irregular**.	woman child person mother-in-law man foot tooth	women children people mothers-in-law men feet teeth
9. Some nouns **do not have a singular form**.	(eye) glasses clothes pants scissors	
10. Some plural nouns are the same as the singular noun.	Chinese fish sheep	Chinese fish sheep

PRONUNCIATION RULES

1. The **final sounds** for regular plural nouns are / **s** /, / **z** /, and / **ɪz** /.	
2. The plural is pronounced / **s** / **after** the **voiceless sounds** / **p** /, / **t** /, / **k** /, / **f** /, and / **ø** /.	cups hats works cuffs myths
3. The plural is pronounced / **z** / **after** the **voiced sounds** / **b** /, / **d** /, / **g** /, / **v** /, / **m** /, / **n** /, / **ŋ** /, / **l** /, / **r** /, and / **ð** /.	crabs cards rugs
4. The plural *s* is pronounced / **z** / **after** all **vowel sounds**.	day days toe toes
5. The plural *s* is pronounced / **ɪz** / **after the sounds** / **s** /, / **z** /, / **ʃ** /, / **ʒ** /, / **ʧ** /, and / **ʤ** /. (This adds another syllable to the word.)	races causes dishes

10 Possessive Nouns

1. Add *'s* to form the possessive of singular nouns.	Lulu**'s** last name is Winston.
2. To form the possessive of plural nouns ending in *s*, add only an **apostrophe (')**.	The girls**'** gym is on this floor. The boys**'** locker room is across the hall.
3. In hyphenated words (*mother-in-law, father-in-law,* etc.) and in phrases showing joint possession, only the last word is possessive in form.	My sister-in-law**'s** apartment is big. Elenore and Pete**'s** apartment is comfortable.
4. To form the possessive of plural nouns that do not end in *s*, add *'s*.	The men**'s** room is next to the water fountain.
5. To form the possessive of one-syllable singular nouns that end in *s*, add *'s*.	**James's** apartment is beautiful.
To form the possessive of words of more than one syllable that end in *s*, add an *'* or an *'s*.	**McCullers's** novels are interesting. OR **McCullers'** novels are interesting.
6. **Be careful!** Don't confuse possessive nouns with the contraction of the verb *be*.	**Carol's** a student. = **Carol** ***is*** a student. **Carol's** book is open. = **Her** book is open.

Common Non-count Nouns*

Liquids	Food		Too Small to Count	School Subjects
milk	bread	ketchup	sugar	math
coffee	cheese	jam	salt	history
oil	lettuce	jelly	pepper	geography
juice	broccoli	fish	cinnamon	biology
soda	ice cream	meat	rice	chemistry
water	butter	sour cream	sand	music
beer	mayonnaise	soup	baking powder	
			cereal	
			spaghetti	
			wheat	
			corn	

City Problems	Weather	Gases	Abstract Ideas	Others
traffic	snow	oxygen	love	money
pollution	rain	carbon	beauty	mail
crime	ice	dioxide	happiness	furniture
	fog	nitrogen	luck	homework
		air	advice	information
			help	jewelry
			noise	garbage
			time	toothpaste
				paper

*Some nouns can be either count or non-count nouns.

I'd like some **chicken**. (non-count)
There were three **chickens** in the yard. (count)

Did you eat any **cake**? (non-count)
I bought a **cake** at the bakery. (count)

Quantifiers: Containers, Measure Words, and Portions

a bottle of (milk, soda, catsup)
a bowl of (cereal, soup, rice)
a can of (soda, beans, tuna fish)
a cup of (hot chocolate, coffee, tea)
a foot of (snow, water)
a gallon of (juice, gas, paint)
a head of (lettuce)
an inch of (snow, rain)
a loaf of (bread)

a pair of (pants, skis, gloves)
a piece of (paper, cake, pie)
a pint of (ice cream, cream)
a quart of (milk)
a roll of (film, toilet paper, paper towels)
a slice of (toast, cheese, meat)
a tablespoon of (flour, sugar, baking soda)
a teaspoon of (sugar, salt, pepper)
a tube of (toothpaste, glue)

Metric Conversion

1 liter	=	.26 gallons or 1.8 pints
1 gallon	=	3.8 liters

1 mile	=	1.6 kilometers
1 kilometer	=	.62 mile
1 foot	=	.30 meter or 30 centimeters
1 meter	=	3.3 feet
1 inch	=	2.54 centimeters

1 ounce	=	28 grams
1 gram	=	.04 ounce
1 pound	=	.45 kilogram
1 kilogram	=	2.2 pounds

12 The Definite Article

1. ***The*** is the **definite article**. You can use ***the*** before **singular count nouns**, **plural count nouns**, and **non-count nouns**.	**The hat** is red. **The hats** are red. **The coffee** is hot.
2. Use ***the*** for **specific things** that the listener and speaker know about.	**A:** How was **the test**? **B:** It was easy. **A:** Would you like to read **the paper**? **B:** Yes, thanks.
3. Use ***the*** when the speaker and listener know there is **only one** of the item.	**A:** Is there a cafeteria in this school? **B:** Yes, **the cafeteria** is on the third floor.
4. Use ***the*** when you are talking about **part of a group**.	Meat is usually expensive, but **the meat** at Ron's Butcher Shop is cheap and delicious.
5. Use ***the*** when you talk about something for the **second time**.	**A:** What did you buy? **B:** Some apples and some pears. **The apples** were bad, but **the pears** were delicious.
6. Use ***the*** before the **plural name** of a whole family.	**The Winstons** live in New York City.
7. Use ***the*** before the names of **oceans**, **rivers**, **mountain ranges**, **seas**, **canals**, **deserts**, and **zoos**.	**The Pacific Ocean** is on the West Coast. **The Mississippi River** is the longest river in the United States. We visited **the Rocky Mountains**. Where is **the Dead Sea**? The boat went through **the Suez Canal**. **The Sahara Desert** is growing. We visited **the San Diego Zoo**.
8. Use ***the*** with phrases with ***of*** when there is **only one** of the item that follows ***the***.	Paris is **the capital of France**. I attended **the University of Michigan**. BUT He drank **a** cup of tea.

1. A **phrasal verb** consists of a verb and a particle. *Away, back, down, in, off, on, out,* and *up* are common particles.* A particle usually changes the meaning of a verb.	He **took** the coat. *(He removed the coat from where it was.)* He **took off** the coat. *(He removed the coat from his body.)* He **took back** the coat. *(He returned the coat.)*
2. Some phrasal verbs have **direct objects**. When the direct object is a noun, it can go after the particle or between the verb and the particle.	verb particle direct object He took off **the coat**.
When the direct object is a pronoun, it always goes between the verb and the particle.	verb direct object particle He took **the coat** off. verb object pronoun particle He took **it** off. NOT: He took ~~off it~~.
3. Some phrasal verbs don't take an object.	His car **broke down** in the middle of the street. Please **come in**.

*Some particles can also be prepositions or adverbs in other sentences. In the sentence, "He walked *up* the hill," *up* is a preposition.

Common Phrasal Verbs That Take Objects

Phrasal Verb	Meaning	Example
bring out	present; show	He **brought out** the wedding cake.
give away	give as a gift	He **gave away** many books when he moved.
give back	return	The sweater was too big, so I **gave** it **back**.
hand in	give some work to a teacher or boss	I **handed in** a ten-page report.
hand out	distribute	They **handed out** papers about the candidates.
put away	return to the place where something is usually kept	Please **put** your clothes **away**.
put off	do later; postpone	We're very busy now, so let's **put off** our vacation for a few weeks.
put on	cover the body with clothes	When I **put** my new boots **on**, I felt a lot warmer.
take back	return	I'd like to **take** those shirts **back**. They're a little tight.
take off	remove from one's body	He **took** his sweater **off** because he was hot.
throw away	put in the garbage	She's sorry that she **threw** those papers **away**.
turn down	lower the volume	The TV is too loud. Please **turn** it **down**.
turn off	stop a machine or electrical item from working	Don't forget to **turn** all the lights **off** before you go to sleep.
turn on	make a machine or electrical item work	The radio is next to you. Please **turn** it **on**.
wrap up	complete	We'll **wrap** the meeting **up** before noon.

COMMON PHRASAL VERBS THAT DON'T TAKE OBJECTS		
Phrasal Verb	**Meaning**	**Example**
break down	stop working	His car **broke down** in the middle of the street.
catch on	become popular; learn	That new style **caught on** very quickly. The new worker **caught on** quickly.
clear up	become clear	In the morning it was foggy, but the weather **cleared up** by noon.
come in	enter	Please **come in**.
come up	arise	That new idea **came up** during the meeting last week.
eat out	eat in a restaurant	Every Sunday they **eat out** at a different restaurant.
grow up	become adult	They **grew up** in the country.
show up	appear	We were surprised when they **showed up** two hours early.
sit down	sit	We **sat down** and had a serious talk about our future.
stand up	stand	After he played the piano, he **stood up** and bowed.

14 Direct and Indirect Objects

Group One								
Subject	Verb	Direct Object	*To*	Indirect Object	Subject	Verb	Indirect Object	Direct Object
She	**sent**	**a gift** **it**	**to**	**us.**	She	**sent**	**us**	**a gift.**

Group Two								
Subject	Verb	Direct Object	*For*	Indirect Object	Subject	Verb	Indirect Object	Direct Object
They	**found**	**a towel** **it**	**for**	**him.**	They	**found**	**him**	**a towel.**

Group Three				
Subject	Verb	Direct Object	*To*	Indirect Object
He	**repeated**	**the question**	**to**	**the class.**

Group Four				
Subject	Verb	Direct Object	*For*	Indirect Object
He	**fixed**	**the shelves**	**for**	**me.**

Group One Verbs (*to*)		Group Two Verbs (*for*)	Group Three Verbs (*to*)	Group Four Verbs (*for*)
e-mail	sell	buy	explain	cash
give	send	build	prove	close
hand	show	find	repeat	fix
lend	teach	get	say	pronounce
owe	tell	make	whisper	translate
pass	throw			
read	write			

(continued)

RULES FOR DIRECT AND INDIRECT OBECTS

1. With **Group One** and **Group Two verbs**, there are **two** possible **sentence patterns** if the **direct object** is a **noun**.	direct object · *to/for* · indirect object I gave the **money to him**. = indirect object · direct object I gave **him the money**. direct object · *to/for* · indirect object We bought **the book for him**. = indirect object · direct object We bought **him the book**.
If the **direct object** is a **pronoun**, it always comes **before the indirect object**.	direct object · *to/for* · indirect object I gave **it to him**. Please get **them for me**. NOT: I gave ~~him it~~. NOT: Please get ~~me them~~.
2. With **Group Three** and **Group Four verbs**, the **direct object** always comes **before the indirect object**.	direct object · *to/for* · indirect object Explain **the sentence to John**. She translated **the letter for us**. NOT: Explain ~~John the sentence~~. NOT: She translated ~~us the letter~~.

15 The Present Progressive: Spelling Rules

1. Add ***-ing*** to the base form of the verb.	drink see eat	drink**ing** see**ing** eat**ing**
2. If a verb ends in a silent ***e***, drop the final ***e*** and add ***-ing***.	smil**e**	smil**ing**
3. If a one-syllable verb ends in a consonant, a vowel, and a consonant **(CVC)**, double the last consonant before adding ***-ing***.	**CVC** sit run	 sit**ting** run**ning**
However, do not double the last consonant if it is a ***w***, ***x***, or ***y***.	sew play mix	se**w**ing pla**y**ing mi**x**ing
4. In words with two or more syllables that end in a consonant, a vowel, and a consonant **(CVC)**, double the last consonant only if the last syllable is stressed.	admít whísper	admi**tt**ing *(stressed)* whispe**r**ing *(not stressed)*

SPELLING RULES FOR THE THIRD-PERSON SINGULAR AFFIRMATIVE

1. Add **-*s*** to form the third-person singular of most verbs.	Pete works. I work too. Doug wears sweatshirts. I wear shirts.
Add **-*es*** to words that end in ***ch***, ***s***, ***sh***, ***x***, or ***z***.	Norma teach**es** Spanish. I teach English. Lulu wash**es** her clothes on Tuesday. Elenore and Pete wash their clothes on Sunday.
2. When a base-form verb ends in a **consonant + *y***, change the ***y*** to ***i*** and add **-*es***.	I study at home. Carol stud**ies** at the library.
Do not change the *y* when the base form ends in a **vowel + *y***. Add **-*s***.	Dan play**s** tennis. I play tennis, too.
3. *Have, do,* and *go* have **irregular forms** for the third-person singular.	I have. He **has**. I do. She **does**. I go. It **goes**.

PRONUNCIATION RULES FOR THE THIRD-PERSON SINGULAR AFFIRMATIVE

1. The **final sound** for the third-person singular form of the simple present tense is pronounced / **s** /, / **z** /, or / **ɪz** /. The final sounds of the third-person singular are the same as the final sounds of plural nouns. See Appendix 9 on pages A-10 and A-11.	/ **s** / talk**s**	/ **z** / love**s**	/ **ɪz** / danc**es**
2. ***Do*** and ***say*** have a change in vowel sound.	I say. / **seɪ** / I do. / **du** /	He say**s**. / **sɛz** / He do**es**. / **dʌz** /	

17 | The Simple Past of Regular Verbs: Spelling and Pronunciation Rules

SPELLING RULES

1. If the verb **ends in an *e***, add ***-d***.	arrive like	arrive**d** like**d**
2. If the verb **ends in a consonant**, add ***-ed***.	rain help	rain**ed** help**ed**
3. If a **one-syllable verb** ends in a consonant, a vowel, and a consonant **(CVC)**, double the last consonant and add ***-ed***.	**CVC** hug rub	 hu**gged** ru**bbed**
However, do not double the last consonant if it is a ***w***, ***x***, or ***y***.	bow mix play	bo**w**ed mi**x**ed pla**y**ed
4. If a **two-syllable verb** ends in a consonant, a vowel, and a consonant **(CVC)**, double the last consonant only if the last syllable is stressed.	refér énter	refe**rr**ed *(stressed)* ente**r**ed *(not stressed)*
5. If the verb ends in a **consonant + *y***, change the ***y*** to ***i*** and add ***-ed***.	worry carry	worr**ied** carr**ied**
6. If the verb ends in a **vowel + *y***, do not change the *y* to *i*. Add ***-ed***.	play annoy	pla**yed** anno**yed**
There are **exceptions** to this rule.	pay lay say	**paid** **laid** **said**

PRONUNCIATION RULES

1. The **final sounds** for regular verbs in the past are / **t** /, / **d** /, and / **ɪd** /.			
2. The final sound is pronounced / **t** / after the **voiceless sounds** / **f** /, / **k** /, / **p** /, / **s** /, / **ʧ** /, and / **ʃ** /.	laug**hed** lic**ked**	sip**ped** mis**sed**	wat**ched** wi**shed**
3. The final sound is pronounced / **d** / **after** the **voiced sounds** / **b** /, / **g** /, / **ʤ** /, / **l** /, / **m** /, / **n** /, / **r** /, / **ŋ** /, / **ð** /, / **ʒ** /, / **v** /, and / **z** /.	ru**bbed** hu**gged** ju**dged** pu**lled**	hu**mmed** ba**nned** occu**rred** ba**nged**	ba**thed** massa**ged** li**ved** surpri**sed**
4. The final sound is pronounced / **d** / **after vowel sounds**.	pla**yed** ski**ed**	ti**ed** sno**wed**	arg**ued**
5. The final sound is pronounced / **ɪd** / after / **t** / and / **d** /. / **ɪd** / adds a syllable.	want instruct rest attend	wan**ted** instruc**ted** res**ted** atten**ded**	

18 Comparisons with Adjectives

Comparative Form (used to compare two people, places, or things)				
Sally	is	**older** **busier** **more industrious**	**than**	her sister.

Superlative Form (used to compare three or more people, places, or things)				
Sally	is	**the**	**busiest** **most industrious**	of the three.

Equative Form (used to show that two people, places, or things are the same)					
Sally	is	**as**	**tall** **busy** **industrious**	**as**	Bob.

SPELLING RULES FOR COMPARATIVE AND SUPERLATIVE ADJECTIVES

1. When a one-syllable adjective ends in a **consonant**, **vowel**, and **consonant (CVC)**, double the last consonant and add ***-er*** or ***-est*** (***hot–hotter–hottest***).	Summers in Miami are **hotter** than summers in San Francisco. July is the **hottest** month of the year.
2. When a two-syllable adjective ends in ***-y***, change the ***y*** to ***i*** and add ***-er*** or ***-est*** (***heavy–heavier–heaviest***; ***easy–easier–easiest***).	Traffic is **heavier** at eight o'clock than it is at noon. Traffic is **the heaviest** on Fridays.

Function	**Modals**	**Examples**
to make polite requests	**Would you (please)** **Could you (please)** **Can you (please)**	**Would you** please lend me your pen? **Could you** please help me? **Can you** please take our picture?
to ask for or give permission	**may** **can**	**May** I use your computer? You **can** return to work on Monday.
to express desire	**would like**	I'**d like** to buy a car. We'**d like** to see you again.
to express possibility (present or future)	**may** **might**	Take an umbrella. It **may** rain. He **might** have a cold.
to express future possibility	**can** **could**	How **can** I get to the library tomorrow? You **could** go by bus or by train.
to talk about the future	**will**	He **will** be three years old next week.
to express present ability	**can**	I **can** type 50 words a minute.
to express past ability	**could**	I **could** run very fast 10 years ago.
to express necessity in the present or future	**must** **have to**	You **must** pay the rent by the first of the month. She **has to** work today.
to express past necessity	**had to**	We **had to** read two new chapters.
to express advisability	**should** **ought to** **had better**	He **should** see a doctor. He doesn't sound very good. We **ought to** study today. They'**d better** return my money.
to promise or assure	**will**	I'**ll be** there at 10:00.
to express strong prohibition	**mustn't**	You **mustn't** smoke near the chemical factory.
to indicate that something is not a requirement	**don't / doesn't have to**	You **don't have to** type your composition. She **doesn't have to** wear a suit at her office.

20 Pronunciation Table

These are the pronunciation symbols used in this text. Listen to the pronunciation of the key words.

Vowels		**Consonants**			
Symbol	**Key Word**	**Symbol**	**Key Word**	**Symbol**	**Key Word**
i	beat, feed	p	pack, happy	ʃ	ship, machine, station, special, discussion
ɪ	bit, did	b	back, rubber	ʒ	measure, vision
eɪ	date, paid	t	tie	h	hot, who
ɛ	bet, bed	d	die	m	men
æ	bat, bad	k	came, key, quick	n	sun, know, pneumonia
ɑ	box, odd, father	g	game, guest	ŋ	sung, ringing
ɔ	bought, dog	tʃ	church, nature, watch	w	wet, white
oʊ	boat, road	dʒ	judge, general, major	l	light, long
ʊ	book, good	f	fan, photograph	r	right, wrong
u	boot, food, student	v	van	y	yes, use, music
ʌ	but, mud, mother	θ	thing, breath		
ə	banana, among	ð	then, breathe		
ɚ	shirt, murder	s	sip, city, psychology		
aɪ	bite, cry, buy, eye	z	zip, please, goes		
aʊ	about, how				
ɔɪ	voice, boy				
ɪr	deer				
ɛr	bare				
ɑr	bar				
ɔr	door				
ʊr	tour				

GLOSSARY OF GRAMMAR TERMS

action verb A verb that describes an action. It can be used in the progressive.

- *Sachiko **is planning** a big party.*

adjective A word that describes (or modifies) a noun or pronoun.

- *That's a **great** idea.*

adverb A word that describes (or modifies) an action verb, an adverb, an adjective, or a sentence.

- *She drives **slowly**.*

adverb of frequency A word that tells the frequency of something.

- *We **usually** eat lunch at noon.*

adverb of manner A word that describes a verb. It usually answers the question *how*.

- *She speaks **clearly**.*

affirmative statement A sentence that does not use a negative verb form *(not)*.

- ***I have a car**.*

apostrophe A punctuation mark used to show possession and to write a short form (contraction).

- *He**'**s in my father**'**s car.*

base form The simple form of the verb without any ending such as *-ing*, *-ed*, or *-s*. It is the same as the infinitive without *to*.

- *Arnold will **come** at 8:00. We should **eat** then.*

***be going to* future** A verb form used to make predictions, express general facts in the future, or talk about definite plans that were made before now.

- *Mei-Ling says it**'s going to be** cold, so she**'s going to take** a coat.*

capital letter The big form of a letter of the alphabet. Sentences start with a capital letter.

- ***A**, **B**, **C**, etc.*

comma Punctuation used to separate single things in a list or parts of a sentence.

- *We went to a restaurant**,** and we ate chicken**,** potatoes**,** and broccoli.*

common noun A noun for a person, place, or thing. It is not capitalized.

- *The **man** got a **book** at the **library**.*

comparative form An adjective or adverb ending in *-er* or following *more*. It is used in comparing two things.

- *My sister is **older** and **more intelligent** than my brother.*
- *But he studies **harder** and **more carefully**.*

consonant The letters *b, c, d, f, g, h, j, k, l, m, n, p, q, r, s, t, v, w, x, y, z*.

contraction A short form of two words. An apostrophe (') replaces the missing letter.

- ***It is** late and **I am** tired. I **should not** stay up so late.*
- ***It's** late and **I'm** tired. I **shouldn't** stay up so late.*

count noun A noun you can count. It usually has a singular and a plural form.

- *In the **park**, there was a **man** with two **children** and a **dog**.*

definite article *The;* It makes a noun specific.

- *We saw a movie. **The** movie starred Sean Penn.*

demonstrative adjective An adjective used to identify the noun that follows.

- ***This** man is resting, but **those** men are busy.*

demonstrative pronoun A pronoun used in place of a demonstrative adjective and the noun that follows.

- ***This** is our classroom, and **these** are my students.*

direct object A noun or pronoun used to receive the action of a verb.

- *She sold a **car**. He bought **it**.*

exclamation point A punctuation mark (!) used at the end of a statement. It shows strong emotion.

- *Help**!** Call the police**!***

formal language Language we usually use in business settings, and academic settings and with people we don't know.

- ***Good morning**, **ladies** and **gentlemen**. **May** we begin?*

gerund The *-ing* form of a verb. It is used as a noun.

- ***Skiing** is fun, but we also enjoy **swimming**.*

imperative A sentence used to give an instruction, a direction, a command, or a suggestion. It uses the base form of the verb. The subject (you) is not a part of the sentence.

- ***Turn** right at the corner. **Drive** to the end of the street. **Stop!***

indefinite article *A* and *an*; used before singular, nonspecific non-count nouns.

- *Jaime brought **a** sandwich and **an** apple for lunch.*

infinitive *To* + the base form of a verb.

- ***To travel** is my dream. I want **to see** the world.*

informal language The language we usually use with family and friends, in e-mail messages, and in other informal settings.

- ***Hey, Doug, what's up?***

inseparable phrasal verb A phrasal verb that cannot have an object between the verb and the particle.

- *She **ran into** John.*

irregular verb A verb that does not form the simple past by adding *-d* or *-ed*.

- *They **ate** a fancy meal last night. The boss **came** to dinner.*

modal A word that comes before the main verb. Modals can express ability, possibility, obligation, and necessity.

- *You **can** come early, but you **mustn't** be late, and you **should** wear a tie.*

negative statement A statement with a negative verb form.

- *He **didn't study**. He **wasn't** ready for the test.*

non-action verb A verb that does not describe an action. It can describe an emotion, a state, a sense, or a mental thought. We usually don't use non-action verbs in the progressive.

- *I **like** that actor. He **is** very famous, and I **believe** he won an Oscar.*

non-count noun A noun we usually do not count. We don't put *a*, *an*, or a number before a non-count noun.

- *All you'll need is **rice**, **water**, **salt**, and **butter**.*

noun A word that refers to a person, animal, place, thing, or idea.

- ***Paula** has a **friend** at the **library**. She gave me a **book** about **birds**.*

noun phrase A phrase formed by a noun and words that describe (modify) it.

- *It was **a dark brown leather jacket**.*

object A noun or pronoun following an action verb. It receives the action of the verb.

- *I sent **a letter**. He read **it**.*

object pronoun A pronoun following a verb or a preposition.

- *We asked **him** to show the photos to **them**.*

period A punctuation mark (.) used at the end of a statement.

- *I'd like you to call on Saturday. We need to talk.*

phrasal verb A two-part (or three-part) verb that combines a verb and a particle. The meaning of the parts together is often different from the meaning of the verb alone.

- *We **put on** our gloves and **picked up** our umbrellas.*

phrase A group of words that can form a grammatical unit.

- *She lost **a red hat**. He found it **under the table**.*

plural The form that means more than one.

- ***We** sat in **our chairs** reading **our books**.*

possessive An adjective, noun, or pronoun that shows possession.

- ***Her** book is in **John's** car. **Mine** is at the office.*

preposition A small word that goes before a noun or pronoun object. A preposition often shows time or place.

- *Maria saw it **on** the table **at** two o'clock.*

prepositional phrase A phrase that consists of a preposition followed by a noun or a noun phrase.

- *Chong-Dae saw it **under the black wooden table**.*

present progressive A verb form that shows an action happening now or planned for the future.

- ***I'm working** hard now, but **I'm taking** a vacation soon.*

pronoun A word that replaces a noun or a noun phrase. There are subject pronouns, object pronouns, possessive pronouns, and demonstrative pronouns.

- ***He** is a friend—I know **him** well. **This** is his coat; **mine** is black.*

proper noun The actual name of a person, place, or thing. A proper noun begins with a capital letter.

- ***Tom** is living in **New York**. He is studying **Russian** at **Columbia University**.*

quantifier A word or phrase that comes before a noun and expresses an amount of that noun.

- *Jeannette used **a little** sugar, **some** flour, **four** eggs, and **a liter of** milk.*

question mark A punctuation mark (?) used at the end of a question.

- *Where are you going**?** When will you be back**?***

quotation marks Punctuation marks (". . .") used before and after the actual words a person says.

- *I said, **"**Where are you going?**"** and **"**When will you be back?**"***

regular verb A verb that forms the simple past by adding *-d* or *-ed*.

- *We **lived** in France. My mother **visited** us there.*

sentence A group of words with a subject and a verb.

- *We opened the window.*
- *Did they paint the house?*

separable phrasal verb A phrasal verb that can have an object between the verb and the particle.

- *She **put on** her coat. She **put** it **on** before he **put** his coat **on**.*

simple past A verb form used to show a completed action or idea in the past.

- *The plane **landed** at 9:00. We **caught** a bus to the hotel.*

simple present A verb form used to show habitual actions or states, general facts, or conditions that are true now.

- *Kemal **loves** to ski, and it **snows** a lot in his area, so he**'s** very happy.*

singular The form that means only one.

- *I put on **my hat** and **coat** and closed the **door**.*

small letter The small form of a letter of the alphabet. We use small letters for most words except for proper nouns and the word that starts a sentence.

- ***a**, **b**, **c**, etc.*

subject The person, place, or thing that a sentence is about.

- ***The children** ate at the mall.*

subject pronoun A pronoun used to replace a subject noun.

- *Irene works hard. **She** loves her work.*

superlative form An adjective or adverb ending in *-est* or following *most*. It is used in comparing three or more things.

- *We climbed the **highest** mountain by the **most dangerous** route.*
- *She drives the **fastest** and the **most carelessly** of all the drivers.*

syllable A group of letters with one vowel sound. Words are made up of one or more syllables.

- *One syllable—**win***
- *Two syllables—**ta ble***
- *Three syllables—**im por tant***

verb A word used to describe an action, a fact, or a state.

- *He **drives** to work now. He **has** a new car, and he **is** a careful driver.*

***wh-* question** A question that asks for information. It begins with *what, when, where, why, which, who, whose,* or *how*.

- ***What**'s your name?*
- ***Where** are you from?*
- ***How** do you feel?*

***will* future** A verb form used to make predictions, to talk about facts in the future, to make promises, to offer something, or to state a decision to do something at the time of speaking.

- *It **will** probably rain, so I**'ll take** an umbrella. I**'ll give** you my extra one.*

***yes/no* question** A question that has a *yes* or a *no* answer.

- *Did you arrive on time? Yes, I did.*
- *Are you from Uruguay? No, I'm not.*
- *Can you swim well? Yes, I can.*

REVIEW TESTS ANSWER KEY

Note: In this answer key, where the contracted verb form is given, it is the preferred form, though the full form is also acceptable. Where the full verb form is given, it is the preferred form, though the contracted form is also acceptable.

PART I

I (Units 1–3)

1. B
2. A
3. D
4. C
5. A

II (Units 1–3)

1. D
2. A
3. C
4. A
5. D
6. B

III (Unit 2)

1. Was it cloudy yesterday?
2. Is it cloudy now?
3. Were you in school last week?

IV (Units 1, 3)

It ~~be~~ *is* cold and rainy. But yesterday *was* beautiful. It *was* sunny all day.

PART II

I (Units 5–7)

1. D
2. B
3. A
4. A
5. D
6. B

II (Units 4–6)

1. B
2. B
3. C
4. D
5. C

III (Unit 4)

1. a, a, a
2. an, a
3. Ø, Ø
4. an
5. a
6. an, an
7. an, a, Ø

IV (Unit 7)

1. Where
2. Who
3. Why
4. What

V (Unit 6)

2. is between the Book Nook and QB Bank.
3. is next to Nina's Hair Salon. OR is next to the post office. OR is next to Fogtown post office
4. is on the corner of Maple Street and Second Avenue. OR is on the corner of Maple and Second.
5. is on Maple Street.

PART III

I (Units 8–10)

1. C
2. B
3. C
4. C
5. C
6. A
7. C

II (Units 8–10)

1. Do, need
2. washes
3. has
4. isn't
5. fixes
6. goes
7. does
8. Does, speak
9. Do, wear
10. don't eat
11. worries
12. lives
13. makes
14. does, come
15. do, keep

III (Unit 8)

1. have
2. needs
3. don't need
4. isn't
5. don't eat
6. live
7. don't play
8. speaks
9. doesn't cook
10. wears

IV (Unit 9)

1. **a.** Do you like
   b. I do
2. **a.** Does he need
   b. he doesn't
3. **a.** Do they speak
   b. they don't
4. **a.** Do I know
   b. you do
5. **a.** Do you remember
   b. I don't
6. **a.** Does it rain
   b. it does
7. **a.** Does your brother live
   b. he doesn't

V (Units 9, 10)

2. **a.** Who always wears a hat?
   b. What does Sachiko always wear?
3. **a.** Does Jasmine get up at nine o'clock?
   b. What time/When does Jasmine get up?
   c. Who gets up at nine o'clock?
4. **a.** Does your friend work at a restaurant?
   b. Who works at a restaurant?
   c. Where does your friend work?
   d. What does your friend do?
5. **a.** Who usually goes to bed after midnight?
   b. What time/When does Bob usually go to bed?

VI (Units 8–10)

1. Dan ^ like soccer.
   doesn't
2. She isn't write to me often.
   need
3. Does your friend needs an umbrella?
   want
4. Do they wants any help?
5. My aunt is teaches Spanish.
6. Who does cooks in your family?
7. They don't work or don't live near the train station.
   does that word mean
8. What means that word?
9. How ^ you spell your name?
   do
10. When does you get up?
11. Why ^ they shop there?
    does he feel
12. How feels he?

PART IV

I (Units 11–14)

1. C
2. D
3. D
4. C
5. D

II (Unit 11)

1. second
2. first
3. seventy-five
4. eleventh

III (Unit 13)

1. This
2. Those
3. that
4. Those
5. these

IV (Unit 14)

1. ones
2. It
3. one
4. It
5. It
6. ones

V (Unit 11)

1. What
2. Whose; Nuray's
3. Where; at
4. When; on
5. What; at
6. Whose; Fiore's

VI (Units 11, 12)

1. When is Uncle Mike's birthday?
2. Where is Scott?
3. What is his aunt's last name?
4. Who is in the living room?
5. Whose car is in the garage?

VII (Unit 12)

1. Her
2. Their
3. His
4. Its
5. Their

PART V

I (Units 15–19)

1. A
2. C
3. D
4. D
5. C
6. C
7. D

II (Units 16–19)

1. a
2. a
3. b
4. a
5. a
6. a
7. b

III (Unit 17)

2. a. Read the directions.
b. Don't start before 10:00.
3. a. Use the side streets.
b. Don't take the highway.
4. a. Wear your jacket.
b. Don't forget your scarf.

IV (Unit 15)

1. are not/aren't/'re not studying
2. is/'s writing
3. is/'s looking
4. are not/aren't/'re not reading
5. are/'re relaxing
6. are/'re taking

V (Units 16–19)

1. A: Is ~~it's~~ *it* raining outside?
2. A: Are they ~~play~~ *playing* soccer?
3. B: He speaks well now, but last year he ~~can't~~ *couldn't* speak at all.
4. A: Why don't we ~~to~~ take a walk?
5. A: Please ~~you are~~ *be* quiet.

PART VI

I (Units 20–22)

1. B
2. B
3. C
4. B
5. B
6. C

II (Unit 22)

1. a
2. c
3. a
4. c
5. b
6. b
7. a
8. b

III (Units 20, 21)

1. lived
2. had
3. loved
4. got
5. decided
6. went
7. chopped
8. saw
9. felt
10. walked
11. went
12. didn't play
13. didn't eat
14. chopped
15. decided
16. walked
17. did
18. chopped
19. said

IV (Units 20–22)

1. a. did arrive
b. forgot
2. a. ate
b. didn't eat
c. don't like
3. a. got
b. sent
4. a. does say
b. missed
5. a. studied
b. did do
c. played
6. a. 's playing (is playing)
b. 's doing (is doing)
c. did
7. a. hid
b. did hide
c. 'm trying (am trying)
d. want

V (Unit 20)

1. Every Monday
2. this morning
3. ago
4. last

PART VII

I (Units 23–25)

1. C
2. B
3. D
4. D
5. C

II (Unit 23)

1. Are there; there are
2. Are there; there aren't
3. Is she; she is
4. Are they; they aren't
5. Is there; there isn't

III (Unit 25)

1. an; an
2. a, a; the, the
3. the; the
4. the
5. a
6. an

IV (Unit 25)

1. any
2. a few
3. much
4. some
5. a
6. a
7. much
8. many

V (Unit 24)

1. b
2. a
3. b
4. b
5. a

PART VIII

I (Units 26–29)

1. D
2. D
3. B
4. D

II (Units 26–29)

1. C
2. C
3. B
4. A

III (Unit 26)

1. b
2. h
3. g
4. e
5. a
6. d
7. f
8. c

IV (Unit 26)

1. Every week they go to the bank. OR They go to the bank every week.
2. She rarely wears jeans.
3. They always watch TV at night.
4. Several times a year we go to rock concerts. OR We go to rock concerts several times a year.
5. He is often late. OR Often he is late. OR He is late often.

V (Unit 26)

1. How often does Ellen call her parents?
2. How often do we get a free lunch?

VI (Units 26, 27)

1. tastes
2. a. are wearing
   b. want
3. Do, remember
4. a. Is, eating
   b. likes
5. do, spell

VII (Units 26–28)

1. are
2. says
3. love
4. living
5. meeting
6. have
7. 're/are reading
8. to go
9. to take
10. 'm/am doing
11. to take
12. want
13. go
14. don't study
15. take
16. talk
17. to introduce
18. love
19. 'm/am wearing
20. feel

VIII (Unit 29)

2. When was he born
3. When did he die
4. Where was he born
5. When did he write the Declaration of Independence
6. How long was he president OR For how many years was he president
7. What was

PART IX

I (Units 30–32)

1. C
2. D
3. A
4. B

II (Units 30–32)

1. c
2. b
3. c
4. b

III (Units 31, 32)

1. may
2. 'll
3. 'll
4. a. may
   b. won't
5. 'll
6. 'll
7. might

IV (Units 30, 31)

1. a. rained
   b. 's raining
   c. 's going to rain
2. a. 'm going to help
   b. 'm getting
3. a. Did, hear
   b. won
   c. think
   d. is, going to do
   e. 's going to visit
   f. 's going to take
4. a. did, return
   b. 'll return
   c. closes
   d. won't

V (Units 30, 31)

1. 'm going to go OR 'm going
2. 'll be back OR 're going to be back
3. may, may OR might, might
4. 'm meeting them (on), OR 'm going to meet them

VI (Units 30–32)

1. *Tomorrow they're*
   ~~They're~~ going to ~~tomorrow~~ start the job. OR They're going to ~~tomorrow~~ start the *tomorrow* job^.
2. *see*
   He's going to ~~sees~~ the art exhibit this afternoon.
3. *will you*
   How ~~you will~~ travel?
4. *be*
   She won't ~~is~~ home this evening.
5. I think they might ~~to~~ buy a car.
6. *Maybe we*
   ~~We maybe~~ will go to the early show.
   may
   OR We ~~maybe will~~ go to the early show.
   might
   OR We ~~maybe will~~ go to the early show.

PART X

I (Units 33–35)

1. B
2. B
3. A
4. B

II (Unit 33)

1. How many
2. How many
3. How much
4. How much

III (Unit 33)

1. **a.** a few
   b. friends
   c. some
2. **a.** any
   b. ice
3. **a.** some
   b. stamps
4. **a.** a little
   b. time
5. **a.** How much
   b. mail
6. **a.** How many
   b. bottles
7. enough cooks
8. enough
9. **a.** How many
   b. days
10. too many
11. too
12. too few

IV (Unit 33)

1. carton
2. bowl
3. cup
4. jar
5. pound
6. piece

V (Unit 35)

1. **a.** you
   b. yours
   c. your
2. **a.** mine
   b. me
   c. my
   d. I
3. **a.** we
   b. Our
   c. us
   d. Ours
4. **a.** Its
   b. It
5. **a.** they
   b. them
   c. their

VI (Units 33–35)

1. *any*
   We didn't buy ~~some~~ bread.
2. *few*
   They need a ~~little~~ more days to finish.
3. *enough chairs*
   We don't have ~~chairs enough~~ for everyone.
4. *much*
   He has too ~~many~~ homework. He can't go out.
5. *much*
   We can't see that movie today. It's ~~very~~ too late. OR It's ~~very~~ late.
   too
6. This isn't my jacket. Mine ~~jacket~~ is in the closet. OR ~~Mine~~ jacket is in the closet. It's probably hers.
   My

PART XI

I (Units 36–39)

1. C
2. A
3. A
4. B
5. A
6. C

II (Units 36–39)

1. to
2. to
4. to
8. to

III (Units 38–39)

1. don't have to
2. should
3. mustn't
4. has to
5. had better ('d better)
6. ought to
7. should
8. had better not ('d better not)
9. don't have to
10. can't

IV (Units 36–39)

1. have to
2. don't have to
3. have
4. can
5. can't
6. can't

V (Unit 37)

1. I'd be glad to.
2. No, thanks. I'm full.
3. I'm sorry. I can't right now.
4. Yes, thanks.
5. Sure.

VI (Units 36–39)

1. What should we ~~doing~~ do about the missing book?
2. She ought to ~~finds~~ find a better job.
3. May I ~~to~~ help you?
4. You mustn't ~~talked~~ talk about that in front of him.
5. Yesterday we ~~have~~ had to work late.
6. Would ~~please~~ you please help me?
7. When do we have to be there?

PART XII

I (Units 40–43)

1. A
2. B
3. C
4. B
5. B
6. A
7. B
8. C
9. A
10. C
11. B

II (Units 41–42)

1. carefully
2. slowly
3. beautiful
4. beautifully
5. well
6. very
7. too
8. good

III (Units 40, 42)

1. than
2. as
3. from
4. as
5. than
6. as

IV (Units 40, 43)

1. the worst
2. worse than
3. the fastest
4. the most interesting
5. funnier than
6. the funniest
7. the best
8. the most industrious
9. older than

V (Units 40–43)

1. He is one of the best ~~student~~ students in the school.
2. Who's the ~~most~~ tallest one in their family?
3. The next level is a lot ~~more~~ harder than this one.
4. We're busier in December ~~as~~ than we are in January.
5. The workbook isn't as expensive as the CD.
6. He works ~~hardly~~ hard.
7. Taxes are ~~highest~~ higher than last year.
8. It tastes ~~deliciously~~ delicious.

INDEX

This Index is for the full and split editions. All entries are in the full book. Entries for Volume A of the split edition are in black. Entries for Volume B are in color.

Notes

Notes

Notes

Notes

Notes

Notes